THE VARIETIES OF GOODNESS

International Library of Philosophy and Scientific Method

EDITOR: TED HONDERICH
ADVISORY EDITOR: BERNARD WILLIAMS

A Catalogue of books already published in the
International Library of Philosophy and Scientific Method
will be found at the end of this volume.

THE VARIETIES
OF GOODNESS

by

Georg Henrik von Wright

LONDON

ROUTLEDGE & KEGAN PAUL

NEW YORK : THE HUMANITIES PRESS

First published 1963
by Routledge & Kegan Paul Ltd
Broadway House, 68–74 Carter Lane
*London, E.C.*4

Printed in Great Britain
by Compton Limited
London & Aylesbury

© *Georg Henrik von Wright* 1963
Second impression 1964
Third impression 1968

SBN 7100 3614 0

PREFACE

IN 1959 and 1960 I gave the Gifford Lectures in the University of St. Andrews. The lectures were called 'Norms and Values, an Inquiry into the Conceptual Foundations of Morals and Legislation'. The present work is substantially the same as the content of the second series of lectures, then advertised under the not very adequate title 'Values'. It is my plan to publish a revised version of the content of the first series of lectures, called 'Norms', as a separate book. The two works will be independent of one another.

I take this opportunity to express my thanks to the University of St. Andrews for honouring me with the invitation to give the Gifford Lectures and to the members of staff and students at St. Andrews, with whom I was able to discuss the content of the lectures when they were in progress. Giving the lectures afforded me with an urge and opportunity to do concentrated research, for which I am deeply grateful.

In the course of revising the contents of my lectures and preparing them for publication I have had the privilege of regular discussions over a long period with Professor Norman Malcolm. I am indebted to him for a number of observations and improvements and, above all, for his forceful challenge to many of my arguments and views.

There is very little explicit reference to current discussion and literature in this book. I hope no one will interpret this as a sign that the author wishes to ignore or belittle the work which is being done by others. It is true, however, that the works of the classics have provided a much stronger stimulus to my thoughts than the writings of my contemporaries. In particular have I learnt from three: Aristotle, Kant, and Moore. I have been successively under the spell of the Kantian idea of duty and the Moorean idea of intrinsic value. In fighting my way against Kant I was led to reject the position sometimes called 'deontologist', and in resisting Moore I became convinced of the untenability of value-objectivism

v

and -intuitionism. In this largely negative way I arrived at a *teleological* position, in which the notions of the beneficial and the harmful and the good of man set the conceptual frame for a moral 'point of view'. Perhaps one could distinguish between two main variants of this position in ethics. The one makes the notion of the good of man relative to a notion of the *nature* of man. The other makes it relative to the needs and wants of individual men. We could call the two variants the 'objectivist' and the 'subjectivist' variant respectively. I think it is right to say that Aristotle favoured the first. Here my position differs from his and is, I think, more akin to that of some writers of the utilitarian tradition.

From what has just been said someone may get the impression that this is a treatise on ethics. It is not. (See Ch. I, sect. 1.) But I think that it contains the germ of an ethics, that a moral philosophy may become extracted from it. This philosophy will hardly strike one as novel in its main features. What may be to some extent new is the *approach* to ethics through a study of the varieties of goodness. I think that this approach is worth being pursued with much more thoroughness than I have been capable of. I hope others would find it inviting to work out in greater detail things, which are here presented in the form of a first sketch.

GEORG HENRIK VON WRIGHT

CONTENTS

CONTENTS

CONTENTS

I

THE VARIETIES OF GOODNESS

1. ETHICS is often said to be the philosophy of morals or 'theory' of morals. Questions of morals are, to a large extent, questions of good and evil and duty. Not all good, however, is morally relevant and not every duty is a moral duty. With the conception of ethics as the philosophy of morals is sometimes associated a view, according to which there is a peculiar *moral* sense of 'good' and 'duty', which is the proper object of ethical study.

I shall refer to this view as the idea of *the conceptual autonomy of morals*. I am referring not so much to a well-defined position as to a certain climate of opinion in moral theory. Nobody, I believe, has contributed more to the creation of this climate of opinion than Kant. One could therefore also refer to it as a Kantian tradition in ethics.

I have no objection to a definition of ethics as the philosophy of morals. There is not much talk in this book of moral concepts or judgments or rules or principles—and the little which there is, is not very systematic. The major part of this book does not treat of morals at all. Therefore the title 'Ethics' would not have been well suited for it.

I do, however, object strongly against the view, which I called that of the conceptual autonomy of morals. As I shall try to argue presently, moral goodness is not a form of the good on a level with certain other basic forms of it, which we are going to distinguish. The so-called *moral* sense of 'good' is a derivative or secondary sense, which must be explained in the terms of non-moral uses of the word. Something similar holds true of the moral sense

1

of 'ought' and 'duty'. For this reason it seems to me that a philosophic understanding of morality must be based on a much more comprehensive study of the good (and of the ought) than has been customary in ethics. The name 'Prolegomena to Ethics' would not be ill-suited for such a study.

I had thought of using this title. But besides the fact that it has been used before, it would be too ambitious. For it is, after all, only an *aspect* of the broader approach needed for ethics, which I have ventured to study with any thoroughness in the present work. What it is and what the other main aspects are, I shall indicate later in this chapter (sect. 4).

2. It has long been current among philosophers to distinguish between normative ethics and ethics which is not normative. Ethics of the first type is supposed to tell what is good and bad and what is our moral duty. Ethics of the second type does not value or prescribe.

The idea of a sharp distinction between ethics which is normative and ethics which is not normative can, I think, be regarded as an off-shoot of a more general idea of a sharp distinction between *norm* and *fact*, between the 'ought' and the 'is'. This second idea has become associated, in particular, with the name of Hume. One could, though with caution, talk of a Humean tradition in moral philosophy.

The distinctions between the ought and the is and between the two types of ethics is commonly understood in such a way that the term 'ought' covers both norms and values and that 'normative' as an attribute of 'ethics' refers both to the prescriptive and to the evaluative. As another off-shoot of the idea of a sharp distinction between the evaluative and prescriptive on the one hand and the factual on the other hand may be regarded the idea that 'science' is value-free (*Die Wertfreiheit der Wissenschaften*).

On the question, what a non-normative study of morals is, there is much obscurity and many divergent opinions. Some philosophers, particularly from the decades round the turn of the century, used to conceive of ethics which is not normative as a *science des mœurs*, *i.e.* as a sociological and/or psychological study of the 'natural history' of moral ideas, codes, and customs.

There is no doubt a way of studying moral phenomena, which is 'detached' and 'scientific' and which can be *sharply* distinguished

2

from normative ethics. But it is at least doubtful whether an empirical study of morals is the only form of ethics which is not normative. Many philosophers would deny this. They would maintain that there is a philosophical study of moral concepts and judgments, which is distinct both from normative ethics and from the empirical study of moral phenomena. For this type of study of morals the term *meta-ethics* has recently become fashionable.

On the further question of the nature of meta-ethics opinions are not settled. Some would call meta-ethics a conceptual or logical study of morals. And some would wish to add that a conceptual study of morals is essentially a logical study of the language of morals. Meta-ethics—this seems to be agreed—does not aim at telling what things *are* good and bad and what *are* our moral duties. It aims at a better understanding of what 'good' and 'bad' and 'duty' *mean*.

All these characterizations are loaded with problems. They do not suffice by themselves for drawing a sharp boundary either between meta-ethics and normative ethics or between meta-ethics and empirical investigation.

The idea of a sharp separation of normative ethics and meta-ethics seems to me to rest on an oversimplified and superficial view of the first and on an insufficient understanding of the nature of the second. The view of normative ethics as (some sort of) moral legislation, perhaps in combination with a criticism of current moral standards, is one-sided. So is the view of normative ethics as casuistry. 'Normative ethics' is not a suitable name for any *one* thing. Those, who use the name, tend to heap under it a number of different philosophic and moralistic activities. *One* of these activities, thus classified as 'normative', I would myself call *conceptual* investigation; and I would not know how to distinguish it sharply from the allegedly non-normative conceptual analysis belonging to meta-ethics.

Anyone who thinks that a sharp distinction can be maintained between meta-ethics and normative ethics is invited to consider the nature of such works as Aristotle's *Nicomachean Ethics*, Kant's *Grundlegung zur Metaphysik der Sitten*, or John Stuart Mill's *Utilitarianism*. Is their contents meta-ethics or normative ethics? Some, I think, would answer that the works mentioned contain elements of both types of ethics and perhaps deplore that their authors did not distinguish more sharply between the two. My own inclination

B

would rather be to say that the difficulties in classification here show the artificiality of the distinction.

3. I would call the investigations conducted in the present work *conceptual*. I would also agree to saying that the subject-matter of conceptual investigations is the *meaning* of certain words and expressions—and not the things and states of affairs themselves about which we talk, when using those words and expressions. Why is it that I nevertheless do not wish to call the inquiry 'meta-ethical' and to regard it as sharply distinguishable from the pursuits of 'normative ethics'?

My hesitation has to do with the question of the nature of a conceptual investigation. This is a question on which I wish I had and could state a clearer view than I have actually been able to form for myself. I shall here in a brief and somewhat dogmatic way try to state my position with regard to some aspects of it.

First of all I think that there are many types of conceptual investigation, many 'methods' in philosophy. The choice of a method may depend upon the nature of the problem to be treated or it may, perhaps, depend upon the temperament of the individual philosopher. I have come to think that the types of conceptual investigation, which are best suited for ethics, are essentially different from the types suited for theory of knowledge or metaphysics. This difference is probably connected with the fact that the aims, as I see them, of so-called practical and so-called theoretical philosophy are intrinsically different.

An urge to do conceptual investigations—and one of the main urges to do philosophy, I think—is *bewilderment* concerning the meaning of some words. With the words in question we are usually familiar. We know on the whole, how and when to use them. But sometimes we are at a loss as to whether a thing should be called by some such word '*x*'. We are at a loss, *not* because we are ignorant as to whether this thing has some feature *y*, which would be a ground for or against calling it '*x*'. We hesitate because we do not know which features of this thing *are* grounds for or against calling it '*x*'. We are challenged to *reflect* on the grounds. Instead of grounds for calling things '*x*', I could also have said *criteria* or *standards* for deciding, whether a thing is *x* or not.

How are grounds or criteria or standards for calling things by words related to *meaning*? This is a complicated problem, on which

4

I shall here only say this much: The meaning of a word has many aspects—and the grounds for calling something by a word I shall call an *aspect* of the meaning of this word. (If someone wants to distinguish here between criteria and meaning, I need not quarrel with him about the meaning of 'meaning'.)

Reflexion on the grounds for calling things by words is a *type* of conceptual investigation. How is such investigation conducted? Here a warning is in place. The aim of the type of investigation, of which I am speaking, is not to 'uncover' the existing meaning (or aspect of meaning) of some word or expression, veiled as it were behind the bewildering complexities of common usage. The idea of the philosopher as a searcher of meanings should not be coupled with an idea or postulate that the searched entities actually *are there*—awaiting the vision of the philosopher. If this picture of the philosopher's pursuit were accurate, then a conceptual investigation would, for all I can see, be an *empirical* inquiry into the actual use of language or the meaning of expressions.

Philosophic reflexion on the grounds for calling a thing '*x*' is challenged in situations, when the grounds have not been fixed, when there is no settled opinion as to what the grounds are. The concept still remains to be *moulded* and therewith its logical connexions with other concepts to be *established*. The words and expressions, the use of which bewilder the philosopher, are so to speak *in search of a meaning*.

I would not wish to maintain that the *only* fruitful way of dealing with the problems here is to mould the unmoulded meanings, to make fixed and sharp that which ordinary usage leaves loose and undetermined. It has seemed to me, however, that conceptual inquiries, which take the form of a moulding or shaping of concepts, are particularly suited for the treatment of problems in ethics and some related branches of philosophy (aesthetics, political philosophy).

Am I saying that such inquiries aim at stipulative definitions and other proposals concerning the use of language? And is it in the 'stipulative' nature of their results that the affinity of these inquiries to 'normative' ethics consists?

I do not know exactly, how to answer the questions. To say that conceptual investigations sometimes end in stipulative definitions may be true—in some peculiar sense of 'stipulative' and in a broad and loose sense of 'definition'. But to say thus would be on

5

the whole more misleading than illuminating. Here it is good to remember that the philosopher seldom deals with a single concept only. He moves in a *field* of concepts. This makes him on the whole more interested in logical *distinctions* and *connexions* between parts of the field than in the 'definitions' of local spots in it.

In ethics, conceptual investigations of the type which I have been sketching are a quest for grounds or standards, whereby to judge of good and bad and duty. To have such standards is important to our orientation in the world as moral agents. As we shape our standards for judging of good and bad and duty differently, we shape the conceptual frame of our moral judgments differently. It does not necessarily follow that the judgments too will be different, although they *may* be. But the grounds on which the judgments are based will be different, and therewith their meaning. Our moral 'points of view' will be different.

With the remarks in this and the preceding section I have not wanted to deny that there is an activity deserving the name 'meta-ethics' and another deserving the name 'normative ethics', such that the two are different in kind and sharply distinguishable. But I have wanted to say that there is also a philosophic pursuit deserving the name 'ethics', which shares with a common conception of 'meta-ethics' the feature of being a *conceptual investigation* and with a common conception of 'normative ethics' the feature of aiming at *directing our lives*.

4. The concepts which are relevant to ethics may, for the purpose of a first approximation, be divided into three main groups.

To the first group belong *value*-concepts. The most important member of this group, which is of interest to ethics, is the concept *good* (and its opposites *bad* and *evil*).

Concepts of the second group I shall call *normative*. Here belong, in the first place, the notions of an obligation, a permission, a prohibition, and a right.

To the third group of concepts belong the notion of a human *act* and the notions which are relevant to action, such as choice, deliberation, intention, motive, reason, and will. Closely related to them are the notions of desire, end, need, and want.

Concepts of the third group are sometimes called 'psychological'. They differ, however, from the psychological concepts studied in epistemology in that they have a 'total' character

6

referring to man 'as a whole'—and not to special faculties such as perception or memory or thinking. Perhaps this is a reason for calling those concepts 'anthropological' rather than 'psychological' and for labelling their study a Philosophical Theory of Man or Philosophical Anthropology.

Next we have to notice that there are concepts or groups of concepts, which fall 'between' the three groups and have a 'foothold' in two or more of them.

Firstly, there are concepts which exhibit affinities both to concepts of the first and to concepts of the second group. Examples are the notions of right and wrong and the idea of justice. The three concepts mentioned can be understood in a 'legal' sense which seems to be purely normative. But they can also be understood in a 'moral' sense which relates them to ideas of good and evil and therewith makes them value-tinged.

Secondly, there are concepts which fall somehow between the first and the third group. For example the notions of pleasure and happiness and their contraries. Is pleasure a value-concept or is it a psychological concept? The question is related to the problem, whether pleasantness is a 'natural' or a 'non-natural' characteristic of things and states.

Thirdly, there are concepts which appear to have a foothold in each of the three primary groups. I am thinking chiefly of the generic notion of a *virtue* and of the various traits of character called virtues—such as courage, generosity, industry, temperance, etc. Because of their connexion with the important notion of character they are anthropological (psychological) concepts. They get a normative tinge from their connexion with ideas of a (choice of) right course of action. And finally they are value-tinged due to the connexion between the virtuous and the good and the vicious and the bad man and life.

By a 'narrow approach' to ethics I shall understand an approach in the Kantian tradition of the conceptual autonomy of morals. (Cf. sect. 1.) With it I would contrast a 'broad approach' to ethics. The latter looks for a place for the moral ideas in the more comprehensive network of concepts of the three basic groups mentioned and the intermediate groups.

One could perhaps distinguish between two main directions, which a broad approach to ethics might take. One can look for a foundation of morals so to speak in a 'vertical' dimension, in the needs and wants of man and in the specific nature of man as agent. On this view, a clarification of the concepts of the third group above, the 'anthropological' or 'psychological' ones, is the most urgent preliminary to moral philosophy. Ethics, one could also say, has to be set in the perspective of a Philosophical Anthropology.

One can, however, also look for a foundation of morals in a 'horizontal' dimension, trying to place the moral notions in a broader setting of value-concepts and normative ideas. Ethics then, as it were, emerges as a special branch of a General Theory of Value and Norm.

I do not wish to maintain that the two methods are exclusive of one another or that they can be sharply distinguished. Nor would I say that one of them must be given priority, if one cannot pursue both. The first may be regarded as the more fundamental in the sense that one cannot study norms and values in isolation from the psychological concepts, whereas one can study the latter in relative isolation from the former.

If the method adopted in this treatise has to be placed in the above typology, we shall have to say that it is of the 'horizontal' rather than of the 'vertical' type. It is, furthermore, an approach to ethics from the side of value rather than from the side of norm. (This last has to do with the view which I tend to take on the mutual relations between norms and values. Cf. Chapter VIII.) More specifically still: it is an approach to ethics from a study of the concept of goodness.

It may be true, as has been said, that a better understanding of the concept of a human act and of the related psychological concepts is needed before we can successfully tackle the problems of ethics. But it seems to me equally true that a necessary preliminary to a successful study of moral action, moral goodness, and moral duty is a study of goodness in all its varieties. I do not know that this study had been systematically undertaken before. A beginning to it is attempted in the present work.

5. By the Varieties of Goodness I understand the multiplicity of uses of the word 'good'. A useful preliminary to the study of this multiplicity is to compile a list of familiar uses of the word and try to group them under some main headings.

We speak of a good knife, watch, hammer, razor, and other

artefacts, which are used as instruments for various purposes. We also speak of good dogs, cows, horses, and other animals, whom man has domesticated for his needs and ends. In this same region belong a good car, a good house, a good harbour. Hither also belong all that can be called 'a good way of doing' something, *e.g.* unlocking a door, making one's bed, or memorizing a poem.

I shall group all these uses of 'good' under the head *instrumental* goodness. It is not maintained that whenever 'good' is used as an attribute of, say, 'dog' or 'house' it connotes instrumental goodness. Which form of goodness is meant cannot be seen from the phrase alone, but must be gathered from its use in a context.

We further talk of a good chess-player, runner, orator, driver, general, business-manager, administrator, carpenter, scientist, and artist. A common characteristic of such men is that they are *good at* something. That at which they are good is usually some activity or art, for which a man may possess a natural talent but in which he will also have to undergo some special training before he can excel in it. I shall coin for this excellence the name *technical* goodness.

There are borderline cases between instrumental and technical goodness, for example, the use of 'good' in 'a good salesman' or 'a good servant' or 'a good soldier'. The goodness of a good achievement or performance is often of the form which is here called technical.

As constituting a group of their own I shall regard the uses of 'good' as an attribute of *organs* of the body and *faculties* of the mind: for example, when we speak of a (in the medical sense) good heart, of good eyes, good sight, good memory. I can suggest no better name for this form of the good than *medical* goodness. It is related to and yet characteristically different from technical goodness. One of the differences comes to light in the relationship which the goodness and badness of organs and faculties have to the notions of *health* and *illness*—and through them to the more comprehensive notion, which I propose to call *the good of a being* or *welfare*.

Medicine is *good for* the sick, exercise for the health, manure for the soil, lubrication for the engine, to have good institutions is good for a country, good habits for everybody. Generally speaking, something is said to be *good for* a being, when the doing or having or happening of this thing affects the *good of* that being favourably. For this form of goodness I shall here reserve the name of the *beneficial*. That again, which affects the good of a being adversely, is called harmful, damaging, injurious, 'a bad thing' or, quite often, an evil.

The beneficial is a sub-category of the *useful* or of that which I shall also call *utilitarian* goodness. Related to the useful are the advantageous and the favourable. When we speak of a good plan, a good opportunity, good advice, good luck, good news, we are usually thinking of something which is useful or advantageous for some purpose or pursuit. The beneficial could be distinguished from the 'merely useful' by saying that the useful is that which favours some end or purpose in general, and beneficial that which promotes the special end which is the good of some being. The good of a being, however, is not only a very special end. It is an 'end' only in a special *sense* of the word. The idea of the good of a being as an end, as far as I can see, is the same as the idea, entertained by many philosophers, of (some) beings as ends in themselves.

In English the *substantive* 'good' has at least three meanings, which it is important to keep apart. By 'the good' we can understand goodness, the concept or idea of good. By 'the good' we can also understand that which we have called the good of a being, and for which 'welfare' is another name. Finally, there is the substantive 'good', which has the plural 'goods'. In German these three meanings of the substantive are very handily distinguished by means of the three words *das Gute*, *das Wohl*, and *das Gut* (pl. *die Güter*).

By 'a good' one can understand anything which is a bearer of the value 'good', in short: anything which is good. This is typically a philosopher's use of the term. I shall not adopt it here. By 'a good', however, one can also understand anything which is an end of action or object of desire or want or need. When, in this treatise, I sometimes use 'good-goods' as a pair of technical terms, I use it in the second of the two senses mentioned. Extensionally, the two senses, as easily noted, are largely overlapping.

An important form of goodness, which has so far not been mentioned at all, is the *hedonic* good. We speak of a good smell or taste, a good apple or wine, a good dinner, a good joke, a good holiday or time, good company, good weather. Not always, when 'good' is used in such phrases as those just enumerated does it stand for that which is here called hedonic goodness. Good weather, for example, is not necessarily agreeable weather, which is a hedonic feature; it can also be favourable, say, for the harvest, which is a utilitarian quality.

As the useful, and its sub-form the beneficial, is related to that which a man *wants* and *needs*, in a similar manner the hedonic good is related to that which a man *enjoys* and *likes*—to get, to have, to do, to be. The hedonic, moreover, has many rather different sub-forms. Sometimes the hedonic is near the aesthetic sphere. What a good smell is to the nose, a nice tune is to the ear and a beautiful sight to the eye. The hedonically good is frequently called amusing or entertaining, sometimes refreshing or exhilarating. It can always, I think, be called pleasant. The philosopher's traditional term for it is, as well known, *pleasure*.

Further, there are the uses of 'good', which refer to matters of conduct and character. A *man* can *be* good and *do* good. Good is usually done *to* somebody. When a man does good to some being, his *acts* or deeds are frequently, though not always, called good as well. An act can be done from a good *motive* or with a good *intention*. There is a feature of character called *benevolence* and a preparedness to act called a *good will*. Of this last one philosopher said that it is the only thing in the world which is 'good without qualification and restriction'. It is the good in matters of conduct and character which is, above all, related to the so-called *moral* life of man.

The enumeration and grouping of uses of 'good' which we have given, is very far from exhaustive. Examples could easily be given of uses which fall either completely outside any of the forms, which we have here tentatively distinguished, or which seem to fall somewhere between them. The reader is invited to consider whether the following typical phrases with the word 'good' in them should be classified with our above forms or where he would wish to place them on the logical map: 'good manners', 'good times', 'good incomes', 'good sleep', 'good appetite', 'good-tempered', 'a good conscience', 'a good reputation', 'good as gold', 'a good specimen (sample, example)', 'a good impression', 'a good view', 'a good reason', 'a good idea', 'a good book (work of art)', 'a good wife'.

What has been said in this section should give the reader an impression of the semantic multiplicity and logical wealth of the phenomenon which I have called the Varieties of Goodness. It should also show the inadequacy and artificiality of such schematisms as, say, the traditional classification of all good—sometimes of all value whatsoever—into *two* main types, *viz*. good as a means and good as an end, instrumental and terminal, extrinsic and intrinsic good. We shall make no use of these dichotomies for our present purposes. But I think it is appropriate to warn us against them once and for all.

6. Is there a *unity* among the Varieties of Goodness? If there is a unity, what is its nature? If there is nothing which unites the various forms of the good, how is it that the word 'good' has come to have this multiplicity of uses?

One way to achieve unity in the variety here would be to view the forms of goodness as *species of a generic good*. This possibility would imply two things. Firstly, that there is some feature which is common to all forms of goodness, something in which they all share or participate. Secondly, that there are distinguishing features which, when added to or combined with the generic feature, mark off the various forms of goodness from one another. The generic feature would explain why, instrumentally, technically, etc. good things are *good*. The specific differences would explain why some good things are *instrumentally*, some *technically*, etc. good.

Man and dog are both species of the genus mammal. Individual men and individual dogs all have the essential characteristics of mammals—'the form of mammalhood'—in common. These features 'make' them *mammals*. Other specific features distinguish them *as men* and *as dogs*. Is the relation of the concepts of man and dog to the concept of mammal the logical pattern for understanding the relation of the forms of goodness to the idea of good?

It is against an affirmative answer to this question that Aristotle, if I understand him rightly, is polemical in the sixth chapter of the first book of the *Nicomachean Ethics*. In opposition to Plato, Aristotle did not acknowledge the existence of an Idea of Good. One of his reasons for not acknowledging this seems to have been his opinion that the things called 'good' did *not* compose a genus by virtue of a common characteristic, their goodness. But the exact nature of Aristotle's own view of that, which could conveniently be called the meaning-pattern of the word 'good', is not at all clear to me.

One could distinguish between the Varieties of Goods, when 'goods' means 'good things' (see above, p. 10), and the varieties of Goodness. That both wines and carpenters and lungs can be

12

good is an example of how diverse good things can be. That 'good' sometimes means 'pleasant to taste', sometimes 'skilful', and sometimes 'healthy' is an example of how varied are the forms of goodness. Aristotle did not distinguish clearly between the two sorts of variety. His argument against the Idea of Good draws support from the Varieties of Goods rather than from the Varieties of Goodness. It is obvious, however, that the former variety is *secondary* to the latter. It is not because the good things are such a mixed bunch, that there are so many forms of goodness; but it is because of the multiform nature of goodness that things of the greatest dissimilarity in kind and category can be good. An argument against the view that there exists a generic good must therefore be based on considerations pertaining to the Varieties of Goodness rather than the Varieties of Goods.

It seems to me certain that the forms of goodness are *not* related to a generic good as species are related to a genus. (This is why I speak of 'forms' and not of 'kinds' or 'species' of goodness.) But I do not know how to argue conclusively for my opinion.

No attempt will be made in this work to make clear the notion of a *form* which I use when speaking of the forms of goodness. The relation of a form of X to X is not that of species to genus, nor that of occurrence to disposition, nor that of token to type, nor that of individual to universal. Which the relation is, we shall not discuss.

Of the forms of goodness I sometimes distinguish sub-forms. Thus, for example, three sub-forms of technical and three of hedonic goodness will be mentioned. It is not maintained that the relation between a sub-form of a form of goodness and this form of goodness were the same as the relation between a form of goodness and goodness itself. The nature of the relation of sub-forms to forms is another question which will not be discussed.

7. It is sometimes said that the word 'good' is 'vague and ambiguous'. Could the notions of vagueness and of ambiguity be used for throwing light upon the phenomenon which we have called the Varieties of Goodness?

It is important to distinguish between vagueness and ambiguity. The first is a feature of some *concepts* or, as one could also say here, *meanings*. The second is a characteristic of some *words* (and phrases). For this reason, to refer to something as being 'vague and

13

ambiguous' is a rather confused mode of speech. But the two suggestions, that the meaning of 'good' is vague and that the word 'good' is ambiguous, are worth serious consideration.

I shall say that a concept is vague when there easily occurs uncertainty, whether a thing should be classified as falling under the concept or not, and when this uncertainty cannot be removed by appealing either to (further) *facts* about the case or to existing *criteria* for the application of the concept. Vagueness, in this sense, is highly characteristic of *some* of the forms of the good which we have distinguished, chiefly, I think, of instrumental and technical goodness. For example: whether a carving-knife is good or not for its proper purpose may be difficult to decide, because of vagueness, and similarly whether a man is a good wrestler or not. But it is not because of a vagueness attaching to the idea of good that both a *knife* and a *wrestler* are capable of falling under the concept of goodness. In other words, the fact that some of the typical uses of 'good' are vague cannot account for the fact that there are these many uses (forms of goodness). The notion of vagueness, therefore, is not relevant to an understanding of the phenomenon, which we here call the Varieties of Goodness.

Ambiguity may be defined as a (logically) accidental identity of words standing for different ideas.[1] The suggestion that the Varieties of Goodness were due to an ambiguity of the word would amount to saying some such thing as that 'good' in 'good knife' and in 'good intention' mean two different things, which by accident only are called by the same name.

When a word for a certain concept in a language is ambiguous, then it is pure coincidence if the word for that same concept in another language is in the same way ambiguous too. If 'good' in English really were an ambiguous word, we must wonder at the fact that *bon* in French, *dobrij* in Russian, and *agathos* in Greek also happen to exhibit the same ambiguities. The range of things and kinds of thing called 'good' in English are much the same as the things and kinds of thing called *dobrij* in Russian. This observation alone can be considered decisive evidence against the suggestion that ambiguity was responsible for the existence of the many forms of goodness.

Just as *ambiguity* must be distinguished from *vagueness*, it must

[1] That which has become known in philosophy as 'systematic ambiguity' is not ambiguity in this sense of the term.

14

also not be confused with *analogy*. 'Port' in English is ambiguous. The etymological fact that the name of the wine derives from the place-name 'Oporto', which in its turn is derived from the same root as the English word for harbour, does not imply an affinity between the two *meanings* of 'port'. The word 'deep' provides a good example of analogy. In 'a deep well' the word is used with that which I shall call its *primary* or literal meaning. In 'a deep thought' it is used with a *secondary* or analogical or metaphorical meaning. Analogies are, on the whole, intra-linguistic. This indicates that they are grounded in affinities between meanings and not, as ambiguities are, on linguistic accidents. It is natural to think of the Varieties of Goodness as a variety of meaning-affinities. The idea that the Varieties of Goodness were due to analogy therefore has a certain plausibility.

It seems to me, however, that there are decisive arguments against the idea that the diversity of the forms of the good were a diversity of analogical meanings of the word 'good'. Analogy pre-supposes a *primary* use of the word, with which we must be familiar before we can understand and make use of the analogy. When a word has analogical meanings, it is usually in the individual case clear whether the word is being used in its primary sense or with an analogical meaning. It is clear that the Ocean is deep literally and a thought 'only' metaphorically, that a face is smiling literally and a corn-field metaphorically. Nobody would maintain the reverse here. But is there a literal sense of 'good', of which the other senses are analogical or metaphorical extensions? Is, *e.g.*, instrumental goodness primary and hedonic secondary, or *vice versa*? Or are not both equally basic ('literal')? Is it only by analogy to a good apple and a good knife that we speak of a good act or a good general?

It is, among other things, the obvious difficulty of singling out one (or some) of the uses of 'good' as primary or literal, which speaks strongly against the idea that the variety of forms of good-ness is a variety of primary and analogical meanings of the word 'good'. With this I have not wished to exclude the possibility that there actually are some analogical uses of 'good'. Some such analogical uses may even be philosophically of great interest. Perhaps goodness as an attribute of a supreme being (God) is analogical.

Wittgenstein, in his later writings, used the idea of what he

15

called *family-resemblance*. The idea is related both to vagueness, ambiguity, and analogy and yet different from them all. Family-resemblance gives unity to such concepts as those of language or sentence or number or—to use one of Wittgenstein's favourite examples—the concept of a game. We may call them family-concepts. The philosophic importance—as I see it—of the idea of family-resemblance is that the insight into the family-character of a concept may make us give up an attempt to hunt for its 'essence', *i.e.* for a common feature of all things falling under this concept which would explain to us why these things are classified together.

There is some suggestion in Wittgenstein's writings that goodness were a family-concept, that all uses of 'good' formed a family of cases. There may be *some* truth in this. But I doubt whether it is a useful suggestion on the whole. The question 'What is good?', even when understood as a conceptual and not as an axiological question, seems to me very unlike the question 'What is language?' or, to take a question bordering on problems of value, 'What is art?'. The notion of art is, I think, typically a family-concept. Many problems of philosophical aesthetics, incidentally, seem to me relevantly connected with this character of concepts.

Often symptomatic of the family-nature of a concept is a bewilderment as to whether something 'really' falls under this concept. Is photography really an art? Or the drawing of cartoons? Is the language of bees really a language? Such questions can express a genuine philosophic puzzlement. If goodness were a family-concept, like art, we should expect bewilderment as to whether some of the *forms* of goodness really are forms of *goodness*. But such puzzlement is apparently not felt. We may feel astonished at the fact that a smell as well as a general, rainfall as well as lungs can be good. It may, that is, be astonishing to consider how diverse good things can be. But we should not hesitate to call the pleasant or the skilful or the useful or the healthy forms of the good.

Another difference between goodness and some typical family-concepts seems to be this: New members of a family may originate in the course of history. New games are invented, new forms of linguistic communication are created or can be imagined, also maybe new forms of art. But the forms of goodness do not seem to be in the same way relatable to temporal changes. Conceptual observations may lead a logician or philosopher to distinguish between uses of 'good', which had before been classified together,

16

and regard them as separate forms or sub-forms of goodness. But the forms or sub-forms, thus distinguished, would not be new inventions but familiar phenomena, among which a new difference was noted.

Observations of the sort, which we have here mentioned, seem to me to speak against the idea that goodness were typically a family-concept.

What I have ventured to say in this and the preceding section about the Varieties of Goodness are essentially negative things. The unity in the variety, if there is one, is not that which a genus gives to the species falling under it. Nor does it appear to be a unity of the sort, for which analogy or family-resemblance can be held responsible. Ambiguity and vagueness again do not account for the variety of the forms of the good. The meaning-pattern of 'good' is peculiar and puzzling. It is worth more attention than it has received on the part of philosophic semanticists.[1] It is not, however, my plan to discuss these aspects of the Varieties of Goodness in the present work. I have only wanted to draw attention to some problems in the region.

8. From the problem of the nature of and reasons for the variety of the forms of goodness one may distinguish the problem of the logical relationships between the forms. The two problems are not unrelated. If it could be shown that there is one basic form of the good, in the terms of which all the others can be defined, then the solution to the problem of relationships between the forms would automatically cater also for the problem of the semantic character of their variety. The same would be the case if it turned out that all forms of the good can be defined in the terms of a small number of more basic notions.

There will be no systematic discussion at all in this work of the question of the definability of 'good'; nor of the related problem, whether 'good' is the name of a 'natural' or 'non-natural' characteristic. Occasionally some observations will be made which are relevant to these issues. 'Good' has a number of partial synonyms, which can replace it in some contexts without change of meaning. 'Pleasant', 'skilful', 'healthy', 'useful' are such words. That which

[1] The semantics of 'good' is discussed interestingly in the recent work by Paul Ziff, *Semantic Analysis* (1960).

17

we are going to say of their relation to 'good' will not, however, bear directly on the question of relationships between the forms nor will it contribute to an explanation of their variety.

Certain affinities between the forms of goodness are striking. One is the relation between that which I have called instrumental and technical goodness. Excellence in a skill is technical goodness. On account of their skills men serve various purposes of society. This gives to their skills an aspect of instrumental goodness. There is further a relationship between technical and medical goodness. Good organs like good artisans and professionals do their proper job well. The proper job of the organs is to serve the good of the body, in the last resort the good of man.

Instrumental and utilitarian goodness are closely related, although not to the point of being indistinguishable. Sometimes instrumental goodness can be called a degree of usefulness (utilitarian goodness). A sub-form of utilitarian goodness is the beneficial. It is related to the notion of the good of a being. In this respect it resembles medical goodness.

The relationships mentioned between forms of the good do not, as far as I can see, open up a possibility of defining some of the forms in the terms of some other forms. The notion of *moral goodness*, however, holds a peculiar position in this regard. *It* craves for a definition. The fact that there has been so much dispute about its nature, and relatively little about the nature of the other forms of the good, may be regarded as symptomatic of this very craving. Some philosophers would perhaps regard the craving as satisfiable only through the insight that moral goodness is *not* definable, but *sui generis*, an irreducible form of the good. I would hold the exact opposite of this view. I shall later (Chapter VI) propose an account of moral goodness (as an attribute of acts and intentions), which defines it in terms of the beneficial. Moral goodness is thus not, logically, on a level with the other forms which we have distinguished. It is a 'secondary' form. I shall prefer not to talk of it as a special form of goodness at all.

18

II

INSTRUMENTAL AND
TECHNICAL GOODNESS

1. IN this chapter we shall deal with two of the uses of the word 'good'—with two forms of goodness. These are the two forms, for which I proposed the names the *instrumental* and the *technical* good.

Instrumental goodness is mainly attributed to implements, instruments, and tools—such as knives, watches, cars, etc. Hence the choice of the term 'instrumental'. Substantially the same form of goodness is also attributed to domestic animals—dogs, cows, and horses. This case, however, I shall not discuss here. Later, when speaking of the goodness of human acts, we shall be concerned with the notion of 'a good way of doing something'. It is, if not identical with, at least closely related to that which is here called instrumental goodness.

The goodness called technical relates to ability or skill. Somebody, we say, is *good at* (doing) this or that. The thing, at which a being is good, can often be called an art in the broad sense of *techne* in Greek. Hence my choice of the attribute 'technical' for this form of goodness.

By calling something 'good' in the instrumental or technical sense we often, though not always or necessarily, say that this thing is *good of its kind*. For example: a good knife is, *as a knife*, good. A good general is somebody, who, *as a general*, is good.

Let 'X' be a variable name of an individual thing and 'K' a variable name of a kind of thing. One could make a distinction in meaning between 'X is good as a K' and 'X is, as a K, good'. Usage may be said to hint at this distinction, but cannot be said to uphold it rigorously. When we say of some thing that it is *good as a K*, we often mean that, although this thing is *not* a K, it nevertheless can be used with some advantage in the way K's are normally used, or performs with some success in the way characteristic of K's. When, on the other hand, we say of a thing that it is, *as a K, good*, we usually mean that this thing *is* a K and, moreover, a good one.

The possibility of making the above distinction shows that not every attribution of instrumental or technical goodness is an attribution of a goodness of its kind to some thing. When 'X is good as a K' is so used as to imply that X is not a K, then the goodness attributed to X in the judgment is not a goodness of X's kind.

It seems to be the case that, *whenever instrumental or technical goodness is in question*, then the judgment that X is a good K attributes to the individual thing a goodness of its kind. The phrase 'X is a good K' may then be regarded as identical in meaning with 'X is, as a K, good'.

It would, however, be a mistake to think that every judgment to the effect that X is a good K attributes to X a goodness of its kind. For example: When we call X a good act or a good habit, we are not saying that X is an act or a habit and *as such* good. The phrase 'X is a good habit' is not identical in meaning with 'X is, as a habit, good'. Nor is 'X is a good act' identical with 'X is, as an act, good'. This is so because, so far as I can see, there exists no (instrumental, technical, or other form of) excellence, which is peculiar to acts *as acts* or to habits *as habits*.

2. To attribute instrumental goodness to some thing is *primarily* to say of this thing that *it serves some purpose well*. An attribution of instrumental goodness *of its kind* to some thing presupposes that there exists some purpose which is, as I shall say, *essentially associated* with the kind and which this thing is thought to serve well. An attribution of instrumental goodness *of its kind* to some thing is thus *secondary* in the sense that it logically presupposes a judgment of goodness *for some purpose*. Not everything which is good for some purpose, also belongs to some kind which is essentially associated with this purpose. Therefore not every primary attribution of instrumental goodness for some purpose to a thing also serves as basis for a secondary attribution of instrumental goodness of its kind to this thing.

20

By calling a purpose (or set of purposes) 'essentially associated' with a kind K I mean that no thing X will qualify as a member of the kind K, unless it *can serve* the purpose (or some of the purposes of the set) in question. Capacity of serving a characteristic purpose, in other words, is a logically necessary condition of membership of the kind.

A purpose (or member of a set of purposes) which is essentially associated with a kind K, I shall call a K-purpose. Ability to serve a K-purpose is a *functional* characteristic of members of the kind K. Beside functional, *morphological* characteristics may be necessary conditions of membership of the kind. Nothing is a hammer unless it can be used for driving in nails. A knife, if it has a thick and heavy handle, may be used for driving in nails and thus used as a hammer. But since the morphological features of knives and hammers are in any case distinct, this use of the knife as hammer does not make it a hammer. Therefore we do not ordinarily say that a knife which serves the purpose of a hammer well is a good hammer, nor do we, on that account, call it a good knife. (But we can quite correctly say that it is good *as* a hammer.)

Assume that there are several purposes, which are essentially associated with the kind K. Then it may happen that a certain X serves some of these K-purposes well, but others not well or even not at all. Can we then call X a good K? Can we say both that X is a good K and that X is not a good K?

Since the possibility, which we have just mentioned, is altogether realistic, consider what we *do say* in such cases. Knives serve many purposes. Some knives are suited for carving meat, others for sharpening a pencil, others for cutting open a book, others for still other purposes. A knife which carves meat well, could perhaps also be used for cutting the pages of a book. But it would hardly serve the second purpose well. A knife suited for cutting paper could probably not be used for cutting meat at all. This inequality in the capacity of serving different purposes is a ground why we distinguish between various kinds of knife, or sub-kinds of the kind 'knife', such as carving-knives, paper-knives, table-knives, razor-knives, etc. according to the specific purposes which they are designed to serve. Is there any limit to this distinction of sub-kinds according to specifications of a generic purpose? Assume that a carving-knife carves mutton well but not pork. Is it then a good carving-knife or is it not a good one? We can call it either, or both.

There is nothing illogical in saying of a knife that it is both good and not good, when this means that it is good in some respect but not good in another. But we can also say of the knife in our example that it is a good mutton-cutting-knife but not a good pork-cutting-knife and regard the two as distinct kinds of knife, essentially associated with two distinct purposes. The criterion of *distinctness* of kind and of purpose would here be the inequality in the goodness of the performances of the two knives.

It would be dogmatic, however, to maintain that every kind K, which is essentially associated with a set of purposes, can be split up into a definite number of sub-kinds $K_1, \ldots, K_n$ such that each sub-kind is essentially associated with at most one purpose.

3. What is the 'opposite' of a *good K*, when 'good' connotes instrumental goodness?

It is noteworthy that the adjective 'good' in English and the corresponding word in many other languages has *several* opposites. I shall not stop to discuss why this is the case. The fact is striking, and its explanation could therefore be interesting.

Two of the opposites of 'good' in English are 'bad' and 'evil'. The opposites of the German 'gut' are 'schlecht' and 'übel'; the opposites of the Finnish 'hyvä' are 'huono' and 'paha'.

In German the opposite of an instrumentally good K would normally be called 'schlecht', and in Finnish it would be called 'huono'. But in English this opposite is *not* ordinarily called 'bad', although 'bad' (not 'evil') in most cases is the English equivalent of 'schlecht' and 'huono'. The normal English word for the opposite of an instrumentally good thing is the adjective '*poor*'.[1]

Thus, for example, tools such as knives and hammers are called 'poor' rather than 'bad', if they do not serve their proper purposes well. Similarly, it would be more natural to call a watch-dog 'poor' than to call it 'bad', if it were unsatisfactory for its purpose. If we called it 'bad', we should thereby imply that the dog is dangerous or a cause of annoyance, *e.g.* because it is ill-tempered and apt to bite members of the family. If, on the other hand, the dog were deaf or blind and did not easily notice approaching strangers, it would be a *poor* watch-dog, not a *bad* one. A hammer, the handle of which easily breaks into pieces, is a poor hammer for the pur-

---

[1] I am indebted for this observation to Professor Norman Malcolm.

pose of driving in big nails in a piece of hard wood. A hammer, which is apt to damage the wood, might be called 'bad', even if it is very efficient for driving in nails.

The use in English of 'bad' and 'poor' in connexion with things, which serve purposes, thus seems to be indicative of a conceptual distinction. By calling an X, which is supposed to serve some purpose, *poor*, we imply that it does not serve its purpose well. This judgment is, so to speak, in the dimension of *instrumental* goodness. By calling an X, which is supposed to serve some purpose, *bad* we imply that apart from the way X serves its purpose—and it may serve this purpose well—X has some other features, which we regard as unwanted or undesirable and which reveal themselves in the use of X. This judgment is *not* in the dimension of instrumental goodness.

4. Granted that the opposite of 'good' in the dimension of instrumental goodness is 'poor' and not 'bad' (or 'evil'), the question may be raised: *How* are the instrumentally good and the instrumentally poor opposed to one another? Do 'good' and 'poor' here name *contraries* or *contradictories*?

Is, for example, a knife which does not serve its proper purpose well, *ipso facto* a poor knife? How do we actually judge of such cases? The practice, it would seem, is not rigorously fixed. But sometimes—I am inclined to say, usually—we do judge in such a way that an instrument, which definitely does not serve its proper purpose well, is thereby said to be poor for this purpose. Under this way of judging, to be instrumentally poor is to fall short of the standards or requirements of instrumental goodness. The poor K is the not-good K. Poorness, on this view, is a *privation*. It consists in the absence of goodness. When one of two terms names the privation, absence, or lack, of the thing named by the other term, then their meanings are contradictorily, and not contrarily, opposed to one another.

What may make us, even accepting the view of instrumental poorness as a privation, yet hesitate to call the instrumentally good and poor contradictorily opposed, is the fact that it may be difficult to judge *definitely* whether a K is, for its proper purpose, good. This is so because of the vagueness of the notion. (We shall discuss the question of vagueness in the next section.) But the fact that the border between the instrumentally good and the instrumentally

23

poor is vague and not sharp is, in my opinion, not an adequate ground for calling the two notions contrarily, and not contradictorily opposed.

It should be added in this place that the negation of the proposition that X is a good K is capable of two interpretations. That X is not a good K can mean either that X is not a K and therefore *a fortiori* not a good K *or* that X is a K though not a good one. If the negative proposition is understood in the first way, then that X is not a good K does not entail that X is a poor K.

Similarly, that X does not serve a certain purpose well can mean either that X does not serve this purpose at all and therefore *a fortiori* does not serve it well *or* that X serves this purpose, though not well. Only when the negative proposition is understood in the second way, does the proposition that X does not serve a certain purpose well entail the proposition that X serves this purpose poorly.

Of the X which is not a K it is true to say, not only that it is not a good K, but also that it is not a poor K. And of the X which does not serve a certain purpose at all it is true to say, not only that it does not serve this purpose well, but also that it does not serve this purpose poorly. The existence of things which are, in the senses explained, both not-good and not-poor constitutes no ground for saying that 'good' and 'poor' are contraries and not contradictories.

5. Are judgments of instrumental goodness 'objectively' true or false? This is a difficult question, worth—I think—a much more thoroughgoing discussion than can be given to it here.

It is convenient to tackle the problem of objectivity first for judgments of instrumental betterness. It is also convenient to distinguish some main types of case, when a thing is judged instrumentally good or better than another. I shall here briefly discuss four cases.

First case. Someone says of one knife that it is better than another. He is asked, why he thinks thus. He answers that the first knife is sharper. But why should the sharper knife be the better knife? All depends upon the purpose for which it is being used. Our man is evidently not using the knife to cut the pages of a book. For then sharpness is no particular virtue of the knife. Assume that he is carving meat. Other things being equal, the sharper the knife, the less will it tear the surface of the slices cut. He wants the slices to be as smooth as possible. *Therefore* the sharper knife is, in his judgment, the better knife.

In this example there are two relationships worth special attention. The one is between the sharpness of the knife-edge and the smoothness of the cut. The other is between the smoothness of the cut and the goodness (or betterness) of the knife. The first—between 'sharper' and 'smoother'—is a *causal* connexion. That the sharper knife should give the smoother cut is no logical necessity. For some materials it may not even be true. The second—between 'smoother' and 'better'—is a *logical* connexion. If the user of the instrument wants to cut the smoothest possible slices, then the knife which cuts more smoothly necessarily serves this purpose better. 'Better knife', one feels inclined to say, here *means* 'smoother-cutting knife'.[1] But then it should be observed that it is only in this particular setting: wanting to cut as smoothly as possible, that there is this meaning-connexion between the two phrases.

It is important to keep these two questions apart: *What* does the subject want to do? and *How* does he want to do this? The answer to the first question is, in the case under discussion, that the subject wants to carve slices of meat. This is the purpose, for which he uses the knife—the *K*-purpose as we called it. The answer to the second question is that he wants the slices to be as smooth as possible. This I propose to call the *subjective setting* of the purpose.

So far as I can see, the phrase 'this is a good *K*' or 'this *K* is better than that other *K*' makes sense only within a given subjective setting of the *K*-purpose. That *X* is a good *K*, we said, means that *X* serves some *K*-purpose well. The word 'well' is an adverb which qualifies the way of serving the purpose. It is natural to think that the meaning of this adverb in the particular case should be given by another adverb or adverbial phrase, which also qualifies a way of serving this same purpose. In our example the key-word, which gave meaning to 'well', was the adverb 'smoothly'.

It should be observed that the man, in our example, who judges

---

[1] Adopting Hare's distinction between *meaning* and *criterion*, we could say that being smoother-cutting is here a criterion of being better, but that nevertheless the meaning of 'smoother-cutting' is different from the meaning of 'better'. Cf. Hare, *The Language of Morals* (1952), Ch. 7. As Hare himself observes (*op. cit.,* p. 110), we commonly call 'meaning' that which he calls 'criterion', when rating the excellence of something. See also above, Ch. I, Sect. 3.

that the sharper knife is better, is here judging that the sharper knife cuts more smoothly. He is not *judging* that the smoother-cutting knife is better; this is presupposed in the judgment. He is judging a causal property of the sharper knife. This judgment of his is 'objectively' true or false. This is: the judgment is true or false—the word 'objectively' is in fact redundant. The man who makes the judgment can be mistaken. Assume that, contrary to what he believed to be the case, the sharper knife does *not* give the smoother cut. Then the sharper knife is not the better knife. His value-judgment was false.

Following an established terminology, I shall call sharpness in our example a *good-making property* of knives. Being sharper can then be called a better-making property. A good- or better-making property of a thing, it should be observed, is thus *causally* related to the goodness or betterness of this thing. It has, however, this relationship by virtue of the fact that it is causally related to some other property which is, in its turn, *logically* related to the goodness or betterness of the thing *within a certain subjective setting of a purpose*.[1]

'Smooth' and also 'sharp' are words with a *vague* meaning. A surface which is judged smooth by one, may be judged rough by another and more demanding judge. And the same holds true for 'sharp' and 'blunt'. This vagueness of the 'descriptive' or 'naturalistic' adjectives will here entail a corresponding vagueness of the value term 'good'. In the case which we are discussing, the goodness of a good knife is exactly as vague as the smoothness of a smooth surface. This is a noteworthy feature. But to call value-judgments 'subjective' because of the vagueness which they often have would, I think, be more misleading than illuminating.

Another noteworthy thing is that, although the absolutes 'smooth' and 'sharp' are words with a *vague* meaning, the compara-

[1] Writers, who have employed the term 'good-making property', have in general not distinguished between such properties, which are *causally*, and such which are *logically* related to the goodness of a thing. Once the distinction has been noted, the question may be raised, to which kind of property the term 'good-making' should apply. This question is here answered by calling the causally relevant properties good-making. We could equally well have decided to call the logically relevant properties by that name, or even let the term cover both kinds of properties. The important thing is not, how we understand the philosopher's term 'good-making', but that we should be aware of the two different ways, the causal and the logical, in which a 'naturalistic' property can be relevant to the goodness of something.

tives 'smoother' and 'sharper' are not. Therefore, when *being better* is logically consequent upon *being smoother*, the comparative value-attribute is not vague either. It seems to be largely true to say that, speaking of instrumental goodness, the absolutes 'good' and 'poor' are vague, whereas the comparatives 'better' and 'poorer' are not vague. But this, it should be noted, depends upon the nature of some 'underlying' naturalistic attribute—such as 'smooth' or 'sharp' or 'rough' or 'blunt'—and not directly upon the nature of instrumental goodness. To think that the meaning of 'good' is intrinsically vague, would seem to me to be a mistake.

Second case. Someone says of one knife that it is better than another. When asked why he judges thus, he says that it cuts more smoothly and that smoothness is what he wants. Here is no mention of a better-making property. Perhaps the user is not aware of one. The two knives are equally sharp, the one just cuts more smoothly than the other. There may exist some explanation for this, some better-making property, but it is not known—at least not to the user.

The absence of reference to a better-making property from the value-judgment does not alter its status with regard to 'objectivity'. What is being judged in the judgment that this is the better knife is simply that this knife cuts more smoothly than the other. (It is again presupposed in the judgment that a smoother-cutting knife *ipso facto* is a better knife.) The judgment can be true or false.

It may be noted in passing that judgments of instrumental goodness usually, even if not necessarily, contain a *conjectural* element. This refers to future uses of the instrument. We would hardly say that this knife *is* better than that other knife, if we happened to be speaking exclusively of its performances in the past. Saying that the knife is better involves some expectations about its future performances. In these expectations we may become disappointed. Should this happen, we may also wish to say that we were mistaken in thinking this the better knife.

Third case. Someone again says of a knife that it is better than another. As a reason for judging thus he gives that the first knife suits *him* better for the purpose for which he is using the knife. He has, let us assume, relatively small hands and the knife, which he thinks better, has a smaller handle than the other knife. Another person, whose hands are bigger, may be better served by the other knife for exactly the same purpose. The value-judgment now contains an implicit reference to the user of the instrument.

The implicit reference to user can be, and often is, made explicit by means of inserting the phrase 'for me' or 'for so-and-so' into the formulation of the value-judgment. 'Better for me', 'better for him', 'better for children' are phrases which make sense, when instrumental goodness is concerned. It should be observed, however, that the sense of the sentence 'this knife is better for me', which we are now discussing, is *not* that this knife serves *my* purposes better than, say, some other man's, but that it serves *me*, but not necessarily another man, better for this very purpose.

The fact that a judgment of instrumental goodness contains reference, explicit or implicit, to a user does not alter its character of an 'objectively' true or false judgment. That my hands are relatively small may be an objective fact about my bodily constitution. Therefore it may also be an objective fact that this knife with the smaller handle is better for me than the one with the bigger handle. In judging that the knife with the smaller handle is better for me I may, however, be mistaken.

Fourth case. A man judges one knife better than another. When asked for reasons he says that he just likes it better, just prefers its use to that of the other knife. Even in this case, our man may be able to give further reasons why he likes the use of the one knife better than the use of the other. But these further reasons, if there are any and there need not be, make no reference to the efficiency with which the instruments serve their purpose. He prefers the one knife, not because it cuts better but, say, because it looks nicer or he has some special attachment to it. (Perhaps the knife belonged to his grandfather.)

In the case now under discussion, I shall call the judgment of value *subjective*. Our man does not judge anything about which he can be mistaken. We could also say that he is not *judging* anything at all, but merely giving verbal expression to his preference or to his liking.

This case, however, when the judgment is subjective, is not a case of instrumental goodness at all. For, that X is a better K than Y should mean, according to the explanation we gave earlier, that X serves some K-purpose better than Y. But here it was assumed that the so-called betterness of the one instrument had nothing at all to do with its superiority in serving a purpose. Hence betterness, which is grounded on sheer preference or liking, is not *instrumental* betterness.

The reason why I nevertheless mention this fourth case, is that although it is in principle distinct from the three first and is not a case of instrumental goodness at all, it may in practice be difficult to know whether a value-judgment is of the fourth type or of one of the three first. Consider a man who says of one knife that it is better than another on the ground that it has a pleasanter feel, at least in his hands. The pleasanter feel could be a better-making property in the sense that it causally affects his results in cutting. He cuts, say, more smoothly with the knife of pleasanter feel— perhaps even with the knife of pleasanter (nicer, more attractive) look. This is not an altogether unrealistic possibility. If it should be true, the case belongs to one of the three first, which we discussed. Then the judgment of betterness is objectively true or false. But the pleasanter feel *need not* causally affect the result in cutting at all. Then the judgment of betterness is, as we have said, subjective, but also no judgment of *instrumental* betterness.

Our conclusion is thus that genuine judgments of instrumental goodness are always objectively true or false judgments. This 'objectivity' of theirs is not contradicted or voided by the facts that in such judgments a subjective setting of the purpose is necessarily presupposed, that they may be vague, and that they may contain reference to a user.

The question may be raised, to what extent is it possible to make and uphold general statements about good-making properties? Is, *e.g.*, the sharper knife *always* the better knife? Certainly not, already for the reason that we are not always using knives for purposes, to which the smoothness of the cut is intrinsically relevant. But even when we *do* use knives for such purposes, is it always the case that, other things being equal, we are better served by the sharper knife? Whether we are may depend upon the material to be cut. But if it is true to say that knives are mostly used for purposes, to the subjective settings of which smoothness of cut is intrinsically relevant, and that sharper knives cut more smoothly through most materials, then it is also true to say that sharpness or being sharper is *on the whole* a good- or better-making property of knives. It is with such rough empirical generalizations that we shall have to be content in matters of instrumental, and many other forms of, goodness.

6. Since judgments of instrumental goodness are true or false, shall we say that sentences expressing such judgments are *descriptive sentences?* The term 'descriptive', when applied to a sentence, strongly suggests a certain *use* of the sentence under consideration, *viz.* for purposes of describing. Now it would not be correct to say that instrumental value-judgments are ordinarily made for the sake of describing or conveying information. Therefore it seems to me misleading to make the 'objectivity' of judgments of instrumental goodness a ground for calling sentences expressing such judgments 'descriptive'.

But even if instrumental value-judgments were never made for the sake of describing, it would be correct to say that they have a *descriptive content* (or force or import)—and that this descriptive content is essential to the use of the corresponding value-sentences. Their descriptive content is the possible fact which, if actually there, makes the judgment true. To call this descriptive content the *sense* (or why not 'meaning'?) of the sentences expressing the judgment seems to me unobjectionable.

Thus, for example, the descriptive content of the judgment 'the sharper knife is better' might be that the sharper knife gives the smoother cut. If it is asked what so-and-so meant by calling the sharper knife better, the answer could very well be that he *meant* that it cut more smoothly.

The account of the sense of value-sentences should, in my opinion, be separated from the account of the use of such sentences. The idea that to give an account of the meaning is to give an account of the use, in combination with the important observation that instrumental and other value-sentences are not ordinarily used for purposes of describing, has encouraged an one-sided view of the semantics and logic of evaluative discourse—one-sided chiefly because it underrates the rôle of truth in connexion with valuations.

7. One of the most important uses of 'good', we are told by many recent philosophers, is for *commending*. One commends the use of a thing for a certain purpose. This is not the only but, I think, the most common case of commending. One would therefore think that there is a specially close connexion between commending and

instrumental goodness. This, I believe, is true. When 'good' is used for commending, it is very frequently instrumental goodness that is in question.

What is the force or rôle of the word 'good' or 'better', when we commend things which are thought to possess some instrumental excellence? One could answer that this rôle would not exist, unless the person, who commends a thing, by calling it 'good' or 'better', states a *reason* why the person whom he addresses should use the commended thing for some purpose of his. But how can the instrumental goodness or betterness of a thing constitute a reason for using it? In the assumption that it constitutes such a reason, two presuppositions may be said to be involved. The first is that the person to whom we commend the thing is actually in pursuit of an end or purpose, which the commended thing, on account of its goodness, is supposed to serve well or at least better than some other thing. The second is that, if a person is in pursuit of an end or purpose, which the use of any one of a number of things will serve, then he will be more inclined to use a thing which serves this purpose better than one which serves it less well. Or to put it otherwise: in commending it is presupposed that, relative to a given purpose, we *prefer* the use of the better instrument and therefore shall, when presented with a choice, choose it. The use of the word 'good' for purposes of commending thus hinges upon a connexion between goodness and *preferential choice*. The nature of this connexion we shall now briefly discuss for the special case of *instrumental* goodness.

8. Is it always and necessarily the case that we prefer the use of the better instrument to the use of the less good one, granting that there is a choice and that we pursue the ends, which the instruments in question serve?

It is easy to think of exceptions. For example: We admit that X is a better K than Y. But we prefer Y, because it is less expensive. Does this not mean that we prefer—indeed very often *have* to prefer—the less good to the better? One could answer as follows: What we prefer here is not the use of Y to that of X *for the purpose* essentially associated with K's. We prefer the use of Y to that of X within a larger setting of purposes. We do not only want to do that for which a K is needed but also things for which a L and a M and a N are needed. If we used the best possible K within our choice

31

for *its* purpose, we could afford the use either of no instruments at all or only of exceedingly poor ones for those other purposes. So the *K* which we choose is, after all, the one which we think on the whole best serves our ends. By admitting that it is less good than another *K*, we are in fact saying that we should, of course, have preferred the second one to the one we actually chose, had considerations relating to those other ends and purposes been immaterial.

I think that the lesson taught by this example can be generalized as follows: Whenever we prefer the use of a *K* which we judge poorer to the use of a *K* which we judge better, there is only an apparent exception to the rule that we always prefer, *for its proper purpose*, the instrumentally better thing. For the purpose, for which we prefer the poorer *K*, is not the *K*-purpose relative to which this *K* is judged less good than some other *K*. It is some other purpose or complex of purposes, which the poorer *K* actually is thought to serve better than the better *K*. Thus of the two *K*'s we in fact chose the better, *viz.* for present purposes, though not the better *K*. Generally speaking: It is not logically possible to choose *with a view to a purpose* the use of an instrument which is *judged* less good for that purpose than another instrument.

This in no way contradicts the fact that it is possible to choose with a view to a purpose something which *is* for that very purpose less good than another thing. We are here confronted with an instance of the distinction between the *real* and the *apparent* good. A man can be mistaken about the goodness of an instrument for some purpose of his. He *judges* (considers, thinks) *X* better than *Y*, and chooses *X*. But *Y is* better.

We can now command a clearer view of the relation between commending and instrumental goodness. Commending on grounds of goodness, we said, would be pointless, if there did not exist a relation between instrumental goodness and preferential choice. This connexion, we have suggested, is *not* that we necessarily prefer the better. It is that we necessarily prefer that which we judge to be better—assuming that the preferential choice is with a view to the purpose involved in the judgment of instrumental betterness.

9. Let us now turn to 'technical goodness'. What is here understood by that name could also be called the goodness of ability or

capacity or skill. I do not wish to say that the last three substantives are always perfect synonyms. But the man who is a technically good so-and-so, is commonly also said to be an able or capable or skilful so-and-so. And here the three last adjectives could be replaced by 'good' without alteration of meaning.

When technical goodness is concerned, the judgment that X is a good K or a better K than Y attributes to the things in question an excellence—higher and lower in the case of the comparative judgment—of their kind. To be a technically good (or better) K is to be a K and good (or better) *as such*. The technically, like the instrumentally, good K is a good-as-a-K K.

When members of a kind K are classified as technically good or not good, better or inferior K's, it is presupposed in the value-judgments that membership of the kind is essentially tied to ability to perform a certain *activity*. That the tie is essential means that any individual, in order to qualify as a member of the kind, must be able to perform, must master this activity. The good K is a K, who is *good at* the proper activity of K's. (The logic of technical goodness, one could therefore also say, is the logical grammar of the phrase 'good at'.)

It follows from what has been said that an attribution of technical goodness *of its kind* to some being is a *secondary* valuation. Its basis, the *primary* valuation, is a judgment to the effect that this being is *good at* something.

Examples of uses of the phrase 'a good K' in the sense now under discussion are provided by what is ordinarily meant when we speak of a good chess-player, runner, car-driver, orator, carpenter, general, business-man, teacher, scientist, etc. The thing which the good K is, as a K, good at doing, is sometimes a fairly simple and well-defined activity, which is named by *one* word in language. A good chess-player is good at playing chess, a good orator good at public speaking. What is a good general good at? To say that he is good at conducting armies would be to take a somewhat over-simplified view of the variegated tasks which generals are supposed to handle. Yet a good general would not be a *good general* ('a good-as-a-general general') unless he were good at just those activities (or some of them), the skilful performing of which constitutes the excellence of generals.

People are, by nature, more or less talented for the art or activity which is essentially connected with a kind K of agents. Some of

33

these activities, for example running or speaking, are such that practically every man learns to perform them. Others are typically such, in which not all men share—for example playing chess or conducting an orchestra. But irrespective of whether the activity belongs to the one category or to the other, it seems to be generally true that a man, whom we call a *K*, must not only be able to perform this activity, but must have undergone some *special* training to acquire and develop the skill or take a *special* interest in exercising it. Not everybody, who can run, is a runner, nor is everybody, who can speak, an orator—not even a poor one. Is everybody, who can play chess, to be termed a chess-player? There are no fixed rules for the use of the word. But by calling a person a chess-player we would normally indicate *more* than merely that he knows how to play chess; say, that he is keen on the game or that he has taken pains to develop his skill at playing it.

It follows from what has been said that in order to qualify as a *K* one must, at least in many cases, not only master the appropriate art or activity, but master it with some degree of distinction or excellence. One cannot become a singer unless one learns to sing *rather well*—or an orator unless one learns to talk eloquently. A good singer is therefore a person who sings well in *two* respects: first as compared to how people in general sing, and second as compared to how singers sing.

There is at this point an analogy between kinds of men, who may be good at something, and kinds of instrument, who may serve a purpose well. Just as nothing is, say, a knife merely on the ground that it *can* be used to serve some of a knife's proper purposes, similarly nobody qualifies, say, as a singer merely because he *can* sing. When we are concerned with kinds, the members of which may excel in instrumental goodness, the additional criteria which the thing has to satisfy are, it would seem, typically morphological criteria—such as the characteristic shape of a certain tool. When again the question is of kinds, the members of which may excel (as members of their kind) in technical goodness, the additional criteria have to do with skill above the average or with social status such as profession or office—for which special training is often prescribed.

10. In the realm of instrumental goodness, we said, the opposite of a *good K* is a *poor K*. An instrument is sometimes also said to be a

34

bad instrument. It seems to be the case, however, that we call instruments bad chiefly on account of some detrimental or otherwise unwanted 'side-effects' of their use—and not on account of a deficiency in the way they serve their proper purposes. This observation can be made a ground for saying that there is no such thing as *instrumental* badness. (Cf. sect. 3.)

It is easily noticed that the opposite of a technically good *K* is sometimes called 'poor' and sometimes 'bad'. The question may now be raised, whether we can make a distinction here between 'poor' and 'bad', which would correspond to the distinction between the two terms in the sphere of instrumental excellence. The answer seems to be that there are no strong reasons for making such a distinction in the sphere of technical excellence. This is so because, although the practising of activities may have unwanted 'side-effects' (*e.g.* on the health of the persons who practise them), we do not make the badness of such effects a ground for calling the agents themselves bad members of their kind. This seems to me a noteworthy difference in the way we attribute badness to instruments and to people.

In the realm of technical excellence, both 'poor' and 'bad' are thus used as genuine opposites of 'good' and may be regarded as synonyms.

Do 'good' on the one hand, 'poor' and 'bad' on the other hand connote contraries or contradictories in the realm of technical goodness? I would answer the question in the same way as the corresponding question about 'good' and 'poor' in the realm of instrumental goodness. The relation between the opposites is one of contradictoriness rather than one of contrariness. The technically not-good *K* is the technically poor or bad *K*, and conversely. But, as in the case of instrumental goodness, the border between the good and the not-good is *vague*.

To be a bad or poor *K* in the technical sense is to suffer a *privation*. A man is a poor chess-player, a bad runner, a poor craftsman if his performance as chess-player, runner, or craftsman is not up to certain standards of excellence. He is not bad or poor by virtue of having some 'excellence in the negative direction'. Only in jest do we say of the unskilful craftsman that he excels in performing his art badly.

11. For measuring excellence in some activity, *i.e.* technical

goodness, certain tests are sometimes available. One may distinguish two main types of test: *competitive* tests and *achievement* tests.

Who, for example, is the better chess-player of two? Playing chess, like many other games, is essentially a competitive activity. Success in competition is therefore here a primary sign of goodness. If X invariably or usually beats Y, he is better at the game. If Y usually beats Z, it is likely but by no means certain that X will usually beat Z and thus be better than Z too. The beating-relation is not necessarily transitive; and to think that the relation of betterness is, or must be, transitive for all forms of goodness would be a distorting rationalization.

Consider next the question, who is the better runner of two. Here we have, in addition to competitive tests, also achievement tests for measuring the goodness of the performance. These latter consist in recording the time which it takes a man to run a certain distance. The two types of test are both used and both useful for the same purpose, *viz.* for the purpose of determining the relative excellence of two or more runners. They are, furthermore, *independent* tests. By this I mean that they need not give concordant results. Assume that a man beats the record, when he runs alone, but is regularly beaten in competition. Maybe his nerves fail him. Is he then a good runner? We could say that he is a good solo-runner but a bad competition-runner, and make the discordance of the results in testing a ground for regarding solo-running and competition-running as two distinct activities.

Whenever there are two or more independent tests for measuring excellence in something, it is possible to regard the tests as measuring excellence in two or more (logically) independent activities. When the tests give concordant results, it is usually not urgent to distinguish the activities. When they give discordant results, it may become urgent to distinguish them—or else we shall have to say that one and the same man is both good and not good at the same thing. But sometimes we prefer to express ourselves thus.

The results of testing can be either *causally* or *logically* related to excellence in the activity. We perform certain measurements on a man and watch him go through certain movements and say: he must be good at long distance running. We then regard certain features and capacities of a man as good-making with a view to some activity. It is clear that judgments of goodness, which are based on such tests, can always be mistaken.

36

Tests of technical goodness, which rely on good-making properties, I shall call *symptom*-tests or tests by symptoms. Such competitive and achievement tests, the results of which bear logically on goodness in the activity, might be called *criteria*-tests or tests by criteria.

Be it mentioned in passing that it is sometimes debatable, whether a given test should be regarded as a test by symptoms or by criteria. A well-known case in point are intelligence-tests. Is the one who scores more points in the test than another *ipso facto* more intelligent, or is his achievement only symptomatic of greater intelligence? When it is said, as has often been done, that intelligence *is* what the intelligence-tests measure, then the results of the tests are regarded as logically connected with the measured ability. The methodological problems connected with intelligence-tests we shall not discuss here however. Goodness of intelligence is not of the variety which I call technical goodness, but of a related variety.

Judgments of technical goodness are objectively true or false in all cases in which there are criteria-tests, *i.e.* tests the results of which are related logically to excellence in the activity. As already noted, there are such tests in *many* cases: in competitive games, for example, and in athletic activities whether competitive or not. But are there in *all* cases?

Consider for example the various skilled professions: soldiers, teachers, doctors, etc. Which tests will decide whether a doctor is good or not, or better than another?

Various so-called tests which a man has to undergo in the course of his training—university examinations and similar things—are primarily tests for measuring whether he has acquired the art in question and is henceforth qualified as being a K: a doctor, teacher, etc. For measuring goodness in the art they may have a secondary value, *viz*. as symptom-tests. The results in these tests do not bear logically on excellence in the activity. 'He must be a good doctor, considering his brilliant records from the medical school' is no logically conclusive argument.

The existence of the various professions answers to various needs of society. Doctors, teachers, etc. serve the ends and purposes of men and institutions. Their goodness as doctors, teachers, etc. depends to a large extent upon how well they do this. But the question, how well they do this, is a question of instrumental goodness. This, I believe, is an important point. To be a technically good K, we have said, requires that there is an activity essentially associated with membership of the kind K. But this activity may in its turn be *essentially* connected with some end or purpose, which members of K can serve thanks to the fact that they master the art of K-ing. Doctors are 'essentially' needed to cure the sick. If they were not, our idea of a good doctor would be quite different from what it is now—the medical profession would, in fact, be a different profession.

When there is this essential tie between activity and purpose, then technical goodness is ultimately measured in the terms of instrumental goodness. This is the case with goodness in most so-called professions. It is appropriate to say that technical goodness is here *secondary* to instrumental goodness, since the first is logically dependent upon the second. But in the case of the good chess-player or the good athlete, technical goodness is *not* secondary to instrumental or to any other form of goodness. Goodness at doing something, which is not assessed ultimately in the terms of some other form of goodness, we may call *pure* technical goodness.

Since judgments of instrumental goodness are objectively true or false, the same will hold good of such judgments of technical goodness, which are, in the sense explained, secondary to judgments of instrumental goodness.

Is it always the case that technical goodness either has criteria-tests of its own or criteria-tests, which are derived from standards of instrumental goodness? Consider, for example, excellence in science, or in philosophy, or arts in the aesthetic sense of the term.

Of those activities, in which excellence has no tests of its own or is not secondary to instrumental goodness, certain features seem to be common and characteristic. *One* is that they exhibit a *creative* aspect, which makes them differently related to teaching and training in comparison with other arts and activities. One can be taught to paint or to compose music, but one cannot be taught to become an artist, and it is the painter or composer *as artist*, whom we valuate when we speak of a good painter or musician.

Highest excellence in the creative arts is called genius. It is noteworthy that we call him, who has it, 'great' rather than 'good'.

The question, to which extent excellence in the creative arts can be 'objectively' assessed, I shall not here discuss.

The observations which we have made in this section may be thought to indicate that the notion of being *good at* covers, not one, but several *forms* of goodness. There is first the excellence, of which skill in a game or game-like activity is the standard example. It can be measured by tests of its own. There is secondly the excellence of the skilled professional. It is, mainly at least, assessed in terms of instrumental goodness. Thirdly, there is excellence in the creative arts. This seems to defy assessment by means of tests and in terms of instrumental (or utilitarian) goodness.

It is not very important, whether we wish to speak of the three types of excellence mentioned as three forms of goodness, or as three sub-forms of one form, *viz*. technical goodness. But it is important to be aware that the corresponding three types of activity are, in a manifold of ways, related to one another. The professional skill, *e.g.* of a doctor or a teacher, may rise to the level of creative genius. And the creative activity, *e.g.* of an artist or a philosopher, has an element of play and can therefore sometimes rightly be called game-like.

12. Is there a connexion between technical goodness and commendation? One recommends the good teacher, the good craftsman, the good scientist for a job. This is done because teachers, craftsmen, scientists have a use, may be put to serve the purposes of individual men or social institutions. If the association between a kind K of man and a purpose for which men of this kind may be used is *essential*, is an intrinsic tie, then the standards whereby the technical goodness and those whereby the instrumental goodness of a K are judged, are bound necessarily to give concordant results. And then judgments of technical goodness have a use for commending too.

When, however, the excellence of a man as member of a kind K is *not* also an instrumental excellence for some purpose, judgments of technical goodness have no direct and obvious use for commending. But 'good' in the sense of pure technical goodness can be said to have a *laudatory* or *praising* function.

Technical goodness, which is not also instrumental, bears no intrinsic relationship to preferential choice. This is so because there is then no such thing as wanting the better K for a given purpose. But there is an *analogue* to preferential choice also for pure technical goodness. What this analogue is I shall try briefly to explain.

A man, who is a K, will normally want to be a good K or want to become a better K. Why should there be this desire for perfection? The possible reasons fall in two groups. Either a man wants this, because being a good or better K serves some ulterior end or purpose of his. This case does not interest us here. Its discussion belongs in the context of instrumental and other forms of goodness. Or a man, who is a K, is craving for perfection because he is *keen on* the activity proper to K's or, as we could also put it, is keen on K-ing.

Being keen on the activity corresponds in the sphere of technical goodness to being in the pursuit of an end or purpose in the realm of instrumental goodness. Within the subjective setting of a purpose a man will, we have said, necessarily prefer the use of an instrument, which he considers better, to the use of one which he considers less good for his purpose. Similarly, he will necessarily want to be as good as possible, aim at perfecting himself, in the activity on which he is keen. Otherwise he simply is not keen. Like the man who cannot afford to buy the best instruments, he may not be able to afford the time or money to train himself to become as good as he might otherwise become. But this does not show that he does not want to become as good as possible. It only shows that other circumstances beside his innate resources of self-development may put a limit to his possibilities of perfecting himself in this or that respect.

One can, for some purpose, want to be a poor K. For example: to be a poor cricketer in order not to become selected for the team. But there is no such thing as wanting to be a poor K for its own sake. For this would mean the same as being keen on doing K poorly and this, as I have tried to explain, is a contradiction in terms.

40

III

UTILITARIAN AND MEDICAL GOODNESS. THE BENEFICIAL AND THE HARMFUL. THE NOTIONS OF HEALTH AND ILLNESS

1. IN this chapter we shall discuss two more uses of the word 'good' or two more forms of goodness. One of them is related to instrumental, the other to technical goodness.

Instances of that use of 'good' which is related to instrumental goodness are provided by many cases, when we say of something that it is *good for* a certain thing or being. For example: Medicine is good for the sick, rain for the crops, lubrication for the car. The reign of a king can be good for a country or people.

Instead of saying that something *is good for* a being or thing, we often also say that it *does good to* the being or thing in question. To take a holiday or to get married will do him good, we say.

That which, in the sense of the above examples, is good for or does good to some being or thing, I shall call *beneficial*.

Related to the category of the beneficial is the category of the *useful* and its sister-categories the advantageous and the favourable. For the last three we shall coin the term *utilitarian goodness*. I shall, however, also frequently employ 'useful' as a common name of the three sister-categories and 'usefulness' as a synonym for 'utilitarian goodness'.

There are typical uses of the phrase 'good for somebody', under

41

which we would not translate 'good' by 'beneficial' but by 'useful'. For example: to know the language of the country in which he is travelling, is a good thing for the tourist—knowing the language he will get more out of the journey. Such knowledge is useful under the circumstances. But we do not normally call it beneficial.

When 'good' in 'be good for somebody' means 'useful', then the whole phrase cannot—as when 'good' means 'beneficial'—be replaced by 'do good to somebody'. But of that which is useful, we often say that it is 'good to be' or 'good to have'. For example: to be courageous or to have courage is a good thing for a man, it is useful in situations, when he is facing danger. Many other states of character, traditionally called virtues, such as temperance or industry, are useful too. But virtues are not normally called beneficial.

Which is the logical relation between the category of the useful (and its sister-categories) on the one hand and the category of the beneficial on the other hand? I think it is right to say that the second is a sub-category of the first, or that beneficiality is a sub-form of utilitarian goodness. Everything beneficial is also useful, but not everything useful is also beneficial. Things which are useful without also being beneficial I shall call 'merely useful'.

On the view which is here taken of the relation between beneficiality and utilitarian goodness, the two must have some feature in common. The beneficial, in addition, must possess some distinguishing feature, which marks the beneficial as that which is *in some special sense* useful, advantageous, or favourable.

The common feature seems to be this: Something is useful or beneficial by virtue of the way in which it *causally affects* something else. I shall call this causal relevance of the useful or beneficial a way of *affecting favourably* the thing in question. The 'logical mechanism' of affecting things favourably will be briefly examined in section 4. This form of causal relevance will be seen to have two main branches. I shall refer to them using the words *promote* and *protect* respectively.

In the case of useful things, which are also called beneficial, that to which the useful is favourably causally relevant—ultimately if not immediately—may be characterized as *the good of some being*. Instead of 'good' we can here also say 'welfare'. Physical exercise, for example, is beneficial, because good for the health. 'Health' is another name for the good (welfare) of the body. The good of the human body is an aspect of the good (welfare) of man. Thus to say that exercise is beneficial is to say that it affects favourably, immediately the good of the body, and ultimately the good of man. Generally speaking: everything which is beneficial affects favourably the good (welfare) of some being.

It appears to be the case that a thing which affects the good of some being protectively rather than promotively, we call (merely) useful rather than (also) beneficial. The reason, for example, why we call the causal relevance of virtues to the good of human beings usefulness rather than beneficiality, seems to be that virtues are protective rather than promotive of this good.

Things are thus sometimes useful without also being beneficial on the ground that they affect favourably the good of some being. In most cases, however, things which are merely useful are this on the ground that they are favourably causally relevant to (the attainment of) some *end of action*. It is convenient, we have said, to call anything which is an end of action *a good*. Accepting this terminology, one could also say that a thing is useful when it is favourably causally relevant to some good; and that it is beneficial when it is promotive of that peculiar good which we call the good of a being.

2. Things which are useful for the attainment of ends are often also said to be *instrumental* to the attainment of those ends.

In view of this common use of the word 'instrumental', it may be asked whether we ought not to have reserved the term 'instrumental goodness' for the category of the useful. This, I think, would correspond to the way in which many philosophers actually have used the term.

The dispute about terminology is futile. It is important, however, to realize that 'good' in 'a good knife' or 'a good watch' or 'a good car' does not ordinarily mean the same as 'useful'. Even a poor knife can, under circumstances, be useful. It is useful, whenever the use of this knife is a good thing. But this usefulness of the knife does not necessarily mean that it is a good *knife*.

The distinction between usefulness and that which I have called instrumental goodness can be illuminated by considering the difference in meaning between the phrases 'be good for a purpose' and 'serve a purpose well'. To say of something that it is good for a purpose ordinarily means that it *can be used* to serve this purpose. If we are in pursuit of the purpose in question, then this thing is useful, a good thing to have. But to say of something that it is a good so-and-so, *e.g.* knife, is to *presuppose* that it can be used for a purpose essentially associated with so-and-sos, and to *say* that it serves this purpose well. (See Ch. II, sect. 2.) The opposite (contradictory) of 'good for this purpose' is 'no good for this purpose', *i.e.* 'cannot be used to serve this purpose' or 'useless for this purpose'. The opposite of 'serves this purpose well' is 'serves this purpose poorly'. Nothing can serve a purpose even poorly unless it can serve it, *i.e.* unless it is *in a sense* good for this purpose.

Instrumental goodness is typically an *excellence* or a notion of *rank* and *grade*, whereas usefulness is not. This is reflected in the different rôle, which absolute and comparative judgments of value play in connexion with instrumental goodness on the one hand and in connexion with the useful or the beneficial on the other hand. We are more often interested in knowing whether one knife is, within a given subjective setting of purpose, better than another, than in knowing whether it is, in that setting, good *simpliciter*. This is so because of the intimate connexion which there is between judgments of instrumental goodness and preferential choice. When judging of usefulness again we are primarily interested in the question whether something can be used or is no good for a certain purpose, and in judging of beneficiality whether something will or will not do a being good—for example whether it will be good for him to go into business. This is not to say that we do not also sometimes grade things as being more or less useful or beneficial. But whereas even the less good of two medicines, which both work to cure an illness, does the patient good and in this sense is beneficial, useful for restoring his health, not even the better of two knives, which can both be used for carving meat, needs be a good carving knife.

To call something an instrumentally good *K* is to say that it is a *K* which is good *as such*, *i.e. as a K*. When 'good' in a phrase 'a good *K*' means useful or beneficial, then, for all I can see, we are not attributing a goodness *of its kind* to the *K*. A good habit, for example, is not good *as* habit. Habits have no special excellence of their kind, as knives or watches or cars have. (Cf. Ch. II, sect. 1.) The logical picture, however, is complicated here by the fact that many kinds, the members of which are judged useful or beneficial in some respect, are also essentially associated with purposes, as *e.g.* medicines with purposes of curing illness. When this is the case, the useful or beneficial thing can also be judged from the point of view of its instrumental goodness. Then the *instrumental goodness* of the thing can be said to measure its *degree of usefulness*.

3. We must now consider the opposites of the useful and its sub-category the beneficial.

One opposite of the useful is the useless. To call something useless can mean several things. It can mean that the thing in question has no use for any purpose whatsoever, or that it cannot be used for a certain purpose. When 'useful' means 'good for this purpose', *i.e.* 'can be used for this purpose', and 'useless' means 'no good for this purpose', *i.e.* 'cannot be used for this purpose', then the useful and the useless are opposed to one another as contradictories, and not as contraries. This seems to be the way the two are normally opposed.

If one had to name the opposite of the beneficial, the first name to suggest itself would probably be the adjective 'harmful'. Others which would also come to the mind are 'detrimental', 'damaging', and 'injurious' or 'injuring'.

The beneficial, we said, is something which is good for or does good to a thing or a being, *i.e.* serves the good of the thing or being in question. Clearly, no thing is harmful merely on the ground that it does no good or does not serve the good of any being. 'Harmful', unlike 'useless', is not a privative term. The harmful which is the opposite of the beneficial is that which affects the good of a being unfavourably, adversely. And to affect the good of a being adversely is not the same as *not* to affect it favourably. If it were, then to be harmless (= not harmful) would be the same as beneficial, which it obviously is not.

Good habits, for example, have beneficial effects on a man, good laws and institutions beneficial effects on a community or country. Bad habits have detrimental effects on the good of a man, *e.g.* because they ruin his bodily health. Similarly bad laws and institutions do harm to the community. But habits can also be harmless without being good, and institutions and laws useless or 'pointless' without being harmful, positively obnoxious. Thus whereas the useful and the useless, and the harmful and the harmless are opposed to one another as contradictories, the beneficial and the harmful are opposed to one another as contraries. They exclude one another, but between them there is a neutral zone.

45

The harmful, when it is the contrary of the beneficial, is also said to be bad, or sometimes evil, for the being whose good it affects unfavourably. It is further said to do bad or evil to this being. It is called a bad thing or maybe even more frequently an evil thing. Often it is called simply an evil. The institution of ostracism, one could say, was an evil to the Athenian republic; the reign of Ahab was an evil to Israel, that of Hitler to Germany and Europe. I find it convenient to adopt the substantive form *an evil* for anything—be it an institution, an act, a state of affairs or of character—which is harmful in that sense of 'harmful', which is the opposite of beneficial, *i.e.* for that which is bad for the good of a being.

The notion of evil, thus defined, is a sub-category of the notion of the harmful. Anything which frustrates or hampers the attainment of some end of human action is harmful or detrimental, *viz.* to the attainment of that end. But not of everything, which is in this sense harmful, do we say that it does evil to the being in pursuit of the end. Sometimes we say that it was good for a man that this or that plan of his became ruined—but that which ruined his plans was nevertheless a harmful thing, *viz.* to his plans. This observation shows that the adjective 'harmful' is commonly used also to mean the opposite of utilitarian goodness in general, and not only to mean the opposite of its sub-category the beneficial.

There are thus two senses of 'harmful' which must be distinguished: 'harmful' in the broad sense, which names the contrary of utilitarian goodness, and 'harmful' in the narrower sense, which names the contrary of the beneficial.

There are also two senses of the word 'evil' to be noted in this connexion. When 'an evil' means something which affects the good of a being adversely, then 'an evil' means something which is a cause of harm (to the being involved). But instead of 'a cause of harm' we can here also say 'a cause of evil'. Thus the word 'evil' sometimes means the cause of harm and sometimes the harm caused. The word 'harm', it would seem, has not the same double meaning. It nearly always means the thing (damage) caused or suffered.

The term 'poor', be it noted in conclusion, is also sometimes used in connexion with assessing utilitarian goodness. Then 'poor' does not mean the same as that which is the ordinary meaning of 'bad' in such contexts. The poor thing, in a utilitarian sense, is to

46

some low degree *favourably* relevant to some end or purpose. It is thus not entirely useless, still less is it harmful, for the end or purpose in question. The poor is some, but very little, use. A poor medicine, for example, still does *some* good. If it affects the patient adversely, it is not called *poor*. But it may be called *bad* in the utilitarian sense of harmful or obnoxious.

4. The property of being useful or harmful, and *a fortiori* also the property of being beneficial or evil, belongs to a thing by virtue of a causal relationship between this thing and something else (cf. sect. 1). In the case of things useful or beneficial this causal relationship is one of affecting *favourably* or being favourably relevant to the other thing in question. In the case of things harmful or evil this relationship is one of affecting *adversely* or *unfavourably* this other thing.

There are two principal ways in which something can be causally favourable to the attainment of an end. Either this thing is favourably relevant to the end by taking us, metaphorically speaking, nearer or even up to this end. Or it is favourably relevant by preventing us, metaphorically speaking, from being taken farther away from the end. We have already (p. 42) coined the terms *promotive* and *protective* for these two forms of favourable causal relevance to ends.

In a similar manner one may distinguish between two main forms of affecting the attainment of ends unfavourably. Something is unfavourably relevant by taking us farther away from the end or goal, or by preventing us from getting nearer to it. When the adverse effect is of the first kind, it is also called *deteriorative*.

The promotive effect of some useful or beneficial thing is sometimes described by saying that it makes *bad better* and sometimes by saying that it makes *good better*. The former type of promotive effect is often also called an effect of *curing* or *healing*.

Take, for example, the case of a beneficial medicine or cure. It serves the good of the being to whom it is administered, by curing some illness and thus restoring health. An illness is an evil, something which affects the good of the body—ultimately the good of a man—adversely. A beneficial medicine or cure thus works for the good of a being by working against an existing evil. Generally speaking: it promotes the good by making bad better.

47

In a similar manner, the deteriorative effect of some harmful or evil thing is sometimes described by saying that it makes *good worse* and sometimes by saying that it makes *bad worse*.

When, for example, the wrong medicine is administered to the ill man making him sicker still, the effect of the harmful consists in making bad worse. When excessive use of tobacco or of alcohol ruins the health of a person, the harmful makes good deteriorate. Bad habits, generally speaking, promote evil by ruining the good of the being who practises them.

It would be an interesting and worthwhile task to investigate the formal logic of these various forms of the causal efficacy of utilitarian goodness and its opposite. The investigation would show, for one thing, in how many different senses something can be a 'cause' of good or of evil. To observe these different senses is essential to any ethics, which measures the moral value or rightness of acts in terms of the consequences of action. Yet it is an observation which traditional ethics has habitually neglected to make.

5. Are value-judgments, of the kind which we are now considering, objectively true or false? In discussing this question it is important to separate judgments which involve the notion of the good of a being, from judgments which do not involve this notion. The case of the latter is much simpler.

In judgments of usefulness and harmfulness, which do not involve the notion of the good of a being, we *judge* the causal relevance of something for some purpose or end which we pursue. The existence of the purpose or end is *presupposed* in the judgment. An end, we said, can also be called 'a good' simply by virtue of being desired. The question, however, whether an end is good or bad in some other sense, *i.e.* the question of the *value* of ends, is totally irrelevant to judgments of usefulness and its opposites. Such judgments are *purely causal*.

For example: A man wants to train himself to become a good runner and deliberates whether he should give up smoking. Is the habit of smoking detrimental, harmful, obnoxious to the attainment of his end? He has to consider the causal effects of smoking upon excellence in running. The problem can be viewed under the various aspects of causal relevance, which we distinguished in the preceding section: does smoking prevent him from improving his talents, or does it positively ruin them? Which aspect of the causal

48

problem that will interest him most, will largely depend upon the state which he has already reached with a view to the end.

Suppose our man arrives at the conclusion that smoking is a bad habit in the sense that it has adverse effects on the attainment of his end. The conclusion is true or false—and in this sense 'objective'. Assume that it is true. Does it then follow that smoking is a bad habit with *every* man who pursues the same end as he?

Obviously, identity of aim or end or purpose is not enough to make the judgment concerning the badness of smoking generalizable. Another man may pursue the same end, but have a different constitution or otherwise be differently circumstanced and therefor 'immune' to the harmful effects of tobacco. What is a bad habit for one man in pursuit of a certain end, need not be a bad habit for another man in pursuit of exactly the same end. With a view to this one may call the value-judgment passed on the habit 'subjective'. But this subjectivity—if it be called by that name—does not remove the judgment from the province of truth and falsehood.

Suppose we generalized the case which we have been discussing, and said that smoking is bad for any man who pursues the same end and is exactly similarly circumstanced. This would be trivial, unless we specified the circumstances, in which case the generalization might easily be false.

If we want to generalize in matters of usefulness and harmfulness, we shall on the whole have to be content with *rough* generalizations of the following schematic type: For most men in circumstances C the thing X is good or bad with a view to the end E. The corresponding holds true also for the special form of the useful, which we call the beneficial, and the special form of the harmful, which we call the evil.

Judgments of utilitarian goodness, which do not involve the notion of the good of a being, are, we said, purely causal judgments, though of limited generalizability. Judgments of the beneficial and the evil, however, are not purely causal. They split in two components. One is causal. It concerns the consequences or effects of certain acts or habits or practices or institutions or what not. The other component could conveniently be called axiological. It concerns the relations of these effects to that which we have termed the good of a being. This is not a causal relation. It is more like a relationship of belonging. We shall later have occasion to investigate the nature of this relationship in more detail.

6. What kinds or species of being have a good? What is the range of significance of '*X*' in the phrase 'the good of *X*'?

Can, for example, artefacts and other inanimate beings have a good? It is not unnatural to say that lubrication is beneficial or good for the car, or that violent shocks will do harm to a watch. The goodness of a car or a watch is itself instrumental goodness for some human purposes. Therefore that which is good for the car or watch is something which will keep it fit or in good order with a view to its serving a purpose well. It may be argued that, since the goodness of the car or watch is relative to human ends and purposes, that which is *good for* the car or watch cannot properly be said to serve the *good of* the car or watch themselves. If it serves anybody's good at all, it will be the good of the human being to whom the instrument belongs or who uses it.

A being, of whose good it is meaningful to talk, is one who can meaningfully be said to be well or ill, to thrive, to flourish, be happy or miserable. These things, no doubt, are sometimes said of artefacts and inanimate objects too—particularly when we feel a strong attachment to them. 'My car does not like the roads of this district very much, as shown by the frequent overhaulings which it needs', we may say. But this is clearly a metaphorical way of speaking.

The attributes, which go along with meaningful use of the phrase 'the good of *X*', may be called *biological* in a broad sense. By this I do not mean that they were terms, of which biologists make frequent use. 'Happiness' and 'welfare' cannot be said to belong to the professional vocabulary of biologists. What I mean by calling the terms 'biological' is that they are used as attributes of beings, of whom it is meaningful to say that they have a *life*. The question 'What kinds or species of being have a good?' is therefore broadly identical with the question 'What kind or species of being have a life?' And one could say that it is *metaphorical* to speak of the good of a being, to the same extent as it is metaphorical to speak of the life of that being.

Artefacts, such as cars and watches, have a life and therefore a good, only metaphorically. Plants and animals have a life in the primary sense. But what shall we say of social units such as the family, the nation, the state? Have they got a life 'literally' or 'metaphorically' only? I shall not attempt to answer these questions. I doubt whether there is any other way of answering them except

50

by pointing out existing analogies of language. It is a fact that we speak about the life and also the good (welfare) of the family, the nation, and the state. This fact about the use of language we must accept and with it the idea that the social units in question *have* a life and a good. What is arguable, however, is whether the life and *a fortiori* also the good (welfare) of a social unit is not somehow 'logically reducible' to the life and therefore the good of the beings —men or animals—who are its members.

It would seem that man, among beings who have a good, holds a position, which is peculiar in two respects.

Man is not the only living being who has a social life. But there are a vast number of social units, which are peculiar to man. These are the units which presuppose a *normative order*. The supreme example of such units is the state. How the good of such 'covenanted', as they may also be called, social units is conceptually related to the good of the human individual, is a major problem of political philosophy.

The other respect in which man holds a peculiar position among beings who have a good, is that he may be regarded as *quasi* composed of parts, of whose independent life and good one can speak. Man is body and mind, one sometimes says. Or one makes a tripartite division of man into body, mind, and soul. It makes sense to speak of the life of the body and also of the welfare of the body. The same holds true for the mind and the soul. The welfare of the body and mind is called (bodily and mental) *health*.

In the rest of this chapter I shall discuss a form of goodness which is connected with that aspect of the good of man, which we call health. We may call this form *medical* goodness.

7. Goodness of the form here called medical is referred to when we speak about a (in the medical sense) good heart, good lungs, or good eyes—but also about a good memory or understanding.

The heart and the lungs are *organs* of the body; memory and understanding are often called *faculties* of the mind. That which is here called medical goodness could also be spoken of as the goodness of organs and faculties.

Are the eyes an organ of the body or of the mind? Perhaps we could say that they are an organ of the body, which serves as the bodily substratum of a faculty of the mind, *viz*. sight. The same holds good of the other so-called sense-organs.

E   51

Organs resemble instruments or tools in that they have both morphological and functional characteristics. Faculties again have no morphological features proper to them; in this and other respects they resemble abilities and skills. The functional characteristics of organs, too, resemble abilities; they consist in things which the organs themselves *do*, such as pumping blood or breathing air, rather than—as is the case with tools—in their usability for various assigned purposes.

In speaking of the goodness of various organs we are primarily concerned with their characteristic functions and not with their morphological features. A deformation of the heart may be a cause why it performs badly and is thus called a bad heart. But if the deformation did not impede the performance of the organ, we should hardly call it bad merely because deformed.

When 'good' in the phrase 'a good K' refers to medical goodness and K thus is some organ or faculty, we have another case of a goodness *of its kind*. In this respect medical goodness resembles instrumental and technical goodness, but differs from utilitarian goodness. (Cf. sect. 2.)

Instrumental goodness of its kind presupposes, we found, an essential connexion between the kind and some purpose; technical goodness again an essential tie between the kind and some activity. In a similar manner, medical goodness of its kind can be said to presuppose the existence of an essential connexion between the kind (of organ or faculty) and some *function*.

There is a conspicuous resemblance between medical and technical goodness by virtue of the fact that both forms of goodness manifest themselves as a certain excellence of performance. But there are noteworthy differences as well. I shall here mention the following three:

The technically good man is *good at* something. But the phrase 'good at' is seldom used in connexion with good organs or faculties. A good heart is not ordinarily said to be good at pumping blood or good lungs to be good at breathing. Good eyes are not said to be good at seeing, nor even the man who has good eyes. But the man of good sight may be good at, say, discerning landmarks at a great distance. The man of good memory may be good at, say, remembering dates or telephone numbers or knowing poems by heart. In these last cases the things at which the man is good is some special activity in which one can train oneself, and not the function, as such, of the organ or faculty concerned.

This observation takes us to a second difference between technical goodness and the goodness of faculties and organs. Activities at which men are said to be good, are for the most part acquired rather than innate. Teaching and training are normally needed to reach technical excellence. The functions of organs and faculties again are substantially *innate*. By training one's body and mind one can, to some extent, develop those functions to greater perfection, and by caring for one's body and mind one can, to some extent, prevent them from decaying and deteriorating. But substantially the goodness of faculties and organs is not dependent upon what a man *does* with a view to perfecting them, but upon what might be called the graces of nature and fate.

The term 'innate', incidentally, must not be misunderstood. It does not mean that all faculties and organs perform their proper functions from the birth of the individual. It may take time for them to mature. Man can quite properly be said to be innately endowed with sight, and yet a newly born baby cannot see.

A third major difference between technical goodness and the goodness of organs and faculties is constituted by the way in which organs and faculties serve the good of the being who has them. A man can use his acquired skills and special talents to promote his good. He need not, however, do this. But good faculties and organs he needs. To have a bad heart or bad lungs or a bad memory is bad for—an evil to—the man who has it, and it is because of the detrimental effects on the good of the whole that we judge the organs or faculties in question bad. (See below, sect. 9.)

Because of the intrinsic connexion which holds between the goodness of organs and faculties and the good of the being to whom they belong, I propose to call the functions, which are proper to the various organs and faculties, *essential functions* of the being, or rather, of the kind or species of which the individual being is a member. The 'essentiality' of the functions does not entail that every individual of the species can actually perform all those functions. But it entails that, if an individual cannot do this 'at the time when by nature it should'—to quote Aristotle—we call it *abnormal* or *defect* or *faulty* or, sometimes, *injured*. It follows by contraposition that the essential functions of the species are functions which any *normal* individual of the species can perform.

The essential functions are needed for that which could conveniently be called a *normal life* of the individual.

The notion of normalcy, as we shall soon see, is of great importance to the understanding of the special form of goodness which belongs to organs and faculties.

8. Medical goodness may be said to be related to the notion of the good of a being thanks to the intermediary rôle of the notions of *health* and *illness*.

An organ which performs its proper function well is said to be good *or* well. It is also often said to be healthy and sometimes said to be in good health. This last, however, is more commonly said of the man, or being, whose organs are concerned.

An organ which does not perform its proper function well is sometimes called *ill* and sometimes *weak*. It is also called *bad* or *poor*. One can distinguish between the meanings of 'ill' and 'weak'. 'Bad' and 'poor' again are used pretty much as synonyms in the field of medical goodness; perhaps one could maintain that 'bad' is more often used for the ill than for the weak, and 'poor' more often for the weak than for the ill organ.

That a man has bad health usually means that he suffers an illness of some or several of his organs. Bad health is also called poor health. If a man is said to be of weak health, this weakness of health must be reflected in the weakness of some or several of his bodily parts. Weak health too is sometimes called poor health.

What is the difference between illness and weakness of organs, or between bodily illness and weakness of health? Ordinary usage can hardly be said to maintain a rigorous distinction between the concepts. But it may be said to hint at a distinction which can be made and maintained with a certain rigour.

Illness, we shall say, is an *actual* and weakness a *potential* evil or cause of harm to the being concerned. The ill or diseased organ causes harm or suffering to the being whose organ it is. The weak organ *may* cause suffering. The meaning of 'may' here is not that of mere physical possibility. The 'may' has to be explained in terms of probability. Roughly speaking: weakness as a potential cause of harm to the body is a probability of illness. How this probability is estimated need not concern us here. Weakness could also be called a disposition or tendency to deteriorate into illness. This holds good both of weakness of organs and of weakness of health.

54

Poor or bad organs thus function in a way which affects health adversely, by being either an actual or potential cause of illness. Shall we say contrarywise that good organs function in a way which affects health favourably, *i.e.* promotes the physical well-being of the being or at least prevents it from deteriorating? It seems to me that it would *not* be correct to say thus. For, let us ask, what is ordinarily meant by 'good eyes', 'good lungs', etc. Primarily, it seems, organs which are *not bad* (poor), *i.e.* neither ill nor weak. 'Good' as an attribute of an organ of the body means very much the same as 'all right'. Organs are good when they are in order, fit, as they should be, normal. Organs which are better than normal are called 'exceptionally good'.

Thus in the case of organs, badness (poorness) appears to be logically primary to goodness. 'Good' is here a privative term. It means 'not bad', 'all right', 'no source of complaint'. If I am not mistaken, this is a logical feature in which the form of goodness, which we are now discussing, differs basically from both instrumental and technical goodness. In their case, 'poor' (for technical goodness also 'bad') is a privative term, 'good' a positive term. The positive is logically primary to the privative.

It follows from the definition of medical goodness as an absence of weakness and illness that 'good' and 'poor' as attributes of organs or of bodily health denote contradictories rather than contraries. But from the definition of weakness as likelihood of illness it also follows that the border separating the good from the poor will be vague. (The meaning of 'likely' is inherently vague.) Because of this vagueness it will frequently be impossible to pronounce definitely on the question whether a certain organ of some individual being should be considered good or not.

If a being is said to be in good bodily health, when its organs perform their proper functions well, and if organs are good, when there is nothing wrong with them, *i.e.* no illness or weakness, then the notion of (good) bodily health too is a privative notion. From this privative notion of health one may distinguish a positive notion of health, which is present when the being positively 'enjoys' good health, feels fit, thrives or flourishes physically. But of the two notions, the privative seems far more important. It would be correct to say of an individual that he is in *perfectly good* bodily health merely on the ground that there is *nothing wrong* with his body and bodily functions.

55

The privative notion of goodness of organs and of bodily health has an interesting connexion with certain ideas relating to causation. If an organ functions unsatisfactorily, *i.e.* suffers from some weakness or illness, we think of this bad as having a *cause*— for example some constitutional morphological defect of the organ or some injury, which has befallen it in the course of the life of the individual. But the normal state of the organ, *i.e.* the state in which it is when it functions satisfactorily, is not in the same sense 'caused'.

The idea that a cause is primarily a cause of harm and thus is an evil, *i.e.* a disturbance of an equilibrium or normal state or good order (a *kosmos* in the literal sense of the Greek word) seems to be the very root, from which the idea of causation as we know it to-day has originated. The Greek word for cause is *aitia*, which also means guilt, *i.e.* responsibility for harm or evil. It is an interesting observation that the Finnish word for cause, *syy*, has precisely the same double meaning as the Greek *aitia*. The received meaning of the term *aetiology* is the study of the causes of diseases, but the literal meaning of the word is science of causes in general.

9. Organs are bad, *i.e.* weak or ill, by virtue of their adverse effects on the being whose organs they are. Briefly speaking: organs are bad because of some bad or evil of which they are the cause. But, as noted in the preceding section, organs are not good, because of some good they cause, but simply by not causing harm.

An organ may be judged diseased on the ground that it exhibits a certain deformation. But, as said before (sect. 7), morphological anomalies can at most be symptoms of badness, not defining criteria. For the deformations are bad only to the extent that they impede the function.

The relation between the *functioning* of an organ and its *effects* on the body is a causal and thus extrinsic relation. But the relation between the *badness* of the effects and the *badness* of the organ, whose functioning is responsible for those effects, is a logical and thus intrinsic relation. The evil which bad organs cause is *constitutive* of the badness of the organs themselves, one could also say.

For example: That the discomfort and fatigue, which a man feels each time he has to climb stairs, should be due to an insufficiency of his heart, is a fact about causation in the human body. But when the heart, because of this and similar effects, is said to be weak or to perform poorly, then the *badness* of the effects is not 'symptomatic', but 'constitutive' of the *weakness* of the organ and *poorness* of its performance.

Which then is the evil or harm, which bad organs cause, actually or potentially?

One basic form of such harm is *pain* or pain-like sensations such as discomfort, ache, nausea. Obviously, the pain caused by a diseased organ need not be continuous, in order that we shall call the organ (continuously) ill. These different relationships to change reflect differences in the logic of the concepts of pain and of illness. For example: a diseased heart need not cause pain when the individual is at rest, but it may cause discomfort when he moves.

Wherein does the evil of pain lie? To ask thus is not to ask a triviality. Pain is evil, I would say, only to the extent that it is disliked or shunned or unwanted. It is a fact that pain is not always disliked. The phrase 'a pleasant pain' is not a contradiction in terms. We shall have to speak more about this in connexion with hedonic goodness.

Do all tests for judging, whether the function of an organ is impeded and the organ thus is weak or ill, depend logically upon the notion of pain?

At first sight there seem to be ways of testing the functioning of organs and therewith their goodness, which are independent of pain—and even of harm generally. Consider, for example, how a doctor tests a man's sight. A man, broadly speaking, is said to have bad or poor eyes (sight), if he cannot, at the appropriate distances, discern things and movements which most men can discern. Here the standard of goodness is set by something, which can be called the *normalcy* of the function.

It would, however, be wrong to think of the test of normalcy as being exclusively a performance-test. If the eyes of a man can see exactly those things which normal eyes are supposed to see at the appropriate distances, but if the use of his eyes to see this causes him pain, his eyes would not be normal. The same would hold true if he could look at things only for a short time without his eyes getting fatigued. Thus the tests of normalcy of performance include, or have to be supplemented by, considerations pertaining to pain or fatigue. (Fatigue is discomfort and can for present purposes be counted a form of pain.) The fact alone that the use of an organ is painful may disqualify it in the normalcy-test.

57

But how shall we judge of a case when the functioning of an organ falls decidedly short of the normal performance, but when there is no pain or bodily discomfort of any kind? Such cases are perhaps rare, but they may occur. Shall we then say that the organ is bad, because its performance is sub-normal, or shall we say that it is all right, since it causes no discomfort?

At this point it is good to remember that a man uses his organs to satisfy various needs and wants of his. If some organ of his performs sub-normally, he can be said to suffer *incapacitation*. This means: there will then be things which he could do if the organ performed normally, but which now he cannot do. Should he want to do these things, the fact that he cannot do them may be a cause of annoyance, frustration, grief, and similar feelings. These phenomena can, with some caution, be termed 'mental pains'. The man who suffers them will then complain of the badness of the organ as a source of his mental discomfort.

But suppose he does not want to do things, which he could do, if the organ functioned normally. *He* will then have no reason to complain of this organ of his either. Shall we nevertheless call it bad? One may hesitate about the answer. It seems to me that, *if* we call the organ bad, *i.e.* weak or ill, it is only because of the fact that men *normally* have the wants and needs, which this particular man happens to be without, and therefore also *normally* would suffer if they had this man's deficiency. A man who does not put some or other of his organs to their normal use, may be said to be abnormal in a certain respect, or be said not to live a normal life. This abnormality of the man or of his life could, for a variety of reasons, be considered a bad thing and even be regarded as a sort of illness. But this badness is clearly logically independent of that of the organ.

The evil or harm which bad organs cause, and which is logically constitutive of their badness, is thus of two principal kinds, *viz.* pain and frustration of wants. Abnormality of performance too is logically constitutive of badness of organs, but only indirectly, *via* the notion of normality of the needs and wants of men. Due to the fact that some men may be lacking in normal needs and wants, it may happen that an organ is 'objectively' diseased but that its badness is not 'subjectively' noted.

10. We have so far been talking explicitly about the goodness (and badness) of organs only. Much the same things can be said

about the goodness of faculties. But there are some noteworthy differences. I shall here touch upon the subject very summarily.

In the case of the faculties too we can distinguish between the ill, the weak, and the good. Calling a faculty bad (or poor) is usually to say that it is *weak*. A bad memory is essentially a weak memory. When faculties completely deteriorate, the being whose faculties they are is often said to be mentally ill or deranged. The faculties themselves are not commonly called ill. It would also not be generally correct to say that a weakness of a faculty, like that of an organ, is a likelihood of illness.

The harm caused by poor faculties cannot, for conceptual reasons, be pain in the primary sense of bodily pain. The harm is here basically suffering due to incapacitation. It is the annoyance, frustration, and grief which the individual will experience as a consequence of not being able to satisfy needs and wants which a man, whose faculties function in the normal way, can satisfy.

As in the case of the organs, the harm which bad faculties may cause to the being is logically constitutive of their badness. If use of memory were not vital to the satisfaction of the needs of a normal life, it is not clear why one should call sub-normal capacity of remembering things 'bad memory'. Perhaps we can imagine a form of life under which that, which *we* call bad memory, would be an altogether good thing to have and therefore would be called good memory. We too sometimes consider it good to forget, though not on a scale which would make us revise our notion of goodness of memory. Perhaps we can also imagine circumstances, under which remembering would be a completely useless activity. To be good at remembering would then be a technical excellence or something like it. People might be keen on remembering, as on playing a game. Their notion, too, of a good or bad memory would be different from ours, *i.e.* their notion would lack a feature which is *essential* to ours.

The harm caused by illness, mental or bodily, is not only a concern of the sick person himself. The ill man may not be able to take care of himself. He has to be helped by others. Thus he easily becomes a burden on his fellow-humans. He can, moreover, also be a menace to the good of others: by spreading contagion, if he is bodily ill, and by harmful acts if he is mentally deranged. The question may be raised, whether the relationship between illness and the harm caused to others by the sick is an intrinsic or extrinsic connexion, *i.e.* whether it is constitutive or not of the notion of *illness of a man*—as distinct from the notion of illness of an organ or faculty by itself.

It seems to me that in this respect there is a conceptual difference between physical and mental illness. It is part of our notion of the latter that it upsets the relations of the sick to his surroundings in a way which, from a social point of view, is unwanted, undesirable. A man could not be said to be bodily ill unless *he*, or at least any *normal* person in his state, suffers pain or discomfort. But the feeble-minded or maniac, who is perfectly content and happy in his state, we still consider ill. This we should hardly think of him if his state were not from a social point of view a bad thing, an evil. We can imagine forms of lunacy—there may even be such forms in actual existence—which lack these obnoxious effects upon social life and which we would regard as blessed states, which we praise, rather than illness which we deplore or pity.

11. Are judgments of medical goodness 'objectively' true or false?

A man who judges of some organ of his that it is diseased on the ground that he feels pain, is not judging that he has pain. What he judges is that the pain he feels is caused by some defect of the organ. In this he may, of course, be mistaken. The judgment is true or false. The fact that pain is a state of consciousness of an individual subject does not detract from or void the 'objectivity' of the judgment.

Shall we say that a man, *e.g.* a doctor, who judges of some organ of another man that it is diseased on the ground that this man complains of pain, is making two judgments—one about the pain of that other man and another about the cause of his pain? I don't think we should say thus. The doctor, who judges about the state of health of the organ on the basis of signs of pain, is presupposing or taking for granted the pain. This presupposition he may have reason to question, say because an examination of the organ does not reveal any functional or morphological anomaly, which were symptomatic of illness. His doubts he may express in a judgment (conjecture) to the effect that the other man actually feels no pain. But the judgment to the effect that an organ of that other man is ill, is a judgment solely to the effect that a *cause* of a given discomfort is to be located to the organ (including its functioning).

In a similar manner, when we judge organs or faculties bad on the ground that they are a source of annoyance, frustration, or grief, we are not judging that a certain mental discomfort or pain occurs, but that it is due to such and such causes. In these judgments, as will be remembered, certain standards of *normalcy* are presupposed. These standards may be vague and they may be difficult to apply—for example because they cannot be applied uniformly to all members of a certain zoological species, but must take account of age and sex and training and, maybe, various external circumstances of life too. But this does not constitute a ground for saying that judgments of goodness or badness, which employ such standards, were 'subjective'.

12. Organs and faculties, we have said, serve the good of a being. The organs of the body, one could say without distorting language, serve *immediately* the good of the body. This good is also called bodily health. The faculties of the mind serve *immediately* the good of the mind, our mental health. *Remotely*, organs and faculties serve the good of man.

The concept of health may be considered a model on a smaller scale of the more comprehensive notion of the good of a being. That is: it may be suggested that one should try to understand this good (welfare) in all its various aspects on the pattern of the notion of health. On such a view, the good of man would be a *medical* notion by analogy, as are the good of the body and of the mind literally.

The conception of the good of man on the basis of medical analogies is characteristic of the ethics and political philosophy of Plato. The idea is profound and, I think, basically sound. It is worth a much more thorough exploration than will be given to it in the present work.

We distinguished above (sect. 8) between a privative and a positive notion of health. The first, we said, is the more basic notion. Health in the privative sense consists in the absence of bodily pain and of pain-like states, which are consequent upon the frustration of needs and wants of a normal life. Health in the positive sense consists in the presence of feelings of fitness and strength and in similar pleasant (agreeable, joyful) states. In the enjoyment of those states the healthy body and mind can be said to flourish.

In a similar manner, welfare may be said to present two aspects. The one, which answers to the privative notion of health, is the basic aspect. It is conceptually allied to the needs and wants of beings and to the notions of the beneficial and harmful. I am not, however, going to suggest that it is a privative idea in the same strong sense in which the basic notion of health seems to be this. The other aspect of welfare, which answers to the positive notion of health, has a primary conceptual alliance with pleasure. Of the being, who enjoys this aspect of its welfare, we say that it is happy. Happiness could also be called the flower of welfare.

IV

THE HEDONIC GOOD

---

1. OUR discussion in Chapter III brought us into touch with the notion of the good of a being. This in its turn was found to be related to the notions of pain and pleasure, *i.e.* to a further form of goodness, which is here called *the hedonic good*.

Our term 'hedonic goodness' is supposed to cover *roughly* the same ground as the word 'pleasure' in ordinary language. But, as we shall soon see, this ground is very heterogeneous and the use of *one* word to cover it may produce an appearance of conceptual homogeneity, by which we must not let ourselves become deluded.

To realize the heterogeneity of the conceptual field, in which we are moving in this chapter, some observations on language may be helpful. In English, one is used to speaking of pleasure and pain as a pair of contraries or opposites. In other languages, *this* contrast is not so clearly marked. In German, for example, the nearest parallel to the *pair* 'pleasure-pain' in ordinary parlance is 'Lust-Unlust'. But the German word for 'pain' is not 'Unlust'. It is 'Schmerz'. The German pair of substantives 'Lust-Unlust' answers in meaning more closely to the English pair of adjectives 'pleasant-unpleasant' than to the substantive-pair 'pleasure-pain'. But this correspondence too is not perfect. The words 'pleasant' and 'unpleasant' in English would most naturally be translated by 'angenehm' and 'unangenehm' in German.

Considering the important rôle which the concept of pleasure has played in ethics all through the history of the subject, it is surprising how little this concept has been made the object of special investigation. Neither Hume, nor the British utilitarians, nor Moore and the critics of ethical naturalism in this century, seem to have been aware of the problematic character of this key-notion

63

of their own writings.[1] Most writers in the past regard pleasure as either some kind of sensation or as something between sensation and emotion. Moore, Broad, and the non-naturalists in general take it for granted that pleasantness is a 'naturalistic' attribute of things and states and not an axiological term.[2] This, I think, is a bad mistake. Some of the orthodox views of pleasure were challenged by Professor Gilbert Ryle in an important essay a few years ago.[3] Since then there is noticeable a new interest in the concept for its own sake—and not merely as an item in the ethicists' discussions of moral value.

Our discussion here of the concept of pleasure can claim neither to be deep-searching nor even very systematic. My own feeling is that I am only scratching a surface, under which important problems lie hidden.

I think it is useful, at least for purposes of a first approximation, to distinguish three main *forms*—as I shall call them—of pleasure.[4]

The first I call *passive pleasure*. It is the pleasure, or better: the pleasantness, which we attribute primarily to sensations and other so-called states of consciousness and secondarily also to their causes in the physical world. Pleasantness as an attribute of sensations can also be spoken of as 'the pleasures of the senses' or as 'sensuous pleasure'. It seems to me that this sub-form of passive pleasure is largely regarded as the prototype of all pleasure whatsoever, and that this one-sided view has been much to the detriment of the philosophic discussion of these topics.

The second form of pleasure I shall call, by contrast, *active pleasure*. It is the pleasure which a man derives from doing things which he is *keen on doing*, *enjoys* doing, or *likes* to do. Active pleasure can also be called 'the pleasures of an active life'. To the discussion of the ethical relevance of pleasure, the pleasures of the active life seem to me to be at least as important as the pleasures of the senses. Yet there are few moralists, apart from Aristotle, who have paid much attention to active pleasure.

[1] Hume calls pleasure and pain alternatingly 'impressions' and 'perceptions', sometimes also 'sensations'. Bentham calls them 'interesting perceptions'.

[2] See *e.g.*, the discussion by Broad in 'Certain Features in Moore's Ethical Doctrines' in *The Philosophy of G. E. Moore* (1942), pp. 57–67 and the reply by Moore, *op. cit.*, especially p. 587.

[3] Gilbert Ryle, *Dilemmas* (1954), pp. 54–67.

[4] Substantially the same distinction between three forms of pleasure is made by Broad in *Five Types of Ethical Theory* (1930), pp. 187 and 191f.

In addition to passive and active pleasure there is that which I shall call the *pleasure of satisfaction* or *contentedness*. It is the pleasure which we feel at getting that which we desire or need or want—irrespective of whether the desired thing by itself gives us pleasure. The pleasure of satisfaction has played, implicitly if not explicitly, a great rôle in the formation and discussion of the doctrine known as *psychological hedonism*.

2. As specimens of the use of 'good' to refer to the sub-form of passive pleasure, which we call sensual, one may offer the phrases 'a good wine' or 'a good apple'. Let us here consider the case of the good apple in some detail.

It should first be noted that there are many points of view, from which the goodness of apples may become assessed. Apples are food. When we say that it is good to eat apples or that apples are good for the children, we are probably thinking of the nourishing value and wholesomeness of apples. This goodness of the fruit is of the form we have called the beneficial. When the beneficial nature of apples is concerned, the attribution of goodness is usually not of an individual apple but of apples as such or of some kind of apple.

When the cultivator or producer of apples judges of the goodness or badness of a kind of apple, he may be thinking of such questions as whether this kind is easy to cultivate or—in a cold climate—is a hardy sort of apple. From the consumer's point of view, some apples are particularly good for storing, others for making jam, others again for eating. When judged from the producer's and the consumer's specific points of view, the goodness of apples is often instrumental or utilitarian goodness for some purpose. When these forms of goodness in apples are concerned, the judgment is usually about a kind of apple and not about individual apples.

Calling an individual apple good is often another way of saying that it is not damaged or decayed or diseased. The apple is then being treated as *quasi* a being, of whose good it makes sense to talk. An apple can be 'healthy' as distinct from 'wholesome'. We need not here stop to consider whether and when such talk is 'reducible' to talk of instrumental and utilitarian goodness.

But calling an individual apple good can also be but another way of saying that we like its taste, that it is good-tasting. *Then* the goodness of the apple is hedonic. When it is hedonic it is, more-over, of the form we called passive and the sub-form we called sensuous.

The hedonic judgment need not be about an individual apple. A person who says that apples are good, may mean that he likes the taste of apples, and from this it would not follow that he will like the taste of all individual apples. A person again, who says of an individual apple, which he is *not* actually tasting, '*this* is a good apple' would almost certainly be pronouncing on a kind of apple, of which this individual is a specimen. He finds the taste of apples of this sort good, but he perhaps dislikes the taste of some other kind of apple. I shall here disregard such *general* or *generalized* hedonic judgments.

Consider the particular judgment expressed in the words 'this apple is good' or 'this is a good apple', when 'good' is meant hedonically. The question may be raised: Of what is goodness here really predicated? On the face of it, goodness is predicated of the apple. It could, however, be suggested that the verbal formulation conceals a primary judgment, the overt formulation of which would run 'the taste of this apple is good' or, alternatively, 'this apple is good-tasting' or 'this apple has a good taste'. According to this suggestion, hedonic goodness belongs primarily to the taste of the apple, and secondarily only to the apple itself. The taste is a sensation, or bundle of sensations; the apple is a physical object. It is a causal or dispositional characteristic of the physical object that it evokes or produces, under specific circumstances, taste-sensations in a sensing subject. These sensations are the primary logical subject of the hedonic value-judgment. The physical thing 'partakes', so to speak, in the goodness of the sensations only by being their cause.

Against this idea of a primary and a secondary attribution of goodness the following objection may be raised: To call a good-tasting apple good is both common and natural. It could hardly be maintained that it were uncommon or unnatural to call its taste good too, this simply is one of the uses of 'good'. But instead of calling the good-tasting apple's taste good, we could also call it agreeable or pleasant, whereas the apple itself would not commonly and naturally be called by those attributes. And now someone might wish to make a subtle distinction and say that 'good' is primarily an attribute of the thing and secondarily of the sensations it produces, 'pleasant' again primarily of the sensations and secondarily, if at all, of the physical object.

There are other senses of 'good' which apply *only* to the object, and not to the sensations it produces. For example: The apple can be good for storing or good for providing us with Vitamin C, but its taste cannot possess such goodness. There are thus, it would seem, a great many more senses in which the apple can be good or bad than in which its taste can be good or bad. But to argue from this that there is no sense of 'good', which applies genuinely or primarily to the taste of an apple (or to a sensation in general), seems to me to be quite wrong. The lesson taught by the use of the word 'pleasant' in the context is not that sensations could not be good in a primary sense, but that the word 'pleasant' is a synonym for the word 'good' in *one* of the latter's primary uses.

I shall accept the view that hedonic goodness of the sub-form, which I have called the pleasure of the senses, is primarily an attribute of sensations and secondarily of the objects which produce those sensations. The sentence 'this taste is good' I shall say expresses a *primary* hedonic value-judgment, and the sentence 'this apple is good', when 'good' is used in the hedonic sense, a *secondary* hedonic value-judgment.

3. In the sensation which a thing, as we say, 'produces' when it affects our senses, we sense one or several qualities of the thing. In tasting sugar, for example, we sense its taste-quality, which is sweetness. In tasting an apple we sense many qualities: a certain juiciness, sourness, maybe sweetness too. We could say that the taste-*quality* of the apple is a bundle or mixture of several qualities. (Not all of these ingredient qualities, by the way, are what we would ordinarily call taste-qualities. Some are olfactory qualities. Is juiciness a taste-quality?) In a similar manner we could say that the taste-*sensation* which we have of the apple is a bundle or mixture of several sensations. The several sensations themselves might be called ingredients, or ingredient sensations, of the total sensation.

Assume that a sensation, which contains several ingredient sensations of different qualities, is judged good or pleasant. Then it may happen that we can point to some of those ingredients and say that we judge the sensation pleasant, because of the presence in it of those very ingredients. The ingredients, thus pointed to, we could call *good-making* ingredients (ingredient sensations); and the qualities of the thing, thus sensed, we could call good-making qualities or properties of the thing. For example: someone may wish to maintain that what makes him like the taste of a certain apple, is the presence in it of a certain juiciness and sourness. Juiciness and sourness would then be good-making qualities of the apple, and the sensations of juiciness and sourness good-making ingredients of the total taste-sensation, which the person has of the apple.

In a sensation judged pleasant several ingredient sensations may thus become distinguished, *i.e.* several sense-qualities sensed. Now it may perhaps be thought that pleasantness itself is *one* such quality, just as for example sweetness is.[1]

The idea that pleasure or pleasantness were a sense-quality, *i.e.* something which we sense, is, I think, a bad confusion. I shall briefly indicate why I think so.

In the sensations we sense qualities; sensations are *of* certain qualities, we also say. Thus, for example, we may have a sensation of redness or sweetness. One sometimes calls a sensation of redness a red sensation. One can do so for the sake of verbal convenience. But it is highly misleading. For it suggests a view of sensations as a kind of thing, of the sensible qualities of which: colour, shape, smell, etc., we can talk. (The talk of the fake-entities called sense-data has, I am afraid, much encouraged this view among philosophers of an earlier generation.) But a sensation of red is not the *sort of entity* which smells or has a colour or can be tasted. One can sense a colour or a smell or a taste, but one cannot sense a sensation. What sort of properties then do sensations have? A sensation can, for example, be intense or vivid or dim or vague, it lasts for some time and then passes away, and it can be pleasant or unpleasant. A pleasant sensation is, I believe, sometimes called a sensation *of* pleasure. Perhaps there is some convenience in this mode of speech. But it should be remembered that 'a sensation of

[1] Passow's well-known *Handwörterbuch der griechischen Sprache* gives for the Greek word ἡδύς, of which 'hedonic' and 'hedonism' are linguistic off-springs, the German equivalents *süss* ('sweet') and *angenehm* ('pleasant') and suggests that the word was originally used for taste. Even if this suggestion be true, it does not follow, however, that the word was used as a name of a sense-quality *as distinct from* a value-attribute of sensations of this quality. The two uses, when speaking of sweet-tasting things, probably merged into one. These observations on the Greek ἡδύς may be said to show how deep-rooted is the tendency to view pleasure as *quasi* a sensible quality.

pleasure' is misleading in much the same way as 'a red sensation' is. That is: just as 'a red sensation' may be regarded as a logically distorted form of 'a sensation of redness', similarly 'a sensation of pleasure' may be regarded as a logical distortion of 'a pleasant sensation'.

But is not a sensation of sweetness a sweet sensation? I would answer: Properly speaking, only when 'sweet' is used in an analogical sense to mean 'pleasant' or something near it. 'Sweet' in English has clear analogical uses as a value attribute. 'How sweet of you', 'How nice of you', 'How good of you', say roughly the same. It is the existence of such analogical uses of 'sweet', I would suggest, which makes it appear more natural to speak of sweet sensations than of red or round sensations. Of the other adjectives for taste-qualities, 'bitter' and 'sour' are also used analogically as value attributes. But 'salt' is not quite in the same way and to the same extent used analogically. This perhaps explains why—at least in my ears—it sounds less natural to call a sensation of something salt a salt sensation than to call a sensation of something sweet or bitter or sour a sweet or bitter or sour sensation.

4. As naming the opposite to the thing named by the substantive 'pleasure', language—i.e. the English language (cf. sect. 1) suggests the substantive 'pain'. 'Unpleasure' is not a word in common use. 'Displeasure' again has to do with anger and trouble. It does not name an opposite to that which we have here called passive pleasure, and of which the sensuous pleasures are a sub-form. If it names an opposite of pleasure at all, then it would be of that form which we have called the pleasure of satisfaction, or of some sub-form of it. The displeased man feels dissatisfaction at or disapproves of something.

The adjective 'pleasant' may be said to have two linguistic opposites, 'unpleasant' and 'painful'.

The same arguments, which may be advanced for showing that pleasure and pleasantness are not sense-qualities, also apply to the unpleasant. But which is the status of the painful in this regard?

We speak of painful sensations. But the phrase 'a sensation of painfulness' sounds unnatural. This would indicate that 'painful' too does not refer to a sense-quality.

On the other hand, we speak of a sensation of pain. We have pain in a tooth or pain in the stomach. But we do not commonly say that we have pleasure in the mouth, when eating an apple. Pain, as has often been observed, is much more sensation-like than pleasure. The word 'pain' has analogical uses, which resemble the use of 'pleasure' in that they make the word a value-attribute. But it seems to me right to say that, *in its primary sense*, 'a pain' refers to a kind of sensation and that 'pain' names a sense-quality, of which, however, there are many shades. In this respect 'pain' is on a different logical level, both as compared with the substantive 'pleasure' and as compared with the adjectives 'pleasant', 'unpleasant', and 'painful'.

Pains which are sensations are 'bodily pains'. So-called 'mental pains' are not sensations. They are therefore 'pains' by analogy only.

That pleasure and pain are not contradictories is trivial. Not trivial, however, is that the two, because of their logical 'asymmetry', are not even contraries in any of the senses of 'contraries', which logicians distinguish. 'Pleasant' and 'unpleasant' denote contraries, likewise 'pleasant' and 'painful' and, when used in the hedonic sense, 'good' and 'bad'. If, furthermore, we regard the painful as a sub-form of the unpleasant, we could perhaps say that 'painful' names a stronger contrary to the pleasant than 'unpleasant'.

Neither 'painful' nor 'pleasant' are privative terms. Between the pleasant and the unpleasant there is a zone of genuinely value-indifferent states, and not merely of states which are left unclassified because of vagueness. This is a feature in which the hedonically good and bad differ from the instrumentally good and poor and from the technically and medically good and bad, but agrees with utilitarian goodness and badness.

Are pain-sensations *ipso facto* painful or, at least, unpleasant? I find the question difficult and puzzling. Since sensations are 'naturalistic' things and unpleasantness is a value-attribute, an affirmative answer would provide us with an interesting example of an *intrinsic* connexion between a section of the world of facts and a section of the realm of values.

It seems to be a *logical feature* of the concept of pain that *most* pain is also painful or unpleasant. This feature is probably logically connected with the facts that bodily injury usually is painful and that severe pain in itself often is injurious, in the sense that it has

70

adverse effects on the possibilities of the individual concerned to satisfy his needs and wants.

Yet, though necessarily *most* pain is painful (unpleasant), *all* pain, it seems, is not. 'A pleasant pain' is not a contradiction in terms, we have said before. (See Ch. III, sect. 9.) Some pain-sensations, moreover, we actually like, judge pleasant. An example would be when a father or mother pinches their child in a playful attitude of love or tenderness.

There can also be sensations which are both pleasant and painful to the same subject on the same occasion. But they must, as far as I can see, be *mixed* sensations—like a bitter sweetness. Thus 'painful pleasures' are sensations or other experiences with pleasant *and* painful ingredients. A 'pleasant pain' is different. It is not a sensation, which is *both* pleasant *and* painful. It is not a painful sensation at all. It is a pain-sensation, which we happen to like, judge pleasant, and *not* painful.

Of the painful pleasures it seems always true to say that their painful parts are something which we would, as such, rather be without than suffer. We endure the pain because the pleasure out-balances it, is greater than it. It, so to speak, *pays* to suffer the pain for the sake of the pleasure. But when the child welcomes a pinch with a laugh, this is not because the pain, though in itself dis-agreeable, were outbalanced by a greater pleasure. A pleasant pain is not a *price* we pay for some greater pleasure, but is itself pleasant.

5. We distinguished (in sect. 2) between primary hedonic judgments, the logical subjects of which are sensations or other states of consciousness, and secondary hedonic judgments, the logical subjects of which are events or things in the physical world. The secondary judgments are capable of *analysis* in terms of primary judgments and causal statements. The pattern of analysis is as follows:

The secondary judgment 'this X is good' has, roughly speaking, the same meaning as 'this X produces or has a disposition or tendency to produce pleasant (agreeable) sensations of such and such a kind'. An instantiation of the pattern would be: 'This apple is good' means 'this apple produces pleasant gustatory sensations'. In ordinary life we should not express ourselves thus, but instead of the last sentence say 'this apple has a good (pleasant) taste'. Let

71

us, however, not *now* mind the suggested piece of a philosopher's jargon. Let us also for the moment forget about the fact that the analysans does not specify about *whose* sensations we are talking, and thus is in an important respect an incomplete statement.

This analysis of secondary hedonic judgments shows a conspicuous resemblance to a well-known attempt at analysing moral judgments. I am thinking of the theory, or a variant of it, commonly known as the emotive theory of ethics.[1] According to this theory, broadly speaking, the sentence 'this *X* is morally good' means the same as the sentence 'this *X* produces or has a disposition or tendency to produce a feeling of moral approval'. The '*X*' usually stands for an arbitrary human act. Some authors speak simply of 'a feeling of approval', omitting the adjective 'moral' from the analysans. This makes their theory simpler, though hardly more plausible.

Our analysis of secondary hedonic judgments may be regarded as a simplified model of the corresponding ethical theory. Some of the logical features of the ethical theory, which have caused dispute, can, I think, be conveniently studied in the simplified model. One such disputed point is whether moral judgments, on the emotivist analysis, are true or false, or whether they merely are verbalized expressions of emotion and therefore lack truth-value. The form of emotive theory, which holds the first opinion, could be called *naturalistic subjectivism*. The form, which holds the second, we shall call *non-cognitivist subjectivism*.

Are hedonic judgments true or false? The secondary judgments involve a causal component. It traces certain sensations back to a physical thing as their cause. This causal component we shall here ignore. If we ignore it, our question reduces to the question whether primary hedonic judgments are true or false. To get a firmer grasp of this second question it will be necessary to distinguish two types of primary hedonic judgments. I shall call them, in a technical sense, *first person judgments* and *third person judgments*.

In a first person hedonic judgment the subject is judging of a sensation, which he is himself now experiencing or having, that it

[1] As a prototype may be taken the theory of Edvard Westermarck, first presented in his monumental work *The Origin and Development of the Moral Ideas* I–II (1906–08) and further developed and defended in *Ethical Relativity* (1932).

is agreeable or pleasant, that he likes experiencing or having it. In a third person hedonic judgment the subject is judging of the past, present, or future sensations of another subject that this other subject found or finds or will find them pleasant. Also the case, when a subject judges of the hedonic quality of his own past or future sensations, will here count as third person judgments. The subject is then, as it were, speaking of himself from outside, in the perspective of time.

Third person hedonic judgments obviously are true or false. That Mr. So-and-so likes or does not like or dislikes the taste of an apple, which he is now eating, is true or false. So are the statements that most people like the taste of this or that sort of apple or that they would, if they tasted it, like this particular apple. The difficulties of coming to know the truth-value may be considerable: when the apple is eaten, how *can* we know whether somebody, who never tasted it, would have liked it? Perhaps the answer is that we cannot *know* this. But from this does not follow that the statement is not true or false.

When ascertaining the truth of a third person hedonic judgment, we largely rely on first person hedonic judgments. Does N. N. like the apple, which he is now eating? We ask him and he replies 'Yes' or 'I like it'. His words express a first person hedonic judgment. It is used for assessing the truth of the third person hedonic judgment that N. N. likes the taste of the apple he is eating or, which means the same, that he finds the taste of the apple he is eating good. We may regard the evidence provided by the first person judgment as being so strong that all doubts about the truth-value of the third person judgment are expelled. But sometimes we do not attach much weight to the evidence, *e.g.* because N. N. is a very polite man and is therefore likely to say of an apple, which we have offered him, that he likes it even when in fact he does not. If this were the case, we should probably, in forming our opinion as to whether he liked the fruit or not, rely more on N. N.'s facial expression, when eating the apple, than on his words.

Do first person hedonic judgments have a truth-value? This is a very difficult question and part of a much larger question pertaining to the logical status of first person present-tense statements in general and first person statements about sensations in particular. One may argue the view—successfully, I think—that in the first person hedonic judgments no statements are made at all, and that

73

the judgments therefore cannot properly be called true or false. When the words 'the taste of this apple is good' are used as a first person judgment, they *express* ('give vent to') my pleasure at the taste and do not *state* that I am pleased or *describe* myself as a being, who approves of the taste.

The same distinction between first person and third person judgments can, of course, also be made for judgments about the occurrence of those more subtle phenomena called 'feelings of moral approval or indignation'. In the case of such feelings, too, it is fairly obvious that the third person judgments are objectively true or false, whereas it is at least arguable that the first person judgments are not true or false *statements about feelings*, but neither true nor false *expressions of feeling*.

One could try to do distributive justice to the claims both of naturalistic and non-cognitivist subjectivism as theories of hedonic value-judgments by apportioning to each theory a due share in the truth—to the first because of the propositional character of the third person judgments, and to the second because of the interjectional character of the first person judgments. But by practising such impartiality one runs risk of obscuring an important point. This point is that the third person judgments, just because of the feature of theirs which makes them true or false, *viz.* that they are about the valuations of other subjects (or about the judging subject's own valuations viewed in the perspective of time), *are no genuine value-judgments at all*. They are no value-judgments, since they do not value, but report or conjecture about human reactions, *i.e.* such reactions which we call valuations. The only genuine value-judgments in the context are the first person judgments. In them the judging subject values his sensations. They are not true or false, and therefore, in *a* sense of the word, no 'judgments' even. For this reason it seems to me fair to say that non-cognitivist subjectivism represents the correct view of hedonic value-judgments, whereas naturalistic subjectivism is not a theory of value-judgments at all.

In their relation to truth (primary) hedonic value-judgments, unless I am badly mistaken, differ importantly from judgments of instrumental, technical, or utilitarian goodness. These latter judgments are true or false; one can always be mistaken in them. The primary hedonic value-judgments are neither true nor false, there is no room for mistake in them. They are, in this peculiar sense, 'subjective'. In their sphere one cannot distinguish between an *apparent* and a *real* good; 'to be good' and 'to be judged (or considered or thought) good' are here one and the same. But judgments in which we affirm or anticipate the occurrence of such and such hedonic valuations in ourselves or in other subjects are, of course, true or false judgments—though not value-judgments.

6. Hedonic goodness of the form which we called passive pleasure, is a value-attribute of sensations and other states of consciousness. To call this form of goodness an attribute or characteristic or property of sensations is useful when we want to explain why pleasure itself is not a sensation or a sense-quality (of a thing, which is sensed in a sensation). But to call hedonic goodness a property can also be misleading.

Sensations are tied to a subject. They are somebody's sensations. If the secondary hedonic judgment expressed in the words 'this apple is good' is analysed in terms of primary judgments about the goodness or pleasantness of some gustatory sensations, the question will instantly arise: Of *whose* sensations are we here talking? The overt form of the sentence, which expresses the secondary judgment, does not give us any guidance, since it does not mention an apple-taster. Nor does the overt form of sentences, which express primary hedonic judgments, always mention a subject. 'The taste of this apple is good' and 'this is a pleasant taste' are complete sentences. But I think it is correct to say that the *sense* of the sentences is incomplete, unless it is understood, from the context or otherwise, whose taste-sensations are meant. If this is true of sentences expressing a primary hedonic judgment, the same will *a fortiori* be true of any sentence expressing a secondary hedonic judgment, into the analysis of which the primary judgment may enter.

How is mention of a sensing subject to be worked into the overt form of a sentence expressing a hedonic judgment about the taste of an apple? Let us assume, for the sake of argument, that the subject is the speaker himself. He might then, instead of 'the taste of this apple is good', say 'I find the taste of this apple good'. Instead of 'find' he may also say 'think' or 'judge' or 'consider'. Perhaps he would use the form of words 'I think that the taste of this apple is good'. But this sounds artificial, at least as an expression of his judgment, when he is actually tasting the apple. (It sounds

75

more like a conjecture that he *will* like the taste.) It would also sound rather artificial to say 'the taste of this apple is good to me'. But to say 'I like the taste of this apple'—thus not using the word 'good' at all—would sound perfectly natural.

It will strike us that a majority of these sentences, which mention a subject, are not of the ordinary subject-predicate form, in which a property is predicated of a thing. It may be questioned whether any of them really is of this form. It may also be questioned whether not the overt subject-predicate form of sentences expressing hedonic judgments with suppressed reference to a sensing subject is really spurious, *viz.* as a reflexion of the judgment's logical form. Among the sentences which we gave as examples, the one which comes nearest to being of the ordinary subject-predicate form is 'the taste of this apple is good to me'. If 'good to me' could be said to name a property, then this sentence could be safely said to be a subject-predicate sentence. But 'good to me' rather suggests a relation between the apple-taster and the apple-taste than a property of the taste-sensation. If it be asked what this relation is, a plausible answer would be that it is the liking-relation, or some relation closely akin to it. The sensing subject likes, enjoys, approves of the taste of the apple. This is what could be reasonably meant by the unnatural-sounding form of words 'the taste of this apple is good to me'.

The sentence 'I think that the taste of this apple is good' contains a subject-predicate sentence as a part, within a 'that'-clause. It is not itself a subject-predicate sentence. As already noted, it has a certain artificiality about itself. It suggests to us that a distinction could be made between the taste's being good—as it were 'in itself'—and somebody's thinking or judging or opining of the taste *that* it is good. I can, of course, think or judge or opine that I shall like the taste of this apple, and perhaps find on tasting it that I was mistaken. But, as we had already occasion to stress, when we were speaking of the subjectivity of hedonic value-judgments, I cannot judge the taste of the apple, which I am now tasting, good and be mistaken. Therefore, to think that the taste is good is not to think that something *is* thus and thus, but *might be* otherwise. The taste, which is the logical subject of the first person judgment, cannot, from the point of view of its hedonic value, *be* anything else but what I *think it is*. The use of 'think that' is here quite unlike the normal use of this phrase.

76

It was this slightly unnatural use of 'that'-clauses in value-sentences which suggested to Moore[1] the following refutation of subjectivism in value-theory: If 'this is good' means the same as 'I think that this is good', then by raising the same question over again for the 'this is good', which occurs inside the 'that'-clause, we get as an answer that 'this is good' means the same as 'I think that I think that this is good', and so on *ad infinitum*. This is a clever point as it stands, but not of much consequence for the task of refuting subjectivism. It only establishes that, if the words 'I think that this is good' are offered as an equivalent of 'this is good', then the 'I think that . . .'-form functions in a peculiar way, which should make its very use here sound suspect to our logical ear. If the subjectivist says that 'this is good' means 'I think this good' or 'I consider this good', omitting the word 'that', he is already better off, and Moore's objection cannot be raised against him.[2]

These considerations, in my opinion, tend to show that hedonic goodness is not a *property* and that the subject-predicate form of sentences, which express hedonic judgments, is a spurious reflexion of the logical form of such judgments, which is the *relational* form. As the logically most satisfactory formulations of such judgments in language I should regard their formulation with the aid of the verb 'to like', as for example in the sentence, 'I like the taste of this apple'. But this, needless to say, does not make the subject-predicate form either useless or incorrect as a shorthand formulation in all those innumerous cases, when mention of a sensing subject is omitted from the sentence. The sentences 'this is a good apple' or 'this is a good taste' are all right as they stand. But they are apt to mislead the philosopher by concealing a logical form.

7. To think of pleasure exclusively in terms of predications of pleasantness to various logical subjects is thus philosophically

---

[1] See *Ethics* (1912), p. 76. Moore, when giving the 'refutation', is immediately dealing with the subjectivist suggestion that 'this is right' meant the same as 'somebody believes that this is right'. But the same argument applies, he maintains, to the suggestion that the rightness of an act meant that the act is thought to be right (p. 80) and also to the corresponding suggestion about goodness (p. 98).

[2] It is significant that Moore, when stating the subjectivist view, often uses the formulation 'thinks it right (good)', but when trying to refute it by means of the argument *ad infinitum* switches to the formulation 'thinks (believes) that it is right (good)'.

misleading. To think of pleasure in terms of liking is philosophically enlightening and helpful. Beside 'like', also 'approve' and 'enjoy' are relational verbs, which may be used for expressing hedonic judgments. That of which we approve is normally said to please us, but is not ordinarily said to give us pleasure. 'Enjoy' is more obviously hedonic than 'approve'; any source of enjoyment can also be called a source of pleasure, and *vice versa*.

Among our likings an important position are held by things we *like to do*. One man likes to watch cricket, another to play chess, a third likes to get up early in the morning.

The way in which liking to do is connected with pleasure is rather different in these three examples. The pleasure of watching a game is mainly, I should think, of the form which we have called passive pleasure. Watching a game means the acquisition of experiences which the man, who likes watching the game, finds pleasant. Is his pleasure that of the senses? There are reasons for saying that it is, since our man is enjoying a sight. There are perhaps even stronger reasons for saying that it is not, since enjoying this sight normally requires both knowledge of the rules of the game and some familiarity with the practice of playing it. The border between sensuous pleasure and other forms of passive pleasure is *very* elastic.

The pleasure of playing a game has many aspects. Sometimes one plays a game just for amusement, as a pastime. Then the pleasure which one derives from playing the game is substantially passive pleasure, *i.e.* the pleasantness of certain experiences. But often we like playing a game, *not* 'for the sake of amusement', but because we are interested in the game, *keen on* the art of playing it. Then the delight we take in the game is of the form which I called active pleasure. The same is the case with any pleasure derived from the practising of any activity, of which it is true to say that we are *keen on* it or that we like it 'for its own sake'. It will occur to us that there is a connexion between technical goodness and the form of hedonic goodness called active pleasure. This connexion may be intrinsic. The two forms of goodness are nevertheless distinct.

Consider next the man who likes to get up early in the morning. Must he find early rising pleasant? *Some* men may rise early for 'hedonic' reasons, *i.e.* in order to enjoy the morning: the freshness of the morning air, the beauty of the sunrise, etc. But rather few,

I think, of those who say they 'like' to get up early, would give such reasons for their liking. Someone may like to get up early because he has so many things to do that, if he stays in bed till late, he will not have time to do them at all, or his afternoon will be badly rushed or he will have to work at night. But he may be completely indifferent to the peculiar pleasures of the early morning hours. Should this man not rather then say that he *wants to* get up early than say that he *likes to* get up early? Or perhaps the suggestion will be that our man should say that he *has to* or *must* get up early, considering that this is not anything which he likes or wants to do 'for its own sake', but something that is forced upon him by the 'practical necessities' of life. (Cf. Ch. VIII.) The answer is that the uses of 'like to do' and 'want to do' and 'have to do' shade into one another, and that we sometimes say that we like to do things, the doing of which is a source neither of passive nor of active pleasure to us.

But is there not at least a remote connexion with pleasure also in this third case which we have been discussing? The man who rises early may want to do so in order to avoid having to rush his day's work, which is an unpleasant thing. Or he may be anxious to finish his set work as early in the day as possible, so that he can relax and do in the afternoon what he 'really likes', *i.e.* that which affords him (active or passive) pleasure. These possibilities are not unrealistic. Now it may be argued that, unless our man has *some* such desire either to avoid something unpleasant or to secure for himself some pleasure, then he could not say truly of himself even that he *wants to* get up early in the morning. To argue thus about the man would be to apply to his case a general philosophic thesis about the nature of man, *viz.* that all action is, in the last resort, necessarily prompted by a desire to secure some pleasure or avoid something unpleasant. This is the thesis, or a version of the thesis, known as *psychological hedonism*. We must here try to form some opinion of its truth.

8. Not everything which a man can be said to do is voluntary action. For example: getting fat or sleeping. And not everything which a man does and which is voluntary action, can he also, on any ordinary understanding of the words, be said to *want to do*. Most things which a man does 'because this is the custom', *e.g.* taking off his hat when greeting a lady, or 'because this is the rule

or law', *e.g.* driving to the left or halting in front of a major road ahead, are not things he 'wants to do', whenever he does them. But some of the things which a man voluntarily does, he also wants to do, and some of the things he wants to do he also likes to do.

To maintain psychological hedonism for all voluntary action is hardly feasible. To maintain it for those acts and activities only which a man enjoys doing or likes to do, may seem too narrow to be of much interest. The exact scope of the claim of psychological hedonism is seldom made clear. I shall here regard it as a thesis concerning *at least* all those things, which a man can be properly said to *want to do*. What does this thesis say? That too is seldom made sufficiently clear. I shall here understand it as saying something which can, for purposes of a first approximation, be stated as follows: If, in an individual case, we raise the question *why* a man wants that which he wants to do, the answer will, if not immediately then after a chain of questions and answers, have to mention something which this man likes, finds pleasant or dislikes, finds unpleasant or painful. This statement is admittedly vague, but I hope the subsequent discussion of it will make its intended meaning clearer. (See also Ch. V, sect. 2.)

A man says he wants to get up early to-morrow morning. Why? Because he wants to see the sunrise. Why? Because he enjoys the sight, likes it. The answer to the further question, why he likes sunrises, is *not* that their sight gives him pleasure. For his liking of the sight of a sunrise and the sight's giving him pleasure are one and the same.

The question may, of course, be raised, why the spectacle pleases him. It is not certain that it can be answered. It would be answered by pointing to some fact in the man's life-history, which tells us what *made him like* ('caused' him to like) sunrises. This question 'Why?' does not ask for a reason or motive, but for a (kind of) causal explanation. The question 'Why?', which is relevant to the thesis of psychological hedonism, is a question concerning reasons for doing, *i.e.* ends in acting.

Our early riser can rightly be called a pleasure-seeker. His action is motivated by a desire to secure for himself a certain pleasant experience. He wants to get up early, not because early rising is, as such or in itself, pleasant to him, but because the act is conducive to pleasure, *i.e.* is a necessary condition for his attaining a pleasant experience in the end.

Consider now the following case: A man wants to get up early some morning to see the sunrise. He has never seen one before, but he has heard many people praise the beauty of the sight. He does not, however, expect that he will particularly like it and he is not anxious to secure for himself a new pleasure. He simply is curious to know what the sight, which so many people praise, looks like. Inquisitiveness can be a thoroughly self-sufficient motive of action. The chain of questions and answers could run as follows: Why does he want to get up early? Because he wants to see the sunrise. Why does he want to see the sunrise? Because he is curious about the sight. Here is no mention of liking or pleasure. Perhaps we can also answer the question: What *made* him curious? and that the answer is: The fact that so many poets, whom he reads, have written enthusiastically about sunrises. This question is causal. The fact that its answer can be said to hint at the likings and pleasures of poets is here irrelevant. Our man could equally well be curious to see something which people notoriously dislike. His inquisitiveness, *not* his desire for some pleasant experience, prompts his action.

I think that the case of the curious man refutes hedonism, but the difficulty is to see that it really does so decisively. For could one not argue as follows:

Our inquisitive man is anxious to satisfy his inquisitiveness. The *satisfaction* of this desire gives him pleasure. If any case of doing that, which one wants to do, can be correctly described as a case of satisfying some desire—and let us not here query the correctness of this view—and if to have one's desires satisfied is a pleasure, is then not psychological hedonism after all right?

Before we answer this question, we must say some words about the relation of pleasure to satisfaction of desire.

Desire is sometimes called a dissatisfaction or discontentedness with a prevailing state of things; it is an impulse or longing to change this state to another. The change, at which a desire aims, could therefore also be characterized as a transition from a present 'unpleasure' to a future pleasure. Here, however, great caution is needed. The phrase 'transition from a present unpleasure to a future pleasure' can mean many things. It can mean that the state in which we are now is judged unpleasant, and the one at which we aim is thought of as pleasant. For example: we feel uncomfortable or bored and want to do something which will make us feel

81

comfortable or which will amuse us, cheer us up. Here unpleasantness and pleasantness are clearly hedonic features of the states. This is a common type of desire-situation. But it is not the only type. The case, *e.g.*, of the man who wants to satisfy his curiosity, is different. To have an unsatisfied curiosity can be agitating, exciting, vexing. It *can* be unpleasant too. But it need not be so. Someone may even think that curiosity is more of a pleasant than an unpleasant feeling. Yet on the other hand: if attempts to satisfy our curiosity fail, we shall probably feel annoyed or grieved or even outraged, and *these* states we should ordinarily judge unpleasant. Something corresponding, it seems, holds good of desire in general: frustration is unpleasant, sometimes to the degree of being painful.

I think it is correct to say that frustration of desire is *intrinsically* unpleasant. We should not say that a desire had become 'frustrated', unless one or several unsuccessful attempts to gratify the desire had not had *some* hedonically bad consequences, such as anger, annoyance, grief, impatience, hurt vanity, or the like.

Similarly, it seems to me right to think that satisfaction of desire is intrinsically pleasant. But the connexion between satisfaction and pleasure is more complicated than the connexion between frustration and hedonic badness. This is due to the fact that the description of a desire involves mention of an *object of desire*. The object is *that which* we desire. The attainment of the object intrinsically, 'by definition', satisfies the desire. Thus attainment of the object is, in a sense, intrinsically satisfying. But from this does not follow that the object itself were intrinsically pleasant or otherwise hedonically good. The hedonically good consequences, which are intrinsically connected with satisfaction of desire, consist in feelings of contentedness or joy or power or relief or something similar. If they are not consequent upon the attainment of the object, we should doubt whether there was any desire at all or whether it had been correctly described as a desire for so-and-so.

It is on the evidence of such hedonically tinged consequences both of frustration and of satisfaction that we often judge the strength of the desire. 'He cannot have wanted it very eagerly, since he was not very glad when he got it'; 'He must have desired it strongly, since failure to get it depressed him so much', we say.

For the pleasure, which is intrinsically connected with satisfaction of desire, we already coined (in section 1) the name *pleasure of satisfaction*. It is the existence of an intrinsic tie between satisfaction and pleasure, I think, which is above all responsible for the strong appearance of truth, which the thesis of psychological hedonism undoubtedly possesses. The refutation of hedonism must therefore not consist in an attempt to deny the existence of this connexion.

Wherein then does the refutation consist? As far as I can see, it consists solely in this:

The pleasure of satisfying a desire can never be an object of that *same* desire. For satisfaction presupposes a desire, and a desire in its turn presupposes something which we desire, an object. Therefore the object of desire must necessarily be different from the pleasure of satisfying *that* desire. But the pleasure drawn from the satisfaction of a desire can itself become the object of a *new* desire. This is perhaps not very common, but it is not an entirely unrealistic possibility. Consider again the man who wants to see the sunrise, because he is curious about the sight. It is conceivable that experience had taught him that satisfying a curiosity is something very pleasant. He is of a peculiar inquisitive disposition or temper. Each time he is curious about something he is extremely tense, and when his curiosity has become satisfied he has an immensely exhilarating and joyful feeling of relief. This man welcomes every opportunity for satisfying a curiosity, *because of the pleasure this gives him*. This pleasure is the passive pleasure of some peculiar experience following upon the satisfaction of a curiosity. There is nothing in the logic of things to prevent it from becoming the object of a new desire, *viz*. the desire for the pleasure of having satisfied a curiosity. But whether the original pleasure of satisfaction will or will not itself thus turn into an object of desire is an entirely *contingent* matter. It is the contingent nature of this fact which, in my opinion, constitutes the refutation of psychological hedonism. The error of hedonism is that it mistakes the necessary connexion, which holds between the satisfaction of desire and pleasure, for a necessary connexion between desire and pleasure *as its object*. This mistake is easy to make, but not quite easy to expose. This is why I have spent so much time here on the refutation of psychological hedonism, although this doctrine is said to have been refuted over and over again in the past. I am not certain that any 'refutation' does full justice to the complications of the theory, and the problems raised by it still continue to vex me.

9. Something can be an object of desire, *although* it is thought unpleasant. The question may be raised whether anything can be an object of desire *because* it is considered unpleasant. Can, in other words, the contrary of pleasure be an object of desire?

A pain can be an object of desire. A man can want to inflict pain upon himself as a chastisement. But he can also want this simply because he likes the pain. This is perhaps perverse, but it is not contrary to logic. It is not illogical, since—as we have said before—a pleasant pain is not a contradiction in terms.

A man can also want something for himself which he finds unpleasant—for example to undergo a surgical operation because he considers it necessary or good for his bodily health or general well-being. A man can desire the unpleasant out of sheer curiosity. 'What will be my reaction? Shall I faint or vomit?' One can be intensely curious about such things. A man could take a perverse pleasure in vomiting, and for the sake of this pleasure want to eat something extremely distasteful. In none of these cases, however, in which something unpleasant is wanted, do we want the unpleasant for the sake of its being unpleasant, but for the sake of something else—some pleasure maybe—to which it is conducive.

The fact that the *contrary of pleasure*, if I am right, thus *necessarily is not* an object of desire, may have contributed to the illusion of psychological hedonism that *pleasure necessarily is* the ultimate end, after which people aspire whenever they want something.

10. A few brief remarks will here be made on the doctrine known as Ethical Hedonism.

We shall distinguish between two principal forms, which this doctrine may assume:

Firstly, Ethical Hedonism can be a theory about the concept of goodness or the meaning of the word 'good'. In its crudest form this theory maintains that any context where the word 'good' is used (not mentioned), either is one from which 'good' can be eliminated by simply substituting for it the word 'pleasant'—as in the phrase 'a good-smelling flower'—or is one from which 'good' can be eliminated by means of an analysis in terms of 'pleasure'—as, on our suggested view of secondary hedonic judgments, it may become eliminated from the phrase 'a good apple'.

Secondly, Ethical Hedonism can be an axiological theory about the character of good things. In its crudest form this theory defends some such view as that those and only those things are good, which either are judged pleasant in themselves, or are (somehow) instrumental or useful for the production of pleasure, *i.e.* causally responsible for the coming into being of pleasant things.

Moore, in his well-known criticism of hedonism, thought that the axiological theory could be refuted on the ground that it conflicts with our value-intuitions and the conceptual theory on the ground that it commits 'the Naturalistic Fallacy'. 'Good' means good, Moore says, and not anything else, *e.g.* pleasant. About this I shall only say that it seems to me just as obvious that 'good' *sometimes* means 'pleasant' or can otherwise become translated into hedonic terms as it seems to me obvious that 'good' does *not always* mean 'pleasant' or can become thus translated. The pleasant, pleasure, we have called a *form* of the good or of goodness. It is equally futile to try to reduce this form to one or several others as it is to try to reduce all other forms to it. But there may exist logical connexions of a more complex and subtle nature between the forms.

If one is aware of the multiform nature of goodness, one will realize that the general question 'Is pleasure good?' is unintelligible, unless the form of goodness is specified. In one sense of 'good' the question is just as empty of content or logically defect as the questions 'Is pleasure pleasant?' or 'Is goodness good?'. When correctly stated, the question must mean something along the following lines: Are the things, which are good hedonically, also good in some other respect? And here this other respect must be specified. The question may be well worth discussing. So may the converse question be: Are the things, which are in such-and-such respect good, also good hedonically? In the case of neither question, however, would an affirmative answer establish that pleasure is the 'sole and ultimate good' in any reasonable sense of those unprecise words.

V

THE GOOD OF MAN

1. THE notion of the good of man, which will be discussed in this chapter, is the central notion of our whole inquiry. The problems connected with it are of the utmost difficulty. Many things which I say about them may well be wrong. Perhaps the best I can hope for is that what I say will be interesting enough to be worth a refutation.

We have previously (Ch. III, sect. 6) discussed the question, what kind of being has a good. We decided that it should make sense to talk of the good of everything, of the *life* of which it is meaningful to speak. On this ruling there can be no doubt that man *has* a good.

Granted that man has a good—what *is* it? The question can be understood in a multitude of senses. It can, for example, be understood as a question of a *name*, a verbal equivalent of that which we *also* call 'the good of man'.

We have already (Ch. I, sect. 5) had occasion to point out that the German equivalent of the English substantive 'good', when this means the good of man or some other being, is *das Wohl*. There is no substantive 'well' with *this* meaning in English. But there are two related substantives, 'well-being' and 'welfare'.

A being who, so to speak, 'has' or 'enjoys' its good, is also said to *be well* and, sometimes, to *do well*.

The notion of being well is related to the notion of health. Often 'to be well' means exactly the same as 'to be in good, bodily and mental, health'. A man is said to be well when he is all right, fit, in good shape generally. These various expressions may be said to refer to minimum requirements of enjoying one's good.

Of the being who does well, we also say that it flourishes, thrives,

86

or prospers. And we call it happy. If health and well-being primarily connote something privative, absence of illness and suffering; happiness and well-doing again primarily refer to something positive, to an overflow or surplus of agreeable states and things.

From these observations on language three candidates for a name of the good of man may be said to emerge. These are 'happiness', 'well-being', and 'welfare'.

The suggestion might be made that 'welfare' is a comprehensive term which covers the whole of that which we also call 'the good of man' and of which happiness and well-being are 'aspects' or 'components' or 'parts'. It could further be suggested that there is a broad sense of 'happiness', and of 'well-being', to mean the same or roughly the same as 'welfare'. So that, on *one* way of understanding them, the three terms could be regarded as rough synonyms and alternative names of the good of man.

The suggestion that 'the good of man' and 'the welfare of man' are synonymous phrases I accept without discussion. That is: I shall use and treat them as synonyms. (Cf. Ch. I, sect. 5; also Ch. III, sect. 1.)

It is hardly to be doubted that 'happiness' is sometimes used as a rough synonym of 'welfare'. More commonly, however, the two words are *not* used as synonyms. Happiness and welfare may, in fact, become distinguished as two concepts of different logical category or type. We shall here mention three features which may be used for differentiating the two concepts logically.

First of all, the two concepts have a primary connexion with two different forms of the good. One could say, though with caution, that happiness is a *hedonic*, welfare again a *utilitarian* notion. Happiness is allied to pleasure, and therewith to such notions as those of enjoyment, gladness, and liking. Happiness has no immediate logical connexion with the beneficial. Welfare again is primarily a matter of things beneficial and harmful, *i.e.* good and bad, for the being concerned. As happiness, through pleasure, is related to that which a man enjoys and likes, in a similar manner welfare, through the beneficial, is connected with that which a man wants and needs. (Cf. Ch. I, sect. 5.)

Further, happiness is more like a 'state' (state of affairs) than welfare is. A man can become happy, be happy, and cease to be happy. He can be happy, and unhappy, more than once in his life. Happiness, like an end, can be achieved and attained. Welfare has

87

not these same relationships to events, processes, and states *in time*.

Finally, a major logical difference between happiness and welfare is their relation to *causality*. Considerations of welfare are essentially considerations of how the doing and happening of various things will causally affect a being. One cannot pronounce on the question whether something is good or bad for a man, without considering the causal connexions in which this thing is or may become embedded. But one can pronounce on the question whether a man is happy or not, without necessarily considering what were the causal antecedents and what will be the consequences of his present situation.

The facts that happiness is primarily a hedonic and welfare primarily a utilitarian notion, and that they have logically different relationships to time and to causality, mark the two concepts as being of that which I have here called 'different logical category or type'. It does not follow, however, that the two concepts are logically entirely unconnected. They are, on the contrary, closely allied. What then is their mutual relation? This is a question, on which I have not been able to form a clear view. Welfare (the good of a being) is, somehow, the broader and more basic notion. (Cf. Ch. III, sect. 12.) It is also the notion which is of greater importance to ethics and to a general study of the varieties of goodness. Calling happiness an 'aspect' or 'component' or 'part' of the good of man is a non-committal mode of speech which is not meant to say more than this. Of happiness I could also say that it is the consummation or crown or flower of welfare. But these are metaphorical terms and do not illuminate the logical relationship between the two concepts.

2. By an end of action we shall understand anything, *for the sake of which* an action is undertaken. If something, which we want to do, is not wanted for the sake of anything else, the act or activity can be called an *end in itself*.

Ends can be intermediate or ultimate. Sometimes a man wants to attain an end for the sake of some further end. Then the first end is *intermediate*. An end, which is not pursued for the sake of any further end, is *ultimate*. We shall call a human act *end-directed*, if it is undertaken either as an end in itself or for the sake of some end.

What is an ultimate end of action is settled by the last answer, which the agent himself can give to the question, *why* he does or intends to do this or that. It is then understood that the question 'Why?' asks for a reason and not for a causal explanation of his behaviour. (Cf. Ch. IV, sect. 8.)

In the terms which have here been introduced, we could re-define Psychological Hedonism as the doctrine that every end-directed human act is undertaken, ultimately, for the sake either of attaining some pleasure or avoiding something unpleasant. The doctrine again that every end-directed human act is undertaken, ultimately, for the sake of the acting agent's happiness we shall call Psychological Eudaimonism. A doctrine to the effect that every end-directed act is ultimately undertaken for the sake of the acting agent's welfare (good) has, to the best of my knowledge, never been defended. We need not here invent a name for it.

Aristotle sometimes talks[1] as though he had subscribed to the doctrine of psychological eudaimonism. If this was his view, he was certainly mistaken and, moreover, contradicting himself. It would be sheer nonsense to maintain that every chain of (non-causal) questions 'Why did you do this?' and answers to them must terminate in a reference to happiness. The view that man, in every-thing he does, is aiming at happiness (and the avoidance of misery) is even more absurd than the doctrine that he, in everything he does, is aiming at pleasure (and the avoidance of pain).

I said that, if Aristotle maintained psychological eudaimonism, he was contradicting himself. (And for this reason I doubt that Aristotle wanted to maintain it, though some of his formulations would indicate that he did.) For Aristotle also admits that there are ends, other than happiness, which we pursue for their own sake. He mentions pleasure and honour among them.[2] Even 'if nothing resulted from them, we should still choose each of them', he says.[3] On the other hand, those other final ends are sometimes desired, *not* for their own sake, but for the sake of something else. Whereas happiness, Aristotle thinks, is *never* desired for the sake of anything else.[4] Pleasure, *e.g.* pleasant amusement, can be desired for

---

[1] See, *e.g., Ethica Nicomachea (EN)*, 1094a 18–21, 1095a 14–20, and 1176b 30–31.

[2] *EN*, 1097b 1–2. See also 1172b 20–23.

[3] *EN*, 1097b 2–3.

[4] *EN*, 1097b 1 and again 1097b 5–6.

relaxation, and relaxation for the sake of continued activity.[1] *Then* pleasure is not a final end.

I would understand Aristotle's so-called eudaimonism in the following light: among possible ends of human action, *eudaimonia* holds a unique position. This unique position is *not* that *eudaimonia* is the final end of all action. It is that *eudaimonia* is the only end that is never anything except final. It is of the nature of *eudaimonia* that it cannot be desired for the sake of anything else. *This* is, so Aristotle seems to think, why *eudaimonia* is the highest good for man.[2]

It is plausible to think that a man can pursue, *i.e.* do things for the sake of promoting or safeguarding, his own happiness only as an ultimate end of his action. A man can also do things for the sake of promoting or safeguarding the happiness of some other being. It may be thought that he can do this only as an intermediate end of his action. The idea has an apparent plausibility, but is nevertheless a mistake. The truth seems to be that a man can pursue the happiness of others either as intermediate *or* as ultimate end.

The delight of a king can be the happiness of his subjects. He gives all his energies and work to the promotion of this end. Maybe he sacrifices his so-called 'personal happiness' for the good of those over whom he is set to rule. Yet, if this is what he likes to do, it is also that in which his happiness consists. To say this is not so distort facts logically. But to say that the king sacrifices himself for the sake of becoming happy and not for the sake of making others happy, would be a distortion. It would be a distortion similar to that of which psychological hedonism is guilty, when it maintains that everything is done for the sake of pleasure, on the ground that all satisfaction of desire may be thought intrinsically pleasant.

Can a man's *welfare* be an end of his own action? The question is equivalent to asking, whether a man can ever be truly said to do things for the sake of promoting or protecting his own good. It is not quite clear which is the correct answer.

---

[1] Cf. *EN*, 1176b 34–35.

[2] There is no phrase in Aristotle's ethics which corresponds to our phrase 'the good of man'. *Eudaimonia* (happiness, well-being) Aristotle also calls the best or the highest good. The notion of a *summum bonum*, however, is not identical with the notion of the good of man as we use it here. But the two notions may be related.

On the view which is here taken of the good of a being, to do something for the sake of promoting one's own good, means to do something *because* one considers doing it *good for* oneself. And to do something for the sake of protecting one's own good means to do something *because* one considers neglecting it bad for oneself.

For all I can see, men sometimes do things for the reasons just mentioned. This would show that a man's welfare *can be* an end of his own action.

Yet the good of a being as an end of action is a very peculiar sort of 'end'. Normally, an end of action is a state of affairs, something which 'is there', when the end has been attained. But welfare is not a state of affairs. (Cf. the discussion in section 1.) For this reason I shall say that welfare, the good of a being, can only in an *oblique* sense be called an end of action.

Obviously, the reason why a man does something, which he considers good for himself, is not always and necessarily *that* he considers doing it good for himself. Similarly, the reason why a man does something, which he considers bad for him to neglect, is not always and necessarily *that* he considers neglecting it bad for himself. This shows that a man's own welfare is not always an ultimate end of his action. It also shows that a man's own welfare is not always an end of his action at all. It does not show, however, that a man's own welfare is sometimes an intermediate end of his action. Whether it *can* be an intermediate end, I shall not attempt to decide. If the answer is negative, it would follow that, when a man's own welfare is an end of his action, it is necessarily an ultimate end.

Sometimes a man does something because he considers doing it good for another being, and neglects something because he considers doing it bad for another being. It is obvious that another man's good can be the *intermediate* end of a man's action. The reason why the master takes heed to promote and protect the welfare of his servants, can be that he expects them to serve him more efficiently if they thrive and are happy. Then his servants' welfare is an intermediate end of the master's. It may be suggested that, when the end of a man's action is another being's welfare, then it is necessarily an intermediate end. This suggestion, I think, is false. We shall return to the topic later (Chapter IX), when discussing egoism and altruism.

Beings can be handled or treated as means to somebody's ends. This is the case, *e.g.*, with domestic animals and slaves. Philosophers have sometimes entertained the idea that beings could also be treated as 'ends' or 'ends in themselves'. It is not clear what it means to say that a being, *e.g.* a man, is an 'end in itself'. But treating a man as an end in itself *could mean*, I suggest, that we do certain things because we consider them good for that man (and for no other ulterior reason) and abstain from doing certain things because we consider them bad for that man. In other words: whenever a being's good is an ultimate end of action, that being is treated as an end in itself. A man can treat other men thus, but also himself. That men *should be* thus treated is an interesting view of the nature of moral duty. We shall briefly talk of this in Chapter X.

In the next five sections of the present chapter we shall be dealing with various aspects of the concept of happiness and in the last five sections with questions relating to the concept of welfare.

3. Happiness, we said, is a hedonic notion. It is, of course, not *the same* as pleasure. Nor can it be defined, as has been suggested, as 'pleasure and the absence of pain'.

Moralists who have written about happiness have sometimes associated the notion more intimately with one, sometimes with another, of the three principal 'forms' of pleasure, which we have in this book distinguished. One could, accordingly, speak of three types of *ideals of happiness* or of the happy life.

The first I shall call *Epicurean ideals*. According to them, 'true happiness' derives above all from *having* things which please. 'Pleasure' need not here be understood in the 'grosser' sense of sensuous pleasure. It includes the enjoyment of agreeable recollections and thoughts, of good company, and of beautiful things. Moore's position in *Principia Ethica* can, I think, be called an Epicureanism in this broad sense.

Can a man find happiness entirely in passive pleasure? *i.e.* can following an Epicurean recipe of living make a man completely happy? I can see no *logical* impossibility in the idea. If a man's supreme desire happened to be to secure for himself a favourable balance of passive pleasure over passive 'unpleasure', *i.e.* of states he enjoys over states he dislikes, and if he were successful in this pursuit of his, then the Epicurean recipe of living would, by definition, make him happy. It may be argued—from considerations pertaining to the contingencies of life—that the chances are strongly against his succeeding. It may also be argued—this time from considerations pertaining to the psychology of human nature —that very few men are such pleasure-lovers that the supreme thing they want for themselves in life is a maximum of passive pleasure. But the facts—if they be facts—that Epicurean ideals are risky and not very commonly pursued throughout a whole life, must not induce us to deny that a man—if there be such a man— who successfully pursued such ideals was genuinely happy and flourishing. To deny this would be to misunderstand the notions of happiness and the good of man and would be symptomatic, I think, of some 'moralistic perversion'.

The second type of ideals of the happy life probably comes nearer than the Epicurean ideals to something which the classical writers of utilitarianism had in mind. It seems to me true to say that the utilitarians thought of happiness, not so much in terms of passive pleasure, as in terms of satisfaction of desire. Happiness, on such a view, is essentially contentedness—an equilibrium between needs and wants on the one hand and satisfaction on the other.

Yet one of the great utilitarians—protesting against unwanted consequences of a view which he was himself, though not whole-heartedly, defending—made the famous *dictum*, 'It is better to be a human being dissatisfied than a pig satisfied'. I am not a utilitarian myself. But I would like to protest, in a sense, against Mill's remark. The ultimate reason why it is not good for man to live like a pig, is that the life of a pig *does not satisfy* man. The dissatisfied Socrates, to whom Mill refers, we may regard as a symbol of man in search of a better and therewith more satisfying form of life. If his cravings were all doomed to be nothing but 'vanity and the vexation of spirit', then to idealize the dissatisfied Socrates would be to cherish a perverted view of the good life.

If one adopts the view that happiness is essentially an equilibrium between desire and satisfaction, one may reach the further conclusion that the safest road to happiness is to have as few and modest wants as possible, thus minimizing the chances of frustration and maximizing those of satisfaction. This recipe of happiness I shall call *the ascetic ideal* of life.[1] When carried to the extreme, this ideal

[1] Asceticism as an abnegation of worldly desire for the sake of the good of the soul must be distinguished from that which I here call asceticism as an ideal of life. To the first, asceticism is no 'end' or 'value' in itself, but an exercise and preparation for the good life.

envisages complete happiness in the total abnegation of all desire whatsoever.

Ascetism, in this sense, can be termed a *crippled* view of happiness. In order to see in which respect it is crippled, it is helpful to consider the contrary of happiness, *i.e.* unhappiness or misery. It would seem that there is a more direct connexion between unhappiness and dissatisfaction of desire than there is between happiness and satisfaction. Frustration of desire is a main source of unhappiness. Never or seldom to get that for which one is craving, never or seldom to have a chance of doing that which one likes to do, *this* is above all what makes a man miserable.

To call extreme ascetism a crippled ideal is to accuse it of a logical mistake. This is the mistake of regarding happiness as the *contradictory*, and not as the *contrary*, of unhappiness. By escaping frustration a man escapes unhappiness—provided, of course, that it does not befall him in the form of such affliction, which accident or illness or the acts of evil neighbours may cause him. The man of *no* wants, if there existed such a creature, would not be unhappy. But it does not follow that he would be happy.

The third type of ideals of the happy life which I wanted to mention here, seeks happiness neither in passive pleasure nor in the satisfaction of desire, but in that which we have called active pleasure, *i.e.* the pleasure of doing that on which we are keen, which for its own sake we like *doing*. In the activities which we are keen on doing, we aim at technical goodness or perfection. (See Ch. II, sect. 12.) The better we are in the art, the more do we enjoy practising it, the happier does it make us. Therefore, the more talented we are by nature for an art, the more can the development of our skill in it contribute to our happiness.

It may be argued—chiefly against Epicureanism I should think —that the pleasures of the active life are those which are best suited to secure the attainment of lasting happiness. It is more risky to be, for one's well-being, dependent upon things we *have* or *get* than upon things we *do* (or *are*). That is: it is more risky to seek happiness in passive than in active pleasure. There is probably a great deal of truth in the argument. But it would certainly be wrong to think that the road to happiness through an active life were completely risk-free.

4. The factors which determine whether a man will become

happy, we shall call *conditions* of happiness. Of such conditions one may distinguish three main groups. Happiness, we shall say, is conditioned partly by *chance* or luck, partly by innate *disposition*, and partly by *action*. 'Action' here means action on the part of the individual concerned himself. That which is *done to* a man may, for present purposes, be counted as chance-factors conditioning his happiness.

Illness can befall a man or he can become bodily or mentally injured without any fault of his own. If such misfortune assumes a certain permanence, it may affect a man's happiness adversely. It may do so either as a cause of pain or as a cause of frustration of desire or because it prevents the victim from engaging in activity which, for its own sake, he enjoys. However, luck may also favour a man's good. The benefit a person draws from good friends or good teachers or financial benefactors has, partly if not wholly, the character of luck. It is something which life has in store for some men but not for others to make them happier, independently of their own doings and precautions.

It is an aspect of that which we called the ascetic ideal of life, that man is well advised to *make* himself as independent as possible of chance and luck as conditions of his happiness. This he can try to do in various ways: by hardening himself to sustain pain, by withdrawing from political and social engagements, or by not aspiring too high even in those activities, which he enjoys for their own sake. The belief that a man could make himself altogether independent of external affectations of his good, is a conceit peculiar to certain 'ascetic' and 'stoic' attitudes to life. It overrates man's possibilities of conditioning his happiness and peace of mind by assuming a certain attitude to contingencies.

The innate dispositions of happiness have to do both with bodily health and with mental equipment and temper. A man of weak health is more exposed to certain risks of becoming unhappy than a man of good health. A man of many talents has more resources of happiness than a man of poor gifts. A man of good temper and cheerful outlook will not let adversities frustrate his efforts as easily as the impatient and gloomy man. To the extent that such temperamental dispositions can be developed or suppressed in a man, they fall under those conditions of happiness which a man controls through his action.

Human action, which is relevant to the happiness of the agent

95

himself, is of two types. Action of the first type are things which the agent does, measures which he takes for the sake of promoting or protecting his happiness. Such action is *causally* relevant to his happiness. Action of the second type are things which the agent does or practises for their own sake, as ends in themselves, *i.e.* simply because he wants to do or likes to do them and for no other reason. Action in which a man delights one could call *constitutive* of his happiness, 'parts' of his happiness.

Now it may happen that action, which is thus constitutive of a man's happiness, *also* affects his happiness causally. It may affect his happiness promotingly, but also affect it adversely. For example: a man is immensely fond of playing various games. He plays and enjoys playing them all day long. In so doing he neglects his education and his social duties and maybe his health too. Thus the very same thing, which is constitutive of his happiness, may, by virtue of its consequences, accumulate clouds of unhappiness over the agent's head, while he is rejoicing in this thing. This possibility is responsible for the major complications, which are connected with a man's own action as a conditioning factor of his happiness and welfare generally.

5. When is a man happy? It is obvious that a man can be truly praised happy, even though many painful and unpleasant things have happened to him in the course of his life. But not if he never had any pleasures. What must the preponderance of the pleasant over the unpleasant be, if he is still to be called happy?

Here it is helpful to consider the states which we call gladness and sadness. They occupy a kind of intermediate position between happiness and unhappiness on the one hand, and pleasure and its contrary on the other hand. It may be suggested that pleasant and unpleasant experiences and activities are constitutive of gladness and sadness in a manner similar to that in which states of joy and depression are constitutive of happiness and unhappiness. A man can be glad although he has toothache, and he can be a happy man even though he chances to be very sad for a time. But he could not be glad if he had no pleasures to compensate such pains as he may have at the time of his gladness; and he cannot be happy if he is not *on the whole* more glad than sad. But we cannot tell exactly what must be the balance.

Pleasure, joy, and happiness are things of increasing degrees of permanence and resistance to changes. Something can please a man without cheering him up, and cheer him up without making him happy. Something can be a terrible blow to a man and make him sad, but whether it makes him unhappy is another matter.

Consider, for example, a man whom we praise happy and who is hit by a sudden blow of bad luck, say, the loss of a child in an accident. He will experience painful agonies and extreme sadness. 'News of the disaster made him dreadfully unhappy,' we might say, thinking of these emotional effects on him. If, however, we were to say that the news made him *an unhappy man*, we should be thinking not only, or maybe even not at all, on those emotional effects, but on effects of a less immediate showing and of a longer lasting. If we can say of him some such things as, 'For years after he was as paralysed; none of the things, which used to delight him, gave him pleasure any longer,' or 'Life seemed to have lost meaning for him,—for a time he even contemplated suicide,' then the accident made him *unhappy* as distinct from merely *sad*. But whether things, bearing on the distinction, can be truly said of the man, is not to be seen in an inkling.

Analogous things can be said about changes in the reverse direction. A piece of news, say of an unexpected inheritance, can make a man jump with joy. But whether it makes him *happy* as distinct from merely *glad* can only be seen from effects of a longer lasting and less obvious showing on his subsequent life.

Should we say 'the *whole* of his subsequent life'? I think not. Happiness is neither a momentary state nor is it a sum total to be found out when we close our life's account. A man can *become* happy, *be* happy, and *change* from happy to unhappy. Thus, in the course of his life, a man can be both happy and unhappy. And he can be happy and unhappy more than once. (See section 1.)

We could make a distinction between a happy *man* and a happy *life* and regard the second as a thing of wider scope. This would make it possible to say of somebody that he had a happy life although, for some time, he was a most unhappy man.

6. A judgment to the effect that some being is happy or is not happy or is unhappy we shall call an *eudaimonic* judgment.

I think it is illuminating to compare the logic of the eudaimonic judgment to the logic of the statement 'This is pleasant'. Of the sentence 'This is pleasant' we said that it conceals a logical form. (See Ch. IV, sect. 6.) It suggests that pleasantness is a property which we attribute to some object or state, whereas in fact to judge something pleasant is to verbalize a relationship in which the judging subject stands to this thing. To judge something hedonically good is to manifest an *attitude*, one could also say, to certain things (activities, sensations, the causes of sensations). The logically most adequate form of the verbalization is therefore, it seems, the relational form 'I like this' or some similar relational form.

In an analogous sense the sentence 'He is happy' may be said, I think, to conceal a logical form. It suggests a view of happiness as a property which the happy individual exhibits—which shines forth from him. Whereas, in fact, to be happy is to be in a certain relationship. A relationship to what? it may be asked. A relationship to one's circumstances of life, I would answer. To say 'He is happy' is similar to saying 'He likes it', the 'it' not meaning this or that particular thing or activity but, so to speak, 'the whole thing'. One could also say, 'He likes his life as it is.'

On this view, if a man says of himself 'I am happy', he manifests in words an attitude which he takes, or a relationship, in which he stands, to his circumstances of life. Happiness *is* not in the circumstances—as it were awaiting the judgment—but springs into being with the relationship. (Just as hedonic goodness does not reside in the taste of an apple, but in somebody's liking the taste of an apple.) To judge oneself happy is to pass judgment on or value one's circumstances of life.

To say 'He is happy' can mean two different things. It can mean that the man, of whom we are talking, is in the relationship to his circumstances which, if *he* were to verbalize his attitude, he could express in the words 'I am happy'. Then 'He is happy' is not a value-judgment. It is a true or false statement to the effect that a certain subject values certain things, *i.e.* his circumstances of life, in a certain way. We could also call it a statement to the effect that a certain valuation *exists* (occurs, takes place).

Quite often, however, 'He is happy' is not a judgment about that which *he is* at all, but about that which *we should be*, if we happened to be in his circumstances. 'He is happy' then means roughly, 'He *must be* happy, *viz*. considering the circumstances he is in.' Such judgments are often an expression of envy. To say with

98

conviction, 'Happy is he, who . . .' is usually to pronounce on that which we think would make ourselves happy.

We shall henceforth disregard the case, when the third person judgment 'He is happy' is only a disguise for our own valuations and thus really is a first person judgment.

7. On the view which I am defending here, judgments of happiness are thus very much like hedonic judgments. The third person judgments are true or false. In them is judged that so-and-so is or is not pleased with his circumstances of life. They are judgments *about* valuations—and therefore are no value-judgments. The first person judgments are not true or false. They *express* a subject's valuations of his own circumstances. They are genuine value-judgments, and yet in an important sense of 'judgment' they are no judgments.

Ultimately, a man is himself judge of his own happiness. By this I mean that any third person judgment which may be passed on his happiness, depends for its truth-value on how *he himself* values his circumstances of life. This is so independently of whether he verbalizes his attitude in a first person judgment or not.

In *a* sense, therefore, a man's own verdict 'I am happy' or 'I am unhappy', should he happen to pass it, will be final—whatever we may think *we* should say, if we were in his circumstances. We must never make the presence or absence of circumstances, which would determine our own first person judgments of happiness, the *criteria* of truth of third person judgments.

What may make it difficult to see clearly this 'subjectivity' of the notion which we are discussing, is the fact that not every man is the best and most competent judge of his *prospects* of happiness. A man may strongly want to do something, think his life worthless if he is not allowed this thing. But another, more experienced man, may warn him that, if he follows his immediate impulses, he will in the end become a most miserable wretch. The more experienced man may be right. But the criterion, which proves him right, is *not* the mere fact that certain things—illness, destitution, and what not—befall this other man as a predicted consequence of his folly and wickedness. The criterion is that these consequences make that other man unhappy. If our fool accepts the consequences with a cheerful heart, the wise man cannot insist that he must be right. He cannot do so on the ground, say, that those same consequences would have made him, or most people, miserable. Nor can he pretend that the lightsome fellow is 'really' unhappy, though unaware of his own misery.

But cannot a man be mistaken in thinking that he *is* happy? In a sense he can *not*, but in another he *can*. 'He says he is happy, but in fact he is not' can express a true proposition. But does not the truth of this proposition entail that the person who professes to be happy is lying? And is this not uninteresting? The answer is that, beside uninteresting lies, there exist profoundly interesting lies in the matters, which we are now discussing. First person judgments of happiness can be insincere, and insincerity may be regarded as a species of lying.

The same, incidentally, holds good for first person hedonic judgments too. A youngster may profess to like the taste of tobacco, which in fact he detests, just for the sake of showing off. He may even make himself believe this, in some involved and twisted sense of 'believe'. A polite man may say he likes the taste of a wine merely to please his host. The insincerity of such first person judgments may be relatively easy to unmask.

In the case of first person judgments of happiness and misery, the problem of sincerity is most difficult—both psychologically and conceptually. I shall not here try to penetrate its logical aspects, which I find very bewildering. (I am not aware of any satisfactory discussion of the topic in the literature.) I shall make a shortcut through the difficulties and only say this much in conclusion:

However thoroughly a man may cheat himself with regard to his own happiness, the criterion of cheat or insincerity must be that *he* admits the fraud. A judgment is insincere when the subject 'in his innermost self' admits that it is not as he says it is. If his lips say 'I am happy' and he is not, then in his heart he must already be saying to himself 'I am not happy'. He, as it were, does not hear the voice of his heart. These are similes, and I am aware of the temptation to misuse them. (They are the same sort of similes that are used and misused in psychoanalysis—the similes of the subconscious, the super-ego, etc.) What I mean by them could perhaps be said most plainly as follows: The fact that first person judgments of happiness can be insincere must not be allowed to conflict logically with the fact that, whether a person is happy or not depends upon *his own* attitude to his circumstances of life. The supreme judge of the case *must be* the subject himself. To think that it could be otherwise is false objectivism.

8. Judgments of the beneficial and the harmful, *i.e.* of that which is good or bad for a man, involve two components. We have called them the *causal* and the *axiological* component. (See Ch. III, sect. 5.) We must now say some words about each of them.

When something happens, *i.e.* the world changes in a certain respect, there will usually also be a number of subsequent changes, which are bound (by so-called 'natural necessity') to come about, once the first change took place. These subsequent changes we here call the *consequences* of the first change. If the first change is of that peculiar kind which we call a human act, then the subsequent changes are *consequences of action*. The change or changes upon which a certain further change is consequent (*i.e.* the consequence of which this further change is) we shall call the *cause(s)* of this further change.

Most things which happen, perhaps all, would not have happened, *unless* certain antecedent changes had taken place in the world. These antecedent changes we shall call the *causal pre-requisites* or *requirements* of the subsequent change. They are sometimes also called 'necessary causes'. The necessary causes may be, but need not be, 'causes' in the sense defined above.

These explanations are very summary. Not least of all considering the importance to ethics of the notion of consequences of action, it is an urgent *desideratum* that the logic of causal relationships be better elaborated than it is. We shall not, however, attempt this here. Only a few observations will be added to the above.

The notions both of consequences and of prerequisites and of causes of a change are relative to the further notion of a *state of the world*. Thus, *e.g.*, a change which is required in order to effect a certain change in the world as it is to-day, may not be required in order to effect this same change in the world as it is to-morrow.

It is sometimes said that every event (change) 'strictly speaking' has an infinite number of consequences throughout the whole of subsequent time, and that for this reason we can never know for certain which all the consequences of a given event are. These statements, if true at all, hold good for some different notion of consequence, but not for the notion with which we are here

101

dealing. Exactly what could be meant by them is not clear. Yet we need not dismiss them as nonsense. When, for example, something which happens to-day is said to be a consequence of something which took place hundreds of years ago, what is meant is perhaps that, if we traced the 'causal history' of this event of to-day we should find among its 'causal ancestry' that event of hundreds of years ago. Here the notions of causal ancestry and causal history could be defined in terms of *our* notions of cause, consequence, and prerequisite and yet it need not follow that, if an event belongs to the causal ancestry of another event, the first must be a cause or prerequisite of the second or the second a consequence of the first. For example: Let event b be a consequence (in our sense) of event a and a causal prerequisite (in our sense) of event c. It would then be reasonable to say that event a is a 'causal ancestor' of event c, or that tracing the 'causal history' of c takes us to a. In some loose sense of the words, a may be said to be a 'cause' of c and c a 'consequence' of a. But in the more precise sense, in which we are here employing the terms, a is not (necessarily) a cause of c, nor c (necessarily) a consequence of a.

The causes and consequences of things which happen, are often insufficiently known and therefore largely a matter of belief and conjecture. Sometimes, however, they *are* known to us. The statement, should it be made, that they *cannot* ('in principle') be known either is false or applies to some different notions of cause and consequence from ours.

By knowledge of the causes and consequences of things which happen, I here mean knowledge relating to *particulars*. An example would be knowledge that the death of N. N. was due to a dose of arsenic, which had been mixed into his food. Such knowledge of particulars is usually grounded on knowledge of general propositions—as for example that a dose of arsenic of a certain strength will (unless certain counteracting causes intervene) 'inevitably' kill a man. Whether all such knowledge of particulars is grounded on general knowledge, we shall not discuss.

When in the sequel we speak of *knowledge* of the causes and consequences of things, or of known causes and consequences, 'knowledge' is short for 'knowledge or belief' and 'known' for 'known or believed'. The consequences which are known (*i.e.* known or believed) at the time when the thing happens, we shall also call *foreseen* consequences.

102

So much for the causal component involved in judgments of the beneficial and the harmful. We now turn to the axiological component. A preliminary task will here be to clarify the notions of a *wanted* and an *unwanted* thing.

9. The notion of a wanted thing, which I shall now try to explain, is not the same as that of an end of action. I shall call it the notion of being *wanted in itself*. How things which are wanted in themselves, are related to things which are wanted as ends of action, will be discussed presently. Correlative with the notion of being wanted in itself is the notion of being *unwanted in itself*. 'Between' the two falls a notion, which we shall call the notion of being *indifferent in itself*.

The notion of being wanted in itself is the nearest equivalent in my treatment here to the notion of *intrinsic value* in Moore and some other writers. Moore, when discussing the notion of intrinsic worth, often resorts to a logical fiction which, *mutatis mutandis*, may be resorted to also for explaining the meaning of a thing being wanted, unwanted, or indifferent 'in itself'.

This fiction is that of a preferential choice between two alternatives. A major difficulty is to formulate the terms of the choice correctly for the purpose of defining the axiological notions under discussion. (Moore's explanation of intrinsic value in terms of betterness of alternatives cannot be regarded as *logically* satisfactory —apart from questions of the meaningfulness of the very notion.[1]) Our proposal here of a solution to the problem is tentative only.

Assume you were offered a thing X which you did not already possess. Would you then rather take it than leave it, rather have it than (continue to) be without it? The offer must be considered apart from questions of causal requirements and of consequences. That is: considerations of things which you will have to do in order to get X, and of things which will happen to you as a consequence of your having got the thing X must not influence your choice. If then you would rather take X than leave it, X is *wanted in itself*. If you have the opposite preference, X is *unwanted in itself*. If you have no preference, X is *indifferent in itself*.

As readily noted, the ideas of the in itself wanted and unwanted, which we have thus tried to explain in terms of a fictitious

---

[1] See *Ethics*, pp. 42–44 and, in particular, Moore's reply to his critics in *The Philosophy of G. E. Moore*, pp. 554–557.

preferential choice, are necessarily relative to a *subject*. Nothing is wanted or unwanted 'in itself', if the words 'in itself' are supposed to mean 'apart from any rating or valuing subject'. The words 'in itself' mean 'causal prerequisites and consequences apart'. A thing, which for one subject is a wanted thing, may be regarded as unwanted by another subject. A thing, furthermore, which is wanted *now*, may be unwanted at another time—the subject being the same. The notion of being wanted or unwanted in itself is thus relative, not only to a subject, but also to a particular time in the life of this subject.

Moore did not think that intrinsic value was relative to subject and time. In this respect his 'objectivist' notion of the intrinsically good and bad differs from our 'subjectivist' notion of the in itself wanted and unwanted.

It is important to note that from our definition of the in itself wanted, unwanted, and indifferent it does not follow that, if X is wanted in itself, then not-X (the absence of X) is unwanted in itself. That not-X is wanted, unwanted, and indifferent in itself corresponds, on our definitions, to the following set of preferences:

Consider a thing X, which you have. Would you rather get rid of it than retain it, rather be without it than (continue to) possess it? The proposal must be considered apart from things which you will have to do in order to get rid of X and from things which will happen to you as a consequence of your having got rid of X. Then not-X is wanted in itself, if you prefer to get rid of X, unwanted in itself, if you prefer to retain X, and indifferent in itself, if you have no preference.

10. Anything which is an—intermediate or ultimate—end of action, can be called *a good* (for the subject in pursuit of the end). (Cf. above Ch. I, sect. 5 and Ch. III, sect. 1.) Anything which is an end of action, can also be said to be *a wanted thing*.

Also every thing, which is wanted in itself, can be called a good (for the subject to whom it is wanted). And every thing, which is unwanted in itself, can be called a bad (for the subject who shuns it).

Ends of action and things wanted in themselves thus both fall under the category 'goods'. Ends of action also fall under the category 'things wanted'.

The question may be raised, how ends of action and things wanted in themselves are mutually related. The question is complicated and I shall not discuss it in detail. It is reasonable to think that only things, which are attainable through action, *can be* ends of action. 'Craving for the moon' is not aiming at an end. But things other than those which are attainable through action, can be wanted in themselves—sunshine on a chilly day, for example. The only simple relationship between ends of action and things wanted in themselves, which I can suggest, is that ultimate ends of action are also things wanted in themselves.

Intermediate ends of action are either things wanted in themselves or things indifferent in themselves or, not infrequently, things unwanted in themselves. To get the in itself unwanted can never be an ultimate end of action, since the assumption that it is involves a contradiction. But to escape the in itself unwanted sometimes is an ultimate end of action. The unwanted is that which we shun, except when occasionally we pursue it as intermediate end for the sake of something else or suffer it as a necessary prerequisite of something coveted.

When a man gets something which is, to him, wanted in itself, without having pursued it as an end, we shall say that this wanted thing *befalls* him. Similarly, when a man gets something which is, to him, unwanted in itself and which he has not pursued as an intermediate end, we shall say that this thing befalls him.

The question may be raised whether a thing which befalls or happens to a man can appropriately be said to be 'wanted'. 'Wanted' in English has many meanings and must therefore be used with caution. Sometimes it means 'desired', sometimes 'needed', sometimes 'wished for'. When the wanted thing is an end of action, the nearest equivalent to 'wanted' is 'desired'. Perhaps things which happen to a man and which satisfy our explanation of the in itself wanted, should better be called 'welcome'. They are things we 'gladly accept' or are 'happy to get'. Often we just call them 'good'. When I here call them 'wanted', it is by contrast to 'unwanted', which word is certainly correctly used for shunned things that befall or happen to a man.

11. Consider something, which an agent pursues as an ultimate end. Assume that he gets it. Attaining the end is usually connected with a number of things as its causal prerequisites and a number of other things as its consequences. Of the things which are thus causally connected with his end, some are perhaps known

and others not known to the agent. Some, moreover, may be known to him already at the time when he pursues the end, others become known to him after he has attained it. That is: their causal relationship to the end is (becomes) known to him.

The thing which the agent pursues as an ultimate end, is to him a good and something he wants in itself. Of those things again which are causally connected—either as prerequisites or as consequences—with his attainment of the end, some are wanted in themselves (by him), others are unwanted in themselves (by him), others indifferent in themselves (to him). The sum total of those things, which are unwanted in themselves, we shall call the *price*, which the agent has to pay for the attainment of his ultimate end.

This notion of 'price', be it observed, includes consequences as well as causal prerequisites. On this definition of the notion, not only those things which the agent has to endure, in order to get his wanted thing, but also those which he has to suffer as a consequence of having got it, count as part of that which he has to *pay* for the good. One can define the notion of a price in different ways—for other purposes. This is how we define the notion for present purposes.

For anything which is wanted in itself, the question may be raised: Is this good worth its price? The question can be raised *prospectively*, with a view to things which have to be gone through as a consequence of starting to pursue this good as an end, or it can be raised *retrospectively*, with a view to things already suffered.

To answer the question whether a certain good is (was) worth its price, is to pass a value-judgment. It is to say of something, a good, that it is better or worse, more or less worth, than something else, its price. How shall this value-judgment be properly articulated?

I think we must resort here, for a second time, to the logical fiction of a preferential choice. We said (in section 9) that things which we do not have, are wanted in themselves when, ignoring their causes and consequences, we would rather get them than continue to be without them, and unwanted in themselves when we would rather continue to be without them than get them. This question of taking or leaving, having or being without, we can also raise for things, *considering their causes and consequences*. A correct way of presenting the choice which we should then be facing, is, I think, as follows:

THE GOOD OF MAN

Assume that X is something, which is not already in our world (life), *i.e.* is something which we do not already possess or which has not already happened or which we have not already done. Would we then want X to become introduced into our world (life), considering also the causal prerequisites of getting (doing) X and the consequences of having got (done) X? Or would we prefer to continue to be without X? In making up our mind we should also have to consider the causal prerequisites and the consequences of *not* having this change in our world (life). It may, for example, be necessary for us to take some in itself unwanted action to prevent X from coming into existence, if we wish to avoid having X, and it may be necessary for us to foresake some other in itself wanted thing Y as a consequence of *not* having had X.

We introduce the symbol '$X+C$' for the complex whole, consisting of X and those other things, which are causally connected with it either as prerequisites or as consequences of its coming into being, *i.e.* of the change from not-X to X. The symbol 'not-$X+C'$' shall stand for the complex whole, consisting of the absence of X and the presence of those things which are causally connected, either as prerequisites or as consequences, with the continued absence of X.

The question which is presented for consideration in the fictitious preferential choice we are discussing, is whether we should prefer $X+C$ to not-$X+C'$ or whether we should have the reverse preference or whether we should be indifferent (have no preference).

Let the answer to the proposal be that we should rather have than continue to be without X, *i.e.* prefer $X+C$ to not-$X+C'$. Then we shall say that $X+C$ or the complex whole, consisting of X and the causal prerequisites and consequences of the coming into being of X, is a *positive constituent* of our good (welfare). Of the thing X itself we say that it is *good for us* or *beneficial*. This we say of X independently of whether X is wanted or unwanted or indifferent in itself.

Let the answer to the proposal be that we should rather continue to forego than have X, *i.e.* prefer not-$X+C'$ to $X+C$. Then we shall say that $X+C$ is a *negative constituent* of our good. Of the thing X itself we say that it is *bad for us* or *harmful*. This we say independently of whether X is wanted or unwanted or indifferent in itself.

The answer can, of course, also be that we should be indifferent to the alternatives. Then $X+C$ is neither a positive nor a negative constituent of our good, and X is neither beneficial nor harmful.

Let us call X the *nucleus* of that complex whole, which consists of X and the causal prerequisites and consequences of the coming into existence of X. We could then say that the things which are beneficial or harmful, good or bad for a man, are nuclei of those complex causal wholes, which are positive or negative constituents of his good (welfare).

We can now state the conditions for answering the question whether a certain good is worth its 'price'. When a certain causal whole is a positive constituent of our good *and* its nucleus is a thing, which is wanted in itself, then we say that this thing or good *is* worth its price. When, however, the whole is a negative constituent of our good, *although* its nucleus is a thing, which is wanted in itself, then we say that this thing or good is *not* worth its price.

From our definitions of the beneficial and the harmful it does *not* follow that, if not-X is harmful, then X is beneficial, and *vice versa*. If, however, not-X is harmful, then X will be called *needed*. The needed is that, the lack or loss of which is a bad thing, an evil. The needed and the harmful are opposed as contradictories, *in the sense* that the contradictory of the needed is harmful, and *vice versa*. The beneficial and the harmful are opposed as contraries.

To provide a being with that which is beneficial for it is to *promote* its welfare. To provide it with that which it needs and to take care that it does not lose the needed is to *protect* its welfare. Things (acts, events) which are protective of a being's welfare are good for the being in the sense of 'good for' which can also be rendered by 'useful', but not in that sense of 'good for' which we call 'beneficial'. (Cf. Ch. III, sect. 1.)

12. The preferential choice, in the terms of which we have defined the notions of the beneficial and the harmful, we have called a 'logical fiction'. That it is a fiction implies two things. First, it implies that we are talking of how a man *would choose*, if he were presented with the choice, and not of what he actually chooses. Secondly, it implies that we assume the causal component involved in the value-judgment to be *completely known* to the subject at the time of the choice. This second assumption entails that there are no imperfections in the subject's knowledge which are such that, if they were detected and corrected, the subject would revise his preferences.

Thus, on our definitions, the answer to the question whether a certain thing is good or bad for a man, is independent of the following two factors: First, it is independent of whether he (or anybody else) *judges* or does not judge of the value of this thing for him. Secondly, it is independent of what he (and everybody else) happens to *know* or not to know about the causal connexions of this thing. Yet, in spite of this independence of judgment and knowledge, the notions of the beneficial and the harmful are in an important sense *subjective*. Their subjectivity consists in their dependence upon the *preferences (wants)* of the subject concerned.

Considering what has just been said, it is clear that we must distinguish between that which *is* good or bad for a man and that which *appears*, *i.e.* is judged or considered or thought (by himself or by others), to be good or bad for him.

Any judgment to the effect that something is good or bad for a man is based on such knowledge of the relevant causal connexions which the judging subject happens to possess. Since this knowledge may be imperfect, the judgment which he actually passes may be different from the judgment which he would pass, if he had perfect knowledge of the causal connexions. When there is this discrepancy between the actual and the potential judgment, we shall say that a man's *apparent* good is being mistaken for his *real* good.

Of certain things it is easier to judge correctly whether they are good or bad for us, than of certain other things. This means: the risks of mistaking our apparent good for our real good are sometimes greater, sometimes less. It is, on the whole, easier to judge correctly in matters relating to a person's health than in matters relating to his future career. For example: the judgment that it will do a man good to take regular exercise is, on the whole, safer than the judgment that it will be better for him to go into business than study medicine. Sometimes the difficulties to judge correctly are so great that it will be altogether idle and useless to try to form a judgment.

Sometimes we know for certain that a choice, which we are facing, is of great *importance* to us in the sense that it will make considerable *difference* to our future life, whether we choose the one or the other of two alternatives. An example could be a choice between getting married or remaining single or between accepting employment in a foreign country or continuing life at home. But certainty that the choice will make a great difference is fully compatible with uncertainty as to whether the difference will be for good or for bad. The feeling that our welfare *may* become radically affected by the choice, can make the choice very agonizing for us.

Also of many things in our past, which we did not deliberately choose, we may know for certain that they have been of great importance to us in the sense that our lives would have been very different, had these things not existed. This could be manifestly true, for example, of the influence which some powerful personality has had on our education or on the formation of our opinions. We may wonder whether it was not bad for us that we should have been so strongly under this influence. Yet, if we know only that our life would have been very different but cannot at all imagine *how* it would have been different, we may also be quite incompetent to form a judgment of the beneficial and harmful nature of this factor in our past history.

It is a deeply impressive fact about the condition of man that it should be difficult, or even humanly impossible, to judge confidently of many things which are known to affect our lives importantly, whether they are good or bad for us. I think that becoming *overwhelmed* by this fact is one of the things which can incline a man towards taking a religious view of life. 'Only God knows what is good or bad for us.' One could say thus—and yet accept that a man's welfare is a subjective notion in the sense that it is determined by what *he* wants and shuns.

13. Are judgments of the beneficial or harmful nature of things objectively true or false? When we try to answer this question, we must again observe the distinction between a first person judgment and a third person judgment. (Cf. Ch. IV, sect. 5 and this chapter, sections 6 and 7.)

When somebody judges of something that it is (was, will be) good or bad for somebody else, the judgment is a third person judgment. It depends for its truth-value on two things. The one is whether certain causal connexions are as the judging subject thinks that they are. The other is whether certain valuations (preferences, wants) of another subject are as the judging subject thinks that they are. Both to judge of causal connexions and to judge of the valuations of other subjects is to judge of empirical matters of fact. The judgment is 'objectively' true or false. It is, properly speaking, not a value-judgment, since the 'axiological' component involved in it is not a valuation but a judgment *about* (the existence or occurrence of) valuations.

The case of the first person judgment is more complicated. Its causal component is a judgment of matters of fact. In this respect the first person judgment is on a level with the third person judgment. Its axiological component, however, is a valuation and not a judgment about valuations. With regard to this component the judgment cannot be true or false. There is no 'room' for mistake concerning its truth-value. In this respect the first person judgment of the beneficial and the harmful is like the first person hedonic or eudaimonic judgment.

Although the first person judgment cannot be false in its axiological component, it can be *insincere*. The problem of sincerity of judgments concerning that which is good or bad for a man is most complicated. It is intimately connected with the problems relating to the notions of *regret* and of *weakness of will*. A few words will be said about them later.

A subject can also make a statement about his own valuations in the past or a conjecture about his valuations in the future. Such a statement or conjecture is, logically, a third person judgment. It is true or false both in its causal and in its axiological component.

Whether a judgment is, *logically*, a first person judgment, cannot be seen from the person and tense of its grammatical form alone. A man says 'This will do me good'. In saying this he could be anticipating certain consequences and *expressing* his valuation of them. But he could also be anticipating certain consequences and *anticipating* his valuation of them. In the first case, the judgment he makes is of the kind which I here call a first person judgment of the beneficial or harmful nature of things. In the second case, the judgment is (logically) a third person judgment. The subject is speaking *about* himself, *i.e.* about his future valuations.

Sometimes a judgment of the beneficial or the harmful is clearly anticipative both of consequences and of valuations. Sometimes it is clearly anticipative with regard to consequences and expressive with regard to valuations. But very often, it seems, the status of the judgment is not clear even to the judging subject himself. The judgment may contain *both* anticipations *and* expressions of valuations. Perhaps it is true to say that men's judgments of what is

111

good or bad for themselves tend on the whole to be anticipative rather than expressive with regard to valuations.

The distinction between the *apparent* and the *real* good, it should be observed, can be upheld both for third person and for first person judgments of the beneficial and the harmful. In this respect judgments of the beneficial and the harmful differ from hedonic and eudaimonic judgments. (For the two last kinds of judgment the distinction vanishes in the first person case, *i.e.* in the genuine value-judgments.) Because of the presence of the causal component in the judgment, a subject can always be mistaken concerning the beneficial or the harmful nature of a thing—even when there is no 'room' for mistake with regard to valuation.

14. A man's answer to the question whether a certain good is worth its price or whether a thing is beneficial or harmful, may undergo alterations in the course of time. Such alterations in his judgments can be due either to changes in his knowledge of the relevant causal connexions or to changes in his valuations. For example: a man attains an end, which he considers worth while to have pursued, until years afterwards he comes to realize that he had to pay for it with the ruin of his health. Then he revises his judgment and *regrets*.

There are two types of regret-situation relating to choices of ends and goods in general. Sometimes the choice can, in principle if not in practice, be repeated. To profess regret is then to say that one would not choose the same thing again next time, when there is an opportunity. But sometimes the choice is not repeatable. The reason for this could be that the consequences, of which one is aware and which are the ground for one's regret, continue to operate throughout one's whole life. There is no opportunity of making good one's folly in the past by acting more wisely in the future. Then to express regret is to pass judgment on one's *life*. It is like saying: If I were to live my life over again, I would, when arrived at the fatal station, act differently.

The value-judgments of regret and no-regret, like hedonic judgments and judgments of happiness, are neither true nor false. But they may be sincere or insincere. A person can say that he regrets, when in fact he does not, and he can stubbornly refuse to admit regret which he 'feels'. How is such insincerity unmasked? For example in this way: If a man, after having suffered the consequences, says he regrets his action, but on a new occasion repeats his previous choice, then we may doubt whether his remorse was not pretence only. He was perhaps annoyed at having had to pay so much for the coveted thing and therefore said it was not worth it, but at the bottom of his heart he was pleased at having got it. These are familiar phenomena.

Yet to think that a repetition of the professed folly were a sure sign of insincere regret, would be to ignore the complications of the practical problems relating to the good of man. A good, if strongly desired in itself and near at hand, may be a temptation to which a man succumbs, when the evil consequences are far ahead and the recollection of having suffered them in the past is perhaps already fading. There is no logical absurdity in the idea that a man sincerely regrets something as having been a mistake, a bad choice with a view to his welfare, *i.e.* with a view to what he 'really' wants for himself, and yet wilfully commits the same mistake over again, whenever there is an opportunity.

When a man succumbs to temptation and chooses a lesser immediate good, *i.e.* thing wanted in itself, rather than escapes a greater future bad, *i.e.* thing unwanted in itself, then he is acting wilfully against the interests of his own good. It is in such situations that those features of character which we call *virtues*, are needed to safeguard a man's welfare. We shall talk about them later (in Chapter VII).

That a man can do evil to himself through ignorance of the consequences of his acts or through negligence is obvious. That he can also harm himself through *akrasia* or weakness of will has a certain appearance of paradox. He then, as it were, both wants and does not want, welcomes and shuns, one and the same thing. When viewed in the short perspective, 'prerequisites and consequences apart', he wants it; when viewed in the prolonged perspective of the appropriate causal setting, he shuns it. One could say that, if he lets himself be carried away by the short perspective, then he was not capable of viewing *clearly* his situation in the long perspective. Or one could say that, if a man has an *articulated grasp* of what he wants, he can never harm himself through weakness of will. But saying this must not encourage an undue optimism about man's possibilities of acting in accordance with cool reasoning.

113

VI

GOOD AND ACTION

1. IN this chapter I shall discuss three typical attributions of goodness: the good act, the good intention or will, and—quite briefly—the good man.

It would seem that 'good' in the phrase 'a good act', unlike 'good' in such phrases as 'a good knife' or 'a good general', does *not* signify a goodness *of its kind*. (Cf. Ch. II, sect. 1.) There is no excellence, which is typical of acts *as* acts, as there is an excellence of knives *as* knives and of generals *as* generals. But acts can participate in several forms of goodness.

There is first to be noted a connexion between acts and *technical goodness*. This last, as we know, is primarily an attribute of agents who are good at some activity. It is, in the last resort, in the skilful performance of some acts that technical goodness reveals itself. Acts are sometimes judged good or bad on the basis of the perfection of their performance. 'Well done', we say of the good performance, and a well done so-and-so we sometimes call a good so-and-so, *e.g.* when speaking of a good ski-jump or a good race.

The goodness, which we attribute to an act on the basis of the excellence of its performance, I shall call the technical goodness of the act. It is an attribute of an act as a member of a kind of act. *It* is typically a goodness *of its kind*. The good ski-jump is *as* ski-jump good. If there existed standards of excellence of performance for *all* kinds of acts, then one could in a secondary sense call the goodness of an act's performance the goodness of the act *qua* act, as a good golfer might also be called a good sportsman.

It should be noted that technical goodness as an attribute of acts is necessarily an attribute of act-individuals, *i.e.* individual performances of acts of some kind, and never an attribute of act-categories or kinds of act.

2. One of the most common and familiar uses of 'good' is its use in the phrase 'a good (bad, better, less good) way of doing something'. Here 'doing something' stands for an arbitrary human act. An act is the bringing about or production at will of a change in the world, *e.g.* the unlocking of a door. The change brought about or effected we call the result of the act, *e.g.* the fact that a certain door, which was locked, is now open. The 'way of doing' again is some act or activity which 'leads up to' the result of an act, *e.g.* the turning of a key and pulling of a handle, which opens the door. The tie between 'way of doing' and 'thing done' is an *intrinsic* connexion between a kind of act or activity and some generic state of affairs. Certain turnings of a key is a way of unlocking a door, only provided it results in the door's being unlocked.

Value-judgments, which are passed on ways of doing things, are usually comparative judgments. That one way of doing something is better than another way of doing the same thing can mean that it is easier or quicker or less expensive or more pleasant or more tidy or is not connected with certain unwanted side-effects, etc. What 'better' means in the individual case, depends upon the aim of the doer, whether he wants to do the thing as cheaply as possible or as quickly or as tidily or what not. This relativity of the goodness of a way of doing to aims of the agent does not, however, mean that 'good' here is an attribute of the individual performance. The very phrase 'way of doing' indicates generality.

It should be observed that also a *bad* way of doing a thing is a *way* of doing it, just as a poor or a bad knife is still a knife. This means that there is a sense of 'good', in which even a bad way of doing something is good, *viz*. 'good' as opposed to 'no good' for the purpose of effecting a certain result. Ways of doing, which are no good in a certain acting situation are (usually) not ways of doing the wanted thing at all—and not *bad* ways of doing something. In all these respects the use of 'good' and 'bad' and 'better' as attributes of ways of doing resembles the use of 'good' and 'poor' (sometimes also 'bad') and 'better' for rating instruments.

3. The attribution of instrumental goodness to ways of doing things must not be confused with the attribution of that which we

have here called *utilitarian* goodness, *i.e.* roughly speaking useful-ness, to acts as means to certain ends.

Means-end relationships, which are relevant to judgments of utilitarian goodness, are causal or extrinsic and not logical or intrinsic relationships. (Cf. above Ch. III, sect. 1 and below Ch. VIII, sect. 5.) An act is good or *useful* for a certain purpose or with a view to a certain end, if the doing of this act promotes or favours this purpose or the attainment of this end. It is bad or *harmful* if it hinders or counteracts the attainment of the end. For example: to disobey the doctor's orders may be a hindrance to quick recovery from an illness. It is a bad thing to do with a view to one's recovery. But we do not, except ironically, call it 'a bad way of recovering'.

'Good ways of doing things' and 'bad ways of doing things', I would say, are opposed to one another as contradictories rather than as contraries. But utilitarian goodness and badness as at-tributes of acts denote contraries and not contradictories. The good act is useful by favouring, the bad act detrimental or harmful by counteracting the attainment of the end. These, clearly, are con-trarily related alternatives. Between them fall the acts, which neither favour nor counteract the attainment of the end.

It is useful to distinguish between the *result* and the *consequences* of an act. The result of an act is that state of affairs which *must* obtain, if we are to say truly that the act has been done. For example: the result of the act of opening a window is that a certain window is open (at least for a short time). The consequences of an act are states of affairs which, by virtue of causal necessity, come about when the act has been done. (Ch. V, sect. 8; see also the discussion in Ch. VIII, sect. 5.) For example: A consequence of the act of opening a window may be that the temperature in the room goes down. The relation between an act and its result is *intrinsic*; the relation between an act and its consequences again is *extrinsic*.

It follows from what has been said that whether an act is good or bad in a utilitarian sense, depends upon its consequences. Which will be the consequences of an act again largely depends upon the circumstances under which the act was done. The circumstances may vary from one individual performance to another of an act of a certain category or kind. For this reason, attributions of utilitarian goodness to acts will often be restricted to act-individuals. But they are not necessarily thus restricted. Sometimes the consequences of individual performances of an act are nearly always the same, independently of variations in circumstances. Then utilitarian goodness may become attributed to the act-category. For example: medicines and drugs have nearly uniform effects on the human body. Hence such general judgments become possible as, say, that taking Vitamin C is good (useful) for preventing colds.

Means are not clearly distinguished in language from ways of doing things. *Sometimes*, it would seem, the phrase 'a good (bad) means' means exactly the same as 'a good (bad) way of doing'. But sometimes 'good (bad) means' refers to some act which is causally connected with some end. In the first case 'good' in 'good means' connoted instrumental, in the second case utilitarian goodness.

It is of some interest to note that, whereas technical goodness can be attributed only to individual acts, *viz*. as performances, and instrumental goodness only to kinds of act or activity, *viz*. as ways of doing, utilitarian goodness may become attributed either to an act-individual or, sometimes, to an act-category.

The utilitarian goodness of an individual act or of an act-category depends solely upon a causal relation to some end of action. It is completely independent of any goodness, which the end may possess, in addition to being 'a good' by virtue of being an end. There can be good means to bad ends and bad means to good ends, just as there can be good ways of doing bad things and bad ways of doing good things.

4. Are acts and activities rated as good or bad according to whether they are wanted (welcomed) or unwanted (shunned) in themselves?

Action can be rated as wanted or unwanted in itself by the agent who performs it, but also by various subjects who 'suffer' it, *i.e.* whose lives are affected by it. The ratings by different subjects of one and the same individual act or of one and the same category of act can, of course, be different.

That an act or activity is in itself wanted by the agent means that it is something which he, its causal requirements and consequences apart, would want to do for its own sake. If an act is in itself wanted, then its *result* is a thing wanted in itself. If again an activity is in itself wanted, then *practising* it is a thing wanted in itself.

117

Practising an activity for its own sake is frequently called by the agent a nice thing or a fine thing or a lovely thing to do. Sometimes it is also called by him a good thing to do. But in calling it good he would usually, I think, be implying that he considers this thing *good for him*, *i.e.* beneficial.

That which an agent does is not very often *in itself*, *i.e.* its consequences apart, a wanted thing for another subject. But it is not infrequently in itself unwanted by others. They find it, say, annoying to hear or disagreeable to watch. Action on the part of other subjects, which *we* consider in itself unwanted, is commonly said to be a nuisance (to us). But we would hesitate to call it bad, unless we consider it positively harmful, obnoxious (for somebody).

By the *intrinsic value* of acts and activities we may understand their character of being wanted or unwanted or indifferent in themselves. Accepting this terminology, we seem entitled to say that judging action good or bad on the basis of its intrinsic value is neither a common nor a very important kind of valuation.

Common, however, is the rating of acts and activities as good or bad according to whether they are (thought) beneficial or harmful. The agent of a beneficial act is said to *do good to* the subject or subjects for whom the act is beneficial. Similarly, the agent of a harmful act is said to *do harm to* the subject(s), for whom the act is harmful. Also the acts themselves are sometimes said to *do* good and harm respectively to the subjects. More commonly, however, they are said to be *good for* and *bad for* those whom they affect.

One and the same (individual) act can be beneficial for one but harmful for another subject. Such acts are sometimes said to be *both* good *and* bad. There is no contradiction in this, as long as we remember the relativity of the beneficial and the harmful to ('suffering') subjects.

An agent can be mistaken in thinking that an act of his is beneficial (harmful) for some other subject. This he can be, because he is ignorant of the (causal prerequisites and) consequences of his act. But he can also be mistaken because he is ignorant of the valuation of his act by the other subject. Perhaps he did something which he was sure his neighbour would welcome. Perhaps he did this even for the sake of promoting his neighbour's good. Yet, if his neighbour sincerely resents what was done to him, including its consequences, the act was not beneficial.

Similarly, a subject can be mistaken in judging of something, which has been done 'to him', that it is good (bad) for him. He can be mistaken, because he is ignorant of the consequences, but also because he fails to anticipate correctly his own valuation of the causal whole, of which the act in question is the 'nucleus'.

Judgments of the goodness or badness of human acts according to how they affect the good of various beings, thus share in the precariousness and uncertainties of judgments of things beneficial and harmful in general.

5. Human acts are perhaps the most important category of things, which are judged good or bad 'in a moral sense' or 'from a moral point of view'.

Is there a special *moral* sense of the word 'good'? Is *moral goodness* a special *form* of the good—on a par with hedonic, technical, utilitarian, etc. goodness?

Moral philosophers often discuss the good and the bad (evil), as though the answer to the above questions were affirmative. Whether they are prepared explicitly to defend such a view is usually not clear from the very scanty treatment which those philosophers give to the other forms of goodness beside the moral. There is a tendency to dismiss the other forms, or some of them, as ethically irrelevant.

My own view of the matter is roughly as follows: Moral goodness is *not* a form of the good on a level with the other forms, which we have distinguished. If it be called a form of goodness at all, it is this in a *secondary* sense. By this I mean that an account of the conceptual nature of moral goodness has to be given in terms of some other form of the good. (Cf. Ch. I, sect. 8.)

I shall here attempt to give such an account. The form of goodness, in the terms of which I propose to explicate the notion of the morally good, is the sub-form of utilitarian goodness which we have called the beneficial. To put my main idea very crudely: Whether an act is morally good or bad depends upon its character of being beneficial or harmful, *i.e.* depends upon the way in which it affects the good of various beings.

There is a *prima facie* objection to an account of moral goodness in terms of the beneficial. It can be framed as follows:

The beneficial and the harmful are relative to subjects. If an act is called good on the ground that it is beneficial, the judgment is incomplete unless we are told *for whom* it is good (beneficial).

119

Similarly, if an act is called bad on the ground that it does some harm, the statement is elliptic unless it is added *for whom* the act is bad. 'Good' when it means 'beneficial' is always 'good for somebody', and 'bad' when it means 'harmful' is always 'bad for somebody'.

The morally good and bad is *not* in this sense relative to subjects. Phrases such as 'morally good for me' or 'morally bad for him' must be dismissed as nonsensical. The fact that an act does harm to somebody may be relevantly connected with the moral badness of the act. But if this act is morally bad, then it is bad *simpliciter*— and not for some subject, as opposed to others. And similarly for moral goodness.

There is thus *one* sense, in which moral goodness is 'absolute' and 'objective' and in which the beneficial is 'relative' and 'subjective'. This marks an important logical distinction between the morally good and bad on the one hand and the beneficial and the harmful on the other hand. Does not this difference between the two 'forms' of goodness doom to failure any attempt to define moral goodness in terms of the beneficial? I hope to be able to show that this is not so.

6. One and the same individual act, we said (p. 118), can affect the good of different beings differently—be beneficial for some and harmful for other beings. The question may be raised whether, taking into consideration all such effects, one could form a *resultant* judgment of the value of the act. If the answer is affirmative, the further question could be raised whether this resultant value of the act, its 'overall character' of beneficial or harmful, could be identified with its *moral* worth.

The question whether a value-resultant can be formed on the basis of the character of an act of being beneficial for some and harmful for other beings, is related to the following more general problem: Can the welfare of one being be 'balanced' against the welfare of another? Does it, for example, make sense to say that the good which an act did to some person was greater than the harm it did to another? Or to say that the total amount of moderate good which an act does to several beings, 'outweighs' the great amount of harm which this same act does to one or a few beings?

It seems to me obvious that, *if* a value-resultant of the ways in which acts affect the welfare of various beings can be formed at all,

120

this can only be done by judging the beneficial or harmful nature of the act from the point of view of *the welfare of a collectivity*, of which the various beings concerned are the individual members. Such judging of acts is, as a matter of fact, often attempted. It is attempted, *e.g.*, when we argue that it is better that one man's interests are sacrificed than that all the members of a community shall suffer. Or when we say that it is better that one man is thrown overboard than that the whole crew shall perish. We are then, as it were, saying: this is how the community would prefer to have it. We compare the community to a man who ponders whether he should undergo a painful operation or do something he dislikes for the sake of his subsequent health or well-being.

Are such arguments logically legitimate? The answer is tied to the problem whether the notion of the good (welfare) of a collectivity or community of men is logically legitimate. I am not suggesting that the answers must be negative. But I am sure that the conditions of estimations of value from the point of view of the good of a community are extremely complicated, and also that the appeal to the welfare of a collectivity over and against the welfare of some of its members is often misused in practice. We are here touching upon a major problem in the ethics of politics. I shall not discuss this problem further in the present work. I leave it open.

In the subsequent discussion I shall disregard the possibility of forming a judgment as to the 'overall' beneficial or harmful character of an act. I shall discuss the notion of moral goodness from what could also be called the point of view of the human individual, as distinct from the point of view of the human community. On the logical complications connected with the second point of view I shall not here touch, nor on the question whether the two points of view can be brought into harmony with one another.

7. We next put forward the following suggestions of how the moral value of a human act may be considered a 'function' of the way in which this act affects the good of various beings favourably or adversely:

>an act is morally good, if and only if it does good to at least one being and does not do bad (harm) to any being; and

>an act is morally bad, if and only if it does bad (harm) to at least one being.

The suggestions are open to a number of objections.

First, it may be objected that an act could not be called *morally* good on the ground that it is beneficial for the agent himself— even if it does not hurt anybody else. Similarly, it is at least doubtful, whether harming oneself could be considered *morally* bad.

If one accepts one or both of these objections as valid, one takes the view that moral action is essentially 'social'. On this view, that part of a man's action which affects solely his own good is morally irrelevant.

There is a certain inclination, it seems to me, to say that harming oneself is morally bad, though doing good to oneself is not morally good. It may be suggested, however, that the foundation of this inclination is the fact that by harming himself a person can hardly fail to become a nuisance to or a burden on his fellow humans. According to this suggestion, the moral badness of doing bad to oneself consists in the bad which the agent (indirectly) causes to others.

We shall not here take a stand on the issue, whether action which solely affects the acting agent's own good is morally relevant or not.

Another objection to the suggested definition of moral goodness runs as follows: An act which does good to some and bad to no being need not have been done for the sake of doing good. The agent may not even be aware of the beneficial nature of what he did. Would it not in either case be absurd to label this act *morally* good?

A similar objection may be raised against our proposed definition of moral badness. If the agent is not aware of the harmful nature of what he did, is his act then *morally* bad?

These objections mean that our proposed definition of moral goodness was too 'lenient' and our proposed definition of moral badness was too 'severe'. The first was too lenient because it was compatible with the possibility that action can be morally good, though no good is intended or even foreseen by the agent. The second again was too severe because according to it action can be morally bad even when no bad is intended or foreseen.

There is, however, also an objection to our proposed definition of moral goodness on the ground that it is too severe, and to the definition of moral badness on the ground that it is too lenient. For, under certain circumstances, is not an intention to do some good enough to warrant the moral goodness of the act, even if no good actually results to anybody? And is not similarly an intention to do some bad enough to label the act as morally bad, even if no harm actually results?

Accepting these objections thus means that our proposed definitions of morally good and bad acts were at once too lenient and too severe.

I think we must accept these objections—or some of them at least. The proposed definitions cannot be regarded as successful attempts to catch hold of the 'essence' of moral goodness and badness. The chief reason why they fail is that they make the moral quality of an act independent of *intentions* in acting and of the *foreseeing* of good and harm to other beings.

Before we revise our proposals for defining moral goodness and badness, some words must be said on the concept of intending.

8. How is intention in acting related to the foreseeing of consequences?

In order to answer the question, we shall have to observe that intention is primarily connected with *results* of action—and *not* with consequences. An intention is an intention *to do something*. That which is intended, the object of intention, is the result of an act.

Suppose that I open a window *with the intention*, as we say, of cooling the room. The cooling of the room is a consequence of the opening of the window. Is not here the object of intention the consequence and not the result of my act? I propose to answer the question as follows:

If I open a window with the intention of cooling the room and the temperature in the room goes down as a consequence of my manipulations with the window, then the question 'What did I *do*?' can also be answered by 'I cooled the room'. Cooling the room is something I can do. There is an act of cooling the room. Its result is that the temperature in the room is now lower than it was before. It is a *different* act from the act of opening the window, to which it has a causal, and not an intrinsic, relation. The act of cooling the room would be different from the act of opening the window, even if opening the window were the *only* means to cooling the room. They are different because the result of the one is a consequence of the result of the other. But the *activity* which I display in performing the two acts, *i.e.* the manipulations with the

123

window, is the same in both. (In this sense the two acts could be said to 'look' the same.)

Suppose a person intends to cool the room and, with a view to this, opens the window. And suppose that he succeeds in making his intention effective. Shall we then say that he *also* intended to open the window? We would certainly call his act of opening the window *intentional*. We may wish to call it *intended*, but we may also wish to reserve this term for acts, the results of which have the character of ultimate ends in acting. Usage seems to be somewhat vacillating at this point, and we need not force ourselves to a decision. But we shall decide to call any act, which is done for the sake of or in order to attain some end, intentional *or* intended.

Be it observed in passing that 'intended' is used both of the act and of the state of affairs which is its result, whereas 'intentional' is normally used only of the act. One suggestion could be that the results both of intended and intentional acts be called 'intended'. I shall adopt this suggestion.

The man who opens the window in order to cool the room, can rightly be said to intend two things 'at once' or to have two intentions—one to have the window open and another to have the temperature lower.

Although everything, which is done for the sake of an end, is also intended (as well as the end), it is certainly not the case that everything, which is a consequence of action, is also intended. If the agent, at the time when he is acting, does not foresee the consequence (or at least realizes the 'serious possibility' that it will happen), then he can, in a sense, not even be rightly said to have *done* the consequent thing. 'Look what you have done!' we sometimes say of such cases—particularly when we consider the consequences undesirable. This is said in order to draw the agent's attention to a causal connexion of which he was not aware. Once he is aware of the connexion he can not, on a new occasion, *do* the first thing without also *doing* the second.

It is here appropriate to make a distinction between *foreseen* and *rightly foreseen* consequences of action. Something is a foreseen consequence, if the agent at the time of acting knows or believes that this thing will happen as a consequence of his action. A foreseen consequence will be called rightly foreseen if it actually happens (as a consequence of action). Agents sometimes foresee consequences of their action which never come true.

124

I shall say that everything which is a *rightly foreseen* consequence of one's action, is also *a thing done*. But I shall *not* say that everything which is a *foreseen* consequence of one's action, is also a thing *intended*. Suppose our man opens a window and that, as a consequence, the temperature in the room goes down. When asked *why* he opened the window, he answers that he did it in order to hear the birds sing. Let us assume that he foresaw that the temperature was going to sink—or at least was aware of the possibility. Then he could *not* say that he lowered the temperature *unintentionally*. But to say that he did not lower the temperature unintentionally and to say that he intentionally lowered it, is not—on the ordinary understanding of the words—to say the same. Of everything which is a rightly foreseen consequence of my action, I can say truly that I *did* this and that I did *not* do it unintentionally. But only of such consequences of my action, which were also ends of action—intermediate or ultimate—can I say truly that I intended them or did them intentionally. That consequences are ends entails that they are foreseen—but not that they are *rightly* foreseen.

This much will have to suffice about the notions of intention and foreseen consequences of action, and the related notions of the intentional, the unintentional, and the not unintentional.

9. Can intentions possess an excellence of their kind, *i.e. as* intentions? Intentions can be firm or vague, strong or weak. To say of a man that he had 'good intentions' or 'the best of intentions' to do a certain thing is, it seems, sometimes another way of saying that he was firmly determined to do this. We should not ordinarily, however, call a vague or weak intention to do something a 'bad intention'.

When 'good' is used as an attribute of intentions to indicate firmness of determination or strength of will, it can perhaps be said to connote a goodness *of its kind*. This is one use of the word 'good'. But it is certainly not *that* use of the word which we have in mind, when we speak of intention as the bearer of moral value or as a component in the moral valuation of acts.

'Good' and 'bad' as moral attributes of intentions do *not* connote goodness or badness *of its kind, i.e.* of intentions as intentions. It would seem, moreover, that 'good' and 'bad' as moral attributes of intentions are in an important sense *secondary*. By this I mean that the primary attribution of 'good' and 'bad' here is not of the intention as such, but of the objects of intention, the intended results of action. Basically, 'good intention' is intention to do (some) good, and 'bad (evil) intention' is intention to do (some) bad or evil. The problem is how to give a satisfactory formulation to the dependence of the value of intention on the value of the intended.

Complications are caused here by the fact that an intention may have several objects, and by the fact that everything which is done in order to attain an intended end of action is also intended. Evidently, these complications cannot be ignored in an attempt to assess the moral worth of intentions. Be it said in passing that Kant's doctrine of the good will seems to me to suffer badly from Kant's ignoring the 'multiplicity of intention', which exists thanks to the fact that human acts have causal relationships of which the agent, in acting, is seldom totally unaware.

By an *intended good* I shall understand an end of action which is judged by the agent to be beneficial for some being. By an *intended bad* I shall understand an end of action which is judged by the agent to be harmful for some being. By a *foreseen bad* I shall understand a result or foreseen consequence of action which is judged by the agent to be harmful for some being. Every intended bad is also a foreseen bad, but not conversely.

An intended good is thus an intended state of affairs, the production of which is thought to affect the good of some being favourably. That this state of affairs is produced and that it affects the good of a being favourably are two logically different things. The first may depend upon the agent alone. The second also depends upon the valuation of the being(s) affected by the agent's action. By calling the state of affairs an intended good we thus attribute *two* objects of intention to the agent. The first is the state of affairs itself. I shall call it his *factual* object of intention. The second is that some being(s) will value this state of affairs as good for him (them). I shall call this the agent's *axiological* object of intention.

An intended good or bad can fail to materialize. This can happen for two chief reasons. The intention may fail in regard to its factual object. Or it may fail in regard to its axiological object.

When the intention fails in regard to its factual object, we sometimes contrast the 'good intention' with the 'poor performance'.

A discrepancy between a professed intention and the actual performance may make us doubt whether the intention was there at all or how firm or strong or serious it was. But if no such doubts occur, mere failure with regard to its factual object would not, it seems, be considered relevant to the question of the moral worth of the intention. One of the reasons for thinking that the moral worth of action resides in the intention alone, is probably the idea that this value must not become affected by adversities in acting or by mistakes in foreseeing consequences. This in no way contradicts the view, which I think we must in any case accept, namely that the moral value of the intention depends upon the value of the thing intended.

There is, however, also the case to be considered when an intention to do good reaches its factual object but fails in regard to its axiological object. We did something for the sake of promoting our neighbour's good, for example, and everything went exactly according to our plans—except that our neighbour strongly resented what we did, thoroughly disliked it, perhaps even badly suffered from it. Should such discrepancy between *apparent* and *real* value, as we could call it, influence our judgment of the goodness of intention?

If by good and bad things we understand things beneficial or harmful, as defined in this inquiry, then to mistake the apparent value of something which has been done for its real value is to make a false judgment or conjecture either about the consequences of the achieved result of action *or* about the valuation of this result and its consequences by some subject(s) *or* about both these things. In a first person judgment 'I like this', 'I would rather have this than be without it', 'No, thank you', the subject is valuing something. Then there is no possibility of mistake and no room for a discrepancy between apparent and real value either. In a third person judgment 'This will do him good', or 'This is bad for him', or 'He will like it', we are not valuing but saying what we think *that* the valuations of subjects are or will be. As far as the value of his acts for others is concerned, the agent's judgment will necessarily be a third person judgment and thus *not* a (genuine) value-judgment. A mistake on his part concerning this value will therefore be a mistake concerning empirical matters of fact.

If we want the moral value of intention to be independent of intellectual mistakes in judging, then we must in the name of

127

consistency admit that mistakes as to the value of the factual objects of our intentions do not 'maculate', *i.e.* spoil the goodness of our intentions. 'He *meant* it well', we often say when a mistake as to value (valuation) has occurred, and since he meant it thus it may seem illogical to blame him *morally* for what he *did*.

But even if, on the ground of the goodness of their intentions, we morally excuse persons for some evil they have done, we nevertheless blame them for *ignorance*—either of consequences of action, or of the beneficial or harmful nature of things, or of both. 'You should have known that this is not the way a man wants to be helped; by what you did you only managed to hurt his feelings', we say of many a case of intended beneficiality. Because of ignorance, much bad is done for good motives. This is an aspect of the matter to which moralists in a Kantian spirit, as far as I can see, have habitually paid but little attention. Yet it is an important aspect of the moral life—or at least of action affecting the good of man. Paying due attention to this aspect need not, however, influence our view as to what constitutes the goodness of intention. But it must lead us to realize clearly that intention to do good is, by itself, of rather limited *utilitarian* value for the promotion of the welfare of man and of human collectivities.

10. An agent, who intends to do good to some being, can do so either for the sake of promoting the good of that being or for some other reason. When doing good to somebody is intended solely for the sake of promoting the good of that being, I shall say that good is intended *for its own sake*.

I now propose the following definition of morally good and bad intention in acting:

the intention in acting is morally good, if and only if, good for somebody is intended for its own sake and harm is not foreseen to follow for anybody from the act; and

the intention in acting is morally bad, if and only if, harm is foreseen to follow for somebody from the act.

I shall not here further discuss the question whether we may include or must exclude the case that the subject, whose good the act is foreseen to affect, is the agent himself. (Cf. sect. 7.)

That the intended good must be intended for its own sake, if the intention in acting is to be called *morally* good, seems fairly obvious. A master who takes good care of his servants, in order

128

that they shall be fitter to work hard for him, cannot be said to have a morally good intention in his treatment of his servants. But, if from an attitude of gratitude or love he is anxious to see his servants flourish or thrive, then we may attribute moral goodness to his intentions.

It seems obvious, too, that the intention in acting is deserving of moral blame, not only on the ground that some harm is intended, but already on the ground that some harm is foreseen in acting. Suppose a person opens a window in order to hear the birds sing. Thereby he cools the room and causes another person, who is present, to catch a cold. He is aware of the fact that opening the window will cool the room and also aware, let us assume, of the serious possibility that the other person will catch a cold. If 'with a clean conscience' he can declare that he opened the window in order to hear the birds and that this was his only end, the only thing he intended beside the opening itself of the window, then the cooling of the room and the cold which the other person caught were *foreseen consequences* of his action but not things he can be said to have *intended* to achieve. Yet it would be reasonable to blame him for having opened the window, since he realized at the time of doing it that he was exposing another person to danger. What he intended to do was morally blameworthy, because of the foreseen harmful consequences, and I see no reason why we should not therefore also say that his intention in acting was *morally bad*. But we could not rightly say that his intention in acting was *malicious*. This we can do only when the foreseen harm of his intended action was also intended and not only foreseen.

Some ethicists may be of the opinion that goodness or badness of intention is the only thing that is morally relevant in action, and that there is no need to distinguish between the moral value of the intention and the moral value of the act. It seems to me, however, that a distinction can be sensibly made.

If the *intention* in acting is morally good but the good, which is for its own sake intended, fails to materialize—either because the intention fails in regard to its factual or in regard to its axiological object—then the *act* is not morally good (but morally neutral). If, on the other hand, the intended good materializes, then the act too may be called morally good.

Similarly, if the intention in acting is morally bad but the harm, which is foreseen, does not come about, then the act is not morally bad (but morally neutral). If, on the other hand, the foreseen harm comes about, then the act too is morally bad.

It is a noteworthy asymmetry between moral goodness and moral badness that the first presupposes that some good should be *intended* and, moreover, intended for its own sake, whereas the second only requires that some bad should be *foreseen* to follow from the act.

It is characteristic of the logical complications of the concepts, which we have been discussing, that the notion of a morally good or bad act is secondary to the notion of a morally good or bad intention (will) in acting, which in its turn is secondary to the notion of a good or bad, *i.e.* beneficial or harmful, thing.

11. In our proposed definition of a morally bad act is tacitly presupposed that in every situation there is a course of action open to the agent, from which he foresees no harm to anybody. The presupposition, in other words, is that the agent is always 'free' to choose a course of action which is not morally bad.

(This presupposition, be it observed, is *not* that there always is a course of action from which no harm actually follows. Harm which follows, but which could not have been foreseen at the time of acting, is not relevant to the question of the moral quality of the act.)

However, the presupposition which we just mentioned is not always fulfilled. Cases may occur in which the agent foresees harm to some being from whatever course of action he chooses. Such cases are not common. But they happen. Their rarity does not nullify the importance which their gravity gives to them.

When harm is (rightly) foreseen to follow from whatever an agent does, I shall say that harm is *unavoidable*. This 'absolute' notion of unavoidable harm must not be confused with the 'relative' notion of unavoidable harm. By the second I mean harm which cannot be avoided, if some particular end of action has to be reached.

It is a logical characteristic of the type of acting-situation, which we are now considering, that there should be some act open to the agent which is such that bad is foreseen to follow both from *doing* and from *forbearing* this act. Forbearing to act, it should be observed, is also action. Forbearing to act can have consequences just as well as acting can have. The consequences of forbearance is the happening of those things which action would have prevented.

130

What one would wish to say from a moral point of view of the type of case under discussion is, I think, the following: In a situation when the agent foresees harm both from doing and from forbearing the very same thing, at least one of the two, acting or forbearing, must be morally excusable. If the harm, which is foreseen to follow from doing, is less than the harm which is foreseen to follow from forbearing, then acting is morally excusable, *i.e.* is not the doing of a morally bad act. If again the harm which is foreseen to follow from forbearing is less, then forbearing is morally excusable. If, finally, the foreseen harm from acting equals the foreseen harm from forbearing, either course of action is morally excusable.

We could call this the rule of minimizing unavoidable harm. It determines under which conditions the causing of bad to some being can be morally excused. The harm, which it exculpates, is unavoidable in the 'absolute' sense. Harm, which is in the 'relative' sense unavoidable, can, on my view, never be morally excused. To argue that it could be excused, is a form of arguing that 'the end justifies the means'. This seems to me the very prototype of immoral argument.

The rule of minimizing unavoidable harm has an obvious plausibility. Yet it takes for granted that a difficult problem can be solved when the rule has to be applied. This is the problem of determining ('measuring') the relative magnitude of harm to various beings. It is not certain that this problem has a significant solution in every case. Let us consider the problem in the light of an example.

A man x can save either the man y or the man z but not both from an impending disaster. y and z are, say, wounded and x can carry one of them at a time but not both of them at once to safety. x foresees that, if he carries away one of the men, the disaster will in the meantime reach the place and consume the remaining man.

We can describe x's possible action in the terms of two choices. His first choice is this: Shall I save one of the two or shall I leave both to perish? If he chooses the second, then by his chosen course of action he, in a sense, becomes responsible for the death or disaster of one man. (x's action is then forbearance.) Or, strictly speaking: x becomes responsible for the disaster of one more man than would have perished, had x acted differently.

Assume that x chooses to do his best and save one of the two. We would all agree, I think, that this choice of his is morally right, and that a choice to abstain from action would have been morally wrong. To let both perish is to cause more bad than to leave one to perish. The general principle for comparing the relative magnitudes of harm can here be formulated as follows: That all of a number of men suffer some harm is worse (a greater bad) than that some only of these men suffer the same harm. (It is essential that the smaller group of people, who suffer harm, should be a subclass of the greater group of people, and that the harm which each one of them suffers as a member of the first group is the very same harm which each one of them suffers as a member of the second group.)

So far the case seems clear. But, having chosen to save one of the two rather than to leave both to suffer, x is faced with a second choice: Shall he save y or z? If he chooses the first, then as a consequence of his chosen course of action z will suffer. If he chooses the second, y will suffer. x, we assume, foresees this quite clearly. x takes y and carries him to safety. Disaster befalls z.

Can this second choice of x's be justified with reference to the rule of minimizing unavoidable harm? There are two ways in which the justification may be attempted. One is to argue that the harm, which follows from leaving z, is neither greater nor less than the harm which follows from leaving y, and that hence x is 'morally free' to choose between saving y or saving z. The other is to argue that more harm follows from leaving y than from leaving z and that x hence is 'morally bound' to choose to save y. Both ways of arguing have to cope with similar logical difficulties. Two examples will be given to show what these difficulties could be and how one might try to cope with them:

y is the commander of a group of men, of which x and z are members. x argues: it is worse *for the group* to lose y than to lose z. x is then contemplating the consequences of his action from the point of view of the good (welfare) of a group (community) of men. His argument is that it is preferable (better) *for the group* to have y without z than to have z without y.

y is head of a family, z is single. x argues: If y is left to suffer or die, a number of other people will suffer heavily too. If z is left, others will not be seriously affected. Assuming that the bad, which y and z are facing, is an equal bad for both, then it is a greater bad that beside y also others should suffer harm than that no one in addition to z himself should suffer.

132

The first way of arguing proceeds on the assumption that an appeal to the good of a community of men over and against the good of its individual members is possible. The second argument assumes that it is possible to 'balance' the good of two or more beings against one another. Both assumptions were briefly discussed in section 6. Of the second we said that it, too, is based on the possibility of appealing to the good of a community over and against the good of its individual members. The logical nature and moral character of this appeal, however, will not be further discussed in the present work. What has been said in this section illustrates the urgency of such discussion.

12. We conclude this chapter with some brief remarks about the use of the word 'good' as an attribute of a man.

If there existed a purpose which were essentially associated with man as a kind, then one could by the phrase 'a good man' understand a human individual, who serves this purpose of the kind well. Some may think that there is such an essential purpose of man, *e.g.* that men exist to serve the purposes of their Creator. We shall not here discuss this view.

Men often become accidentally associated with purposes, *i.e.* they are needed and used to serve the purposes of other men or of human institutions. The phrase 'he is a good man' is very commonly used to mean that a man fits or serves some such purpose or task well. The man, who is thus judged instrumentally good, is usually also in some respect technically good, *viz.* as a member of a professional class. Such instrumental or technical goodness of a man, however, does not mean that he were, *as a man*, good, even if it is natural to call him *a good man*.

The idea that there is an activity essentially associated with man as man, may be considered inherently more plausible than the idea that there existed some purpose thus associated with him. The function proper to man, Aristotle thought[1] is activity in accordance with a rational principle or life according to reason. The better a man performs this proper function of his, the better he is, *as a man*. This is a clear use of 'good' and 'better' to attribute to a man a goodness *of its kind*. I shall not here discuss Aristotle's idea. It seems to me that, even if it were true to say that there is an activity which is essential to man, *e.g.* reasoning, it would be

[1] See especially the discussion in *EN*, Bk. I, Ch. 7.

doubtful whether this activity is of the sort *at which* a being can be said to be good or bad. To say that a man lives or does not live in accordance with reason is vague, but we understand *roughly* what it means. But to say that a man is 'good at' living in accordance with reason, would seem to require a *special interpretation* of 'good at', which conceptually distinguishes this case from other cases of that which I have here called technical goodness.

When the phrase 'a good man' is used, *not* in the sense of instrumental or technical goodness but with a moral tinge, it is related to the notions of doing good and of having good intentions. But it has no clear and distinct relationship to these notions.

A man who is intent on doing good is often called *benevolent*. A man can be a 'benefactor' without being benevolent, *e.g.* if he does good to others mainly for the sake of promoting his own social prestige. A true benefactor must be a man who does good (to others), but he need not be that which is ordinarily called a good man.

I am not suggesting that there is a common and important use of the phrase 'a good man' to mean the same as 'a benevolent man'. But I think it is true to say that when the phrase 'a good man' is used with a so-called moral meaning, it is *related* to our idea of a benevolent man. It is of some interest in this connexion to notice that the opposite to a benevolent man, *i.e.* a malevolent man or a man who is intent on doing evil or mischief, is quite commonly and naturally also called, in a moral sense, 'a bad man'.

One affinity between the morally relevant notion of a good man and the notion of a benevolent man is in any case that both notions have to do with features of human *character*. A man may do some bad acts and even entertain some evil intentions—and yet be a good man. But the bad he does or intends must count as an occasional aberration. Or it must have some special excuse. If we were asked how much evil the good man can be 'allowed', we could, of course, not answer by giving an exact measure—'hereunto and no further'. But we could give an inexact and yet significant measure by saying that the bad he does or intends must not affect our judgment of his character. A good man may do some mischief, or revenge a wrong which he has suffered from another man, or tell a lie. But he cannot be mischievous or revengeful or untruthful.

With this last remark we are also touching upon one of the differences between goodness and benevolence as attributes of men. A benevolent man is not necessarily a virtuous man, and he may be lacking in a sense of justice. Virtue and justice are two prominent features in our picture of moral excellence. Until we have discussed them, our notion of the good man will remain insufficiently clarified.

VII

VIRTUE

1. VIRTUE is a neglected topic in modern ethics. The only full-scale modern treatment of it, known to me, is by Nicolai Hartmann. When one compares the place accorded to virtue in modern moral philosophy with that accorded to it in traditional moral philosophy, one may get the impression that virtue as a topic of philosophic discussion has become obsolete, outmoded. This impression may gain additional strength from the fact that traditional discussion has—with rather few notable exceptions—followed the footsteps of Aristotle without much variation or innovation or controversy. Kant's famous *dictum* that formal logic had made no appreciable progress since Aristotle, could be paraphrased and applied—with at least equally good justification—to the ethics of virtue.

Kant thought that the reason why there had been so little progress in logic (as he saw it), was that Aristotle had accomplished most of what there was to be done in the field. As we know now, Kant was badly mistaken. It would be unwise to prophesy a renaissance for the ethics of virtue, comparable to the renaissance which we have in this century witnessed in logic. But I think the time has come when the impression which the discussion of virtue in traditional moral philosophy conveys to the modern spectator, should no longer be that of something accomplished or obsolete, but rather that of a subject awaiting fresh developments.

The relative neglect of the discussion of virtue is certainly connected with the predominance, for a long period, of that which could be called the (purely) *axiological* and *deontological* aspects of moral philosophy. Good and bad and evil are value-terms. Right and wrong and duty are normative terms. But courage, temperance, and truthfulness we would not ordinarily call value-concepts nor

136

normative concepts. Some people would call them psychological concepts, but this too is not a very fitting name. (Cf. Ch. I, sect. 4.)

The discipline known as General Theory of Value, now much in fashion, tries to cater among other things for those aspects of traditional moral theory which are concerned with value—the axiological aspects. Since virtue is not prominent among them, the ethics of virtue has stayed aside from these developments towards greater generality. There is another discipline of recent origin which also has a wider scope than traditional ethics and within which a discussion of virtue could claim for itself a natural place. This is the discipline sometimes called Philosophical Anthropology. Yet it, too, as far as I know, has not so far paid much attention to the topic of virtue.

2. The Latin word *virtus*, of which 'virtue' is a derivation, has a rather more restricted connotation than the English *virtue*. Its original meaning is perhaps best rendered into English by words such as 'manlihood' or 'prowess' or 'valour'. The Greek *arete* again, which it has become customary to translate by 'virtue', has a much wider connotation than the English word. Its primary and original meaning is the excellence or goodness of any thing whatsoever according to its kind or for its proper purpose. The word 'virtue' too is often used with this meaning. We tend, however, to regard this as a secondary or analogical use. We have an idea of what could be meant by the virtues of a good knife. We easily say such things as that so-and-so had all the virtues of a great general— without wishing to call him 'virtuous' in the common understanding of that word. Then we are using *virtue* in a secondary sense—as the Greeks would have used *arete* in a primary sense.

When, however, we call courage, temperance, generosity, or justice virtues, we are using the word 'virtue' *very* differently from that meaning of *arete*, which refers to an excellence of its kind. To see this clearly is, I think, of some importance. Aristotle, I would suggest, did not see *quite* clearly at this point. He was misled by peculiarities of the Greek language into thinking that those features of human character, which are called virtues, are more closely similar than they actually are to abilities and skills, in which a man can possess that which I have previously called *technical goodness*.

137

I shall not maintain, however, that our word 'virtue', when used with a primary meaning, stands for *one* sharply bounded concept. For this it obviously does not do.

There is first to be noted a feature of our use of the word 'virtue', which comes near to being an ambiguity.[1] There is one meaning of 'virtue', which admits of a plural, 'virtues'. This meaning is in question, for example, when we call courage *a virtue*. There is another meaning of 'virtue', which lacks the plural. This is (usually) in question, when *virtue* is contrasted with *vice*, or when—as is sometimes done—to do one's duty is said to be virtue. Virtue in this second sense comes near to being an axiological or a normative attribute—or a mixture of both.[2] It has definitely a moral tinge. It is related to goodness and rightness and to that which in the Bible is called righteousness. With this meaning of 'virtue', be it observed, we are not at all concerned here. One could also say that we are here not concerned with the meaning of 'virtue', but with the meaning of 'a virtue'. Therefore we are here also dealing with that meaning of 'virtuous', which is the display or practising of virtues, and not (directly) with that which is virtuous as opposed to vicious conduct or character.

Although our notion of a virtue obviously possesses a greater 'logical homogeneity' than the notion of an *arete* with the Ancients, not even *it* can be said to be sharply bounded. Courage, temperance, and industry, for example, seem to me to be virtues in a rather different *sense* from, say, piety or obedience or justice. I am not at all certain that those features which, as I view it, mark the first three as virtues also hold good for the second three.

Considering both the unstable usage of the word and the unsatisfactory state of the subject, the task before us could be described as one of moulding or giving shape to *a* concept of a virtue. We cannot claim that everything which is commonly and naturally called a virtue falls under the concept as shaped by us. But, unless I am badly mistaken, some of the most obvious and uncontroversial examples of virtues *do* fall under it. It is therefore perhaps not vain to hope that our shaping process will contribute

[1] I am indebted to Mr. F. Kemp for having drawn my attention to this distinction.

[2] Kant uses *Tugend* mainly to mean virtue in this sense. Kant also calls it *Sittlichkeit* or *moralische Gesinnung*. The best English translation is perhaps 'morality'.

to a better understanding at least of *one* important aspect of the question, what a virtue is.

3. As a first step towards shaping a concept of virtue I shall say that a virtue is neither an acquired nor an innate skill in any particular *activity*. 'To be courageous' or 'to show courage' do not name an activity in the same sense in which 'to breathe' or 'to walk' or 'to chop wood' name activities. If I ask a person who is engaged in some activity, 'What are you doing?' and he answers, 'I am courageous; this is very dangerous,' he may be speaking the truth, but he is not telling me what he is doing.

The lack of an essential tie between a specific virtue and a specific activity distinguishes virtue from that which we have called technical goodness. We attribute technical goodness or excellence to a man on the ground that he is *good at* some activity. But there is no specific activity at which, say, the courageous man must be good—as the skilled chess-player must be good at playing chess and the skilful teacher must be good at teaching. There is no art of 'couraging', in which the brave man excels.

Nor is a virtue a goodness of the sort which we attribute to faculties (or organs) and which, as we have said before, is related to technical goodness. The virtues are not to be classified along with good sight or memory or ratiocination.

One difference between virtues and faculties is that virtues are acquired rather than innate. In this respect virtues resemble technical excellence. Both of the, in some respect, virtuous man and of the man who is skilled in an art, it makes sense to ask, '*What has he learnt*?' The significance of the question is not minimized by the fact that men are by nature more or less *talented* for various arts and also more or less *disposed* towards various virtues. Sometimes a man can be truly said to be skilled or virtuous without any or much previous education and training. But this is the exception rather than the rule. Contrarywise, a man of good sight has not learnt to see well and a man of good memory is not commonly said to have learnt to remember well. This must not be interpreted as meaning that the faculties of man were not *to some extent* capable of being improved by training.

Yet there is another regard in which virtues are more akin to faculties than to skill in activities. This similarity is their relation to the good of man.

139

To do that on which one is keen or which one does well is a source of active pleasure and may, on that ground, be a 'positive constituent' of a man's good. This is *one* reason why it is important that a man should, if possible, be trained in a profession which answers to his natural gifts and interests. But none of the various professions which a man may choose, and the various skills in which he may be trained and may come to excel, is, by itself, *needed* for the good of man.

With the faculties it is different. (Cf. Ch. III, sect. 7.) Sight and hearing, memory and ratiocination are part of a normal individual's equipment for a normal life. Loss of one of the faculties can be disastrous, weakness of some or several of them is usually to some extent detrimental to the well-being of a man. This, of course, does not exclude that one can make up for the loss or weakness of some faculty. And some men are more dependent for their well-being upon one faculty than upon another. For example: some men need good eyes more than other men, and some men need the use of their eyes and ears more than the use of their brains. Such individual differences depend upon differences in profession and upon other contingencies of life.

Virtues, like faculties, are needed in the service of the good of man. This usefulness of theirs is their meaning and purpose, I would say. How virtues fulfil their natural purpose I shall try to show presently. Be it here only remarked that, just as the contingencies of life can make a man more dependent upon some of his faculties than upon others, in a similar manner can contingencies make the acquisition of one virtue be of the utmost importance to a man and the possession of another of relatively little value. Sometimes the factors, which determine the relative utility of the various virtues, have the character of contingencies in the history of society or of mankind rather than in the life of individual men. In a warlike society, such as perhaps were ancient Sparta or Rome of the Republic, courage is more important for the individual man than, say, chastity or modesty. There is then more demand, so to speak, for brave than for modest men. The different ratings, which moralists of different ages and societies have given to the various virtues reflect, sometimes at least, such contingencies in the conditions under which these moralists themselves have lived. (Cf. sect. 9.)

140

4. It is important to distinguish between *acts* and *activities*. Acts are named after that which I have called the *results* of action, *i.e.* states of affairs brought about or produced by the agent in performing the acts. Acts leave an 'imprint', as it were, on the world; when activities cease, no 'traces' of them need remain. Lighting a cigarette, *e.g.*, is an act; it results in a cigarette being lit. Smoking is an activity.

Acts named after the same generic state of affairs are said to form an act-category. The individual performances of acts again we have called act-individuals. The lighting of a cigarette by a certain agent on a certain occasion is an individual act of the category labelled 'lighting a cigarette'.

As a first step towards shaping the notion of a virtue we said that to the specific virtues there do not answer specific activities. As a further step we shall now say that to the specific virtues there do not answer specific act-categories either.

Of the man of whom a certain virtue is characteristic, acts of a certain kind are also characteristic. But these acts do not constitute an act-category in the sense here defined. They are named after the virtue from which they spring, and not after the states in which they result. There is nothing wrong about saying that a courageous man often does courageous acts. But it is not very illuminating. It becomes misleading if it makes us think that we could define the virtues in terms of certain achievements in acting.

There are at least two reasons why the question, which acts are courageous, cannot be answered by pointing to results achieved in the successful performance of courageous acts. The first is that the results of all courageously performed acts need not have any 'outward' feature in common. Killing a tiger and jumping into cold water can both be acts of courage, though 'outwardly' most dissimilar. No list of achievements could possibly exhaust the range of results in courageous action. The second reason why brave acts do not form an act-category is that the result of any courageous act could also have been achieved through action which was not courageous. Not even to have killed a tiger is a sure proof that a man is courageous.

What is true of courage in the said respect is also true of the other virtues. Virtuous acts cannot be characterized in terms of their results, and therefore virtues not in terms of achievements. We can express this insight in many ways. We could say that the

141

notion of a brave, generous, temperate, etc. act is secondary to the notion of a brave, generous, temperate, etc. man. Or that virtuous action is secondary to virtue. Or that a virtue is an 'inner' quality of an agent and of his acts, and not an 'outer' feature of his conduct. But all these modes of expression are also in various ways misleading, and they should therefore either not be used at all or with great caution only.

One of the things which is most commonly said about virtues, particularly in modern books on ethics, is that the virtues are *dispositions*. Here a warning is in place. It has to do with the fact that to the specific virtues do not answer specific act-categories.

What is a disposition? The term has become something of a catch-word. As catch-words generally, it can mean almost anything—and therefore often means nothing.

When is a man, in ordinary parlance, said to have a disposition towards something? One typical case is when we are talking of matters relating to *health*. A man can have a disposition to catch colds, for example. Or he can have a hereditary disposition for headaches. So-called allergic diseases are typically dispositional. A man is, *e.g.*, sensitive to the scent of horses—whenever he comes near a horse, he begins to sneeze or to breathe heavily.

The word 'disposition' is also commonly used in connexion with so-called states of *temper*. If a man easily gets angry or upset or moved to tears or sad, we may speak of him as having a certain disposition.

Dispositions both of health and of temper can be called *latent* traits which, under specific circumstances, *manifest* themselves in characteristic signs—such as sneezing or shedding tears. The appearance, with some regularity, of these signs in the appropriate circumstances *decides* whether there is a disposition or not. Dispositions are typically 'inward' things with 'outward' criteria. They are that, which the virtues would be, if there existed act-categories or specified activities answering to virtues.

I do not insist upon a common meaning of the term 'disposition' for all the cases in which this word is ordinarily used. But I would maintain that there is no current sense of the word 'disposition', in which the various virtues could be said to be dispositions. The philosopher who calls them dispositions is therefore giving to the term 'disposition' a novel use. This he is entitled to do. But then he must explain what this novel use is. This I have never seen done.

142

The nearest equivalent in matters of conduct to 'dispositions' in matters relating to health and temper are *habits*, I would say. A habit may be defined as a certain acquired regularity of acting. A habit manifests itself in the doing of a characteristic act or in the performing of a characteristic activity under recurrent conditions. A habit can be to take a nap after lunch or a whisky before bed-time. Habits, like virtues, are greatly relevant to questions of good and evil. They differ from virtues in that to them always corresponds either a specific activity or a specific act. This is of the essence of habits, and is reflected in the fact that habits are nearly always named after acts or activities, which can be performed independently of the existence of the habit.

To regard virtues as habits would be to misunderstand the nature of virtues completely. One may even go as far as to saying that, if virtuous conduct assumes the aspect of habitual performance, this is a sign that virtue is absent. But if somebody were to say that the acquisition or learning of a virtue is, partly at least, a matter of *habituation*, *i.e.* of getting used to something, then he would probably be hinting at some important truth.

5. We have so far mainly said negative things about the virtues. Virtues are not associated with specific activities; therefore virtue is different from technical goodness and the genus of the virtues is not the genus skill. The virtues are not associated with categories of acts; therefore their genus is neither that of disposition nor that of habit. The question may be raised: Can the virtues become specified within a genus at all? If so, what *is* the genus of the virtues?

The master philosopher in the field in which we are now moving, did not think that the virtues were all of one genus. His opinion, no doubt, was partly influenced by the obvious logical inhomogeneity of the meaning of *arete* in Greek. It has also to do with his division of the virtues of man into the two groups, which are usually called in English by the names *moral* and *intellectual* virtues respectively.

The intellectual virtues with Aristotle are a very mixed bunch. None of them is what *we* would without hesitation call a virtue. This negative trait seems to be nearly the only thing that is common to them all. Among the intellectual virtues Aristotle counts 'art' (in Greek *techne*) or 'knowledge of how to make things'.[1] Excellence

[1] *EN*, Bk. VI, Ch. 4.

in such virtue is not identical with, but related to, that which we have called technical goodness. Among the intellectual virtue he further counts demonstrative knowledge and intuitive grasp of first principles. Excellence in such virtue again is more like the goodness of a faculty. Yet it would not be right to think of them as intellectual endowments or gifts. For intellectual virtue, according to Aristotle, is acquired. It 'owes both its birth and its growth to teaching', he says.[1]

Finally, Aristotle's list of intellectual virtues mentions practical wisdom (*phronesis*) and the related 'minor intellectual virtues' of deliberation, understanding, and judgment. Practical wisdom is knowledge of how to secure the ends of human life, or 'a reasoned and true state of capacity to act with regard to human goods'.[2] It is not, however, knowledge of how to secure ends in general. Rather it is capacity to act with regard to that which is, in our terminology, beneficial or harmful, *i.e.* good or bad for us.[3] This establishes a link between practical wisdom and the moral virtues. (See below, sect. 7.)

To call the second group of virtues with Aristotle 'moral', as has become the custom, is rather misleading. The Greek word is *ethikos*. What it points to in the context is not so much that which we regard as the ethical or moral flavour of the virtues concerned, as another trait which, on Aristotle's view, distinguishes them from the intellectual virtues. This trait is that they are acquired, not as the intellectual virtues through teaching alone, but through teaching in combination with *habituation* or the practising of virtue.

Aristotle thought that his second group of virtues, the 'ethical' or 'moral' ones, fall under a genus. This genus of theirs is *state* or *trait of character*. This, I think, hits the nail on the head. Not skills, not dispositions, not habits, not features of temperament, but traits of character is what the virtues are.

I shall not here discuss the concept of character. It is one of the obviously most important but at the same time most strangely neglected concepts of moral philosophy. It can be said with some, though hardly undue, exaggeration that only two philosophers

[1] *EN*, 1103ª 15.

[2] *EN*, 1140ᵇ 20–21.

[3] In *EN*, 1140ᵇ 4–5 Aristotle calls practical wisdom 'a true and reasoned state of capacity to act with regard to the things that are good and bad for man'

have dug deep into the nature of this concept. One is Aristotle, who thought that character is acquired rather than inborn, and that it is capable of becoming moulded and developed according to human design and not only mutable according to the ordinances of natural necessity. The other is Schopenhauer. To him character seemed inborn and immutable. On Schopenhauer's view there is no moulding of character according to human design. Yet, on a transcendental plane, man is responsible for the *choice* of his character—a strange opinion, but not entirely unlike the views of another profound searcher of human nature, Plato.

6. 'Virtue', *i.e.* moral virtue, Aristotle goes on to say, 'is a state of character concerned with choice, lying in a mean . . ., this being determined by a rational principle.'[1]

The idea that the path of virtue is a *via media aurea* between two extremes, I shall not discuss. It is a fine conceptual observation, and has nothing to do with philistine mediocrity, as has sometimes been maintained. It may, however, be doubted whether it has the general validity which Aristotle asserted for it. Aristotle himself seems to have had doubts about this.

The idea that virtue is concerned with choice seems to me to hint at something more essential than the idea that virtue lies in the mean. I propose to make the following use of it:

Virtues are essentially connected with action. This connexion, however, is with act-individuals and not with act-categories. In Aristotelian phraseology, virtues have an essential and peculiar connexion with *particulars*. It is here that *choice* enters the picture. One could also put it as follows: Because of the lack of an essential tie between a virtue and an act-category, *the path of virtue is never laid out in advance*. It is for the man of virtue to determine where it goes in the particular case. This determination can be called a choice, but we must not necessarily think of it as a choice between alternatives. (Aristotle's notion of *prohairesis* is therefore, perhaps, not altogether adequate to the logical nature of the case.)

The choice connected with a virtue could also be termed a choice of *right* course of action. But then the question will arise: 'right' in which respect or 'right' with a view to what? To answer: right with a view to meeting the demands of virtue, is no help. We must look out for a better answer.

[1] *EN*, 1106[b] 36.

By no means every choice-situation is one in which there is room for practising some virtue. Normally, when I choose a dish from the menu, virtue is not called upon to be displayed. But when I deliberate whether to have another helping of a dish of which I have already had three helpings, virtue may be needed for choosing rightly.

What then is characteristic of a choice-situation, in which a virtue becomes relevant? Briefly speaking: That the case should be one in which the good of some being—either the choosing agent's own good or the good of some other being or beings—is at stake, *i.e.* is likely to become affected by the choice. To have another helping of a delicious dish is tempting, but may cause indigestion. Here *temperance* is needed for choosing rightly. Or, if I provide myself with a third helping, some other person at the table may be deprived of the possibility of having a second helping. Then *consideration* is required.

We can now answer the question, with regard to what the choice, for which a virtue is needed, is right. It is right, we could say, with a view to the good of some being involved.

To further problems connected with the distinction between the case, when the good at stake is the choosing agent's own good and when it is somebody else's, we shall return presently. First, we must try to get a clearer view of the rôle of a virtue, as such, in a choice.

7. In the sentence, which we quoted from Aristotle, mentioning state of character, choice, and the mean as characteristics of virtue, there is also mention of a 'rational principle' determining the choice. This mention of a rational principle refers to the rôle of the intellectual virtue, which Aristotle calls practical wisdom, in the exercise or practising of any moral virtue.

We shall not here discuss Aristotle's view of the relation of knowledge to virtuous action. (Aristotle's theory of *phronesis* is one of the most difficult and obscure, perhaps also one of the most profound, chapters of his ethics.) I think we must accept the idea that in action in accordance with virtue (or perhaps rather: in the right choice behind such action) a kind of knowledge is involved. This, as I see it, is essentially knowledge relating to the beneficial and the harmful, *i.e.* to that which is good or bad for a being. 'Practical knowledge' is not ill-suited as a name for such insight. It could also be called 'knowledge of good and evil'.

146

In the sentence which we quoted, there is no mention of *one* essential feature which is still missing from our logical picture of a virtue. (I am not suggesting that Aristotle himself did not, elsewhere, pay due attention to it.) It can be called an emotion or feeling or passion. This feeling 'contends' in the choice of the right course of action with our rational insight into good and evil. It tends to eclipse or obscure our judgment both as regards consequences and as regards wants (valuations). The rôle of a virtue, to put it briefly, is to counteract, eliminate, rule out the obscuring effects which emotion may have on our practical judgment, *i.e.* judgment relating to the beneficial and harmful nature of a chosen course of action.

Action in accordance with virtue may thus be said to be the outcome of a contest between 'reason' and 'passion'. If we raise the question: What has the man of virtue *learnt*?—and this question, we have said, always makes sense—the general form of the answer is: He has learnt to conquer the obscuring effects of passion upon his judgments of good and evil, *i.e.* of the beneficial and the harmful, in situations when he is acting.

In the case of every specific virtue there is some specific passion which the man of that virtue has learnt to master. In the case of courage, for example, the passion is fear in the face of danger. In the case of temperance it is lust for pleasure.

Consider, *e.g.*, courage. In courage the good of man is involved *via* the notion of *danger*. Danger may be defined as an impending bad or evil, *i.e.* as something which threatens a being with harm.

If we ask what the courageous man has learnt, the answer is not primarily that he has learnt to estimate and to cope with danger, but that he has learnt to conquer or control or master or subdue his *fear*, when facing danger.

What does it mean that the courageous man has learnt to conquer his fear? It does *not* mean that he no longer feels fear when facing danger. The brave man is not necessarily 'fearless' in the sense that he knows no fear. Some courageous men may even feel fear intensely.

Considering this, what then does the brave man's conquest of fear amount to? Here we have to note the fact that men's conduct, when facing danger, is often *influenced* by fear. Fear can paralyse a man so that he becomes unable to do anything to meet the danger.

Or it makes him run away panic-stricken. Fear may thus be *a bad thing* due to its influence on a man's conduct. He who has conquered fear has learnt not to let fear, should he feel it, do him harm. He has learnt not to let fear paralyse him, not to get panic-stricken, not to lose his head because of fear, but to act coolly when facing danger. In short: he has learnt not to let fear obscure his judgment as to what is the right course of action for him. When he has learnt this, he has learnt courage.

It should be observed that the course of action, which is the virtuous man's choice in the particular case, is not necessarily that which we call *a virtuous act* or *an act of virtue*. A man of courage, for example, may sometimes rightly choose to retreat from danger rather than to fight it. Similarly, a temperate man may sometimes rightly choose to have for himself 'another helping of pleasure'; and an industrious man may rightly choose to 'take a day off from work'. Such choices, however, do not terminate in acts called after the virtues. To retreat from danger is never an act of courage, to enjoy pleasure never an act of temperance, and to rest never a display of industry. This is, I think, an observation of some importance. It shows a new sense, in which a virtue is an 'inward' trait of character rather than an 'outward' feature of conduct. The *right choice* in a situation, when a virtue is involved, need not be the choice of a so-called *virtuous act*.

8. In this place it is pertinent to say a few words about a problem which much occupied Plato and to a lesser extent Aristotle, too, in their thinking about the virtues. It could be called the problem of the *unity* of virtue. Are not all virtues substantially the same frame or state of character—and their diversity due only to the diversity of passions which the virtuous man has to master, or perhaps to typical differences in the acting-situations in which virtue is displayed?

It seems to me that there is some foundation for the statement that there is, fundamentally, but *one* virtue. What would then be a suitable name for it, if we do not simply call it 'virtue'? The question of a name, it would seem, is of some importance here. For if we cannot call this master virtue by another name but 'virtue', then to say that *all virtues* are but forms of *one virtue* is an uninteresting tautology. It would also lead to confusion with that

148

sense of the word 'virtue', which is the opposite of vice, and which does not admit of a plural. (See above, sect. 2.)

On the view which we have taken here of the various virtues, the name of the master virtue could not be 'justice'. It is, for one thing, doubtful whether justice fits the conceptual pattern of a virtue, which I have here been outlining, and thus also doubtful whether justice, on our definition, is to be counted as one of the virtues at all.

But another name comes to mind: *self-control*. The various virtues, it may be said, are so many forms of self-control. For what is self-control but the feature of character which helps a man never to lose his head, be it for fear of pain or for lust after pleasure, and always let his action be guided by a dispassionate judgment as to that which is the right thing for him to do. The untranslatable Greek word *sophrosyne*, which was sometimes called the master virtue or harmony and unity of all virtues, may have connoted something similar to this all-embracing virtue of self-control.

It is inviting to compare *by analogy* self-control to justice—independently of the question whether justice is a 'virtue' in the same sense as self-control or not. *I.e.*: it is inviting to compare the man who rules his passions by self-control, to the state in which justice reigns. This analogy between 'the state within us' and 'the state without', as is well known, is fundamental to Plato's political philosophy.

9. The man of virtue, we have said, has learnt to conquer some passion.

The conquest of passion presupposes that one has been susceptible to its influence—at least to some extent. If this condition is not fulfilled, one's conduct in the relevant situations may be exactly similar to the virtuous man's conduct. Yet one could not be said to possess virtue—except in a purely 'external' regard. A man who is totally insensitive to the temptations of pleasure could not be temperate, and a man with no amorous passions could not be chaste, although 'outwardly' his conduct could be the very paragon of temperance and chastity. It may seem more difficult to admit that a man who never experienced fear and thus was literally fearless, could not, strictly speaking, be brave. But this is probably because fear is such a fundamental passion that its total absence in a man comes near to being a mental defect. Halfwits, who do not grasp danger as normal men do, can show the most astonishing fearlessness, *e.g.* in battle. But there need not be any false resentment behind the hesitation we naturally feel to call such men brave.

How does one achieve the conquest of passion, which is a necessary condition of acquiring a virtue? This question is certainly not important only to educationists and psychologists. Its conceptual aspects are interesting too. I shall here touch upon them very lightly only.

According to the explanation of a virtue, which we have given, the conquest of passion means that the 'obscuring' influence of passion on the practical judgment in particular acting-situations has become eliminated. To call the influence 'obscuring' is to say that it induces us to make wrong choices, *i.e.* choices which we later have reason to regret and of which we can subsequently say 'had I surveyed the situation and its implications clearly, I should have acted differently'. (Not always, of course, when we can speak thus, is it because some *passion* has obscured our insight; the mistake we made can, *e.g.*, have been a 'purely intellectual' mistake about the consequences of our actions.)

The conquest of passion, which is the road to a virtue, is thus also a *gain* with a view to our welfare. To subdue passion, in that sense of 'subdue' and 'conquer' of which we are now speaking, is *a useful thing*. Awareness of this usefulness, it seems to me, must be an important factor in the education to virtues.

How does one become aware of the usefulness of conquering passion? It is by no means *obvious* that passions must have detrimental influences. To argue that passions, too, basically serve the good of man does not seem unplausible. Could one not say, *e.g.*, that the natural and proper function of fear is to warn of impending danger; fear holds us back and makes us take precautions, where otherwise we should easily run into disaster? The question is a little bewildering, and from the fact that *some* passions may have an obvious usefulness it does not follow that they *all* have. I shall not here try to argue the general question of the usefulness of the passions. It suffices for present purposes to note that there is nothing obviously bad about them and that our natural inclination certainly is to follow their impetus and not to go against it. To realize the usefulness of conquering passion may therefore be connected with considerable difficulties.

A man may come to realize the usefulness of temperance from having suffered the pains consequent upon overeating, or the usefulness of industry from having witnessed the miseries of destitution. This is not to say that only through 'vice' can one learn 'virtue'. Only in exceptional cases does the vicious man turn virtuous. But some foretaste of the life of the wicked may be effective and even necessary as a means in the education to a virtue. This foretaste is often provided in the form of discouraging or deterrent examples. A whole *genre* of literature is concerned with the fictitious setting up of such anti-models of virtues. Its educational or edifying value is often disputed. I shall not enter the disputes of educationists. I shall only say that I think it of some importance for educationists of a certain bent of mind to remember that virtues are no ends in themselves but instruments in the service of the good of man, and for educationists of a certain other bent of mind not to lose sight of the fact that it is only by being aware of harmful consequences of yielding to passion that man has a rational ground for aspiring after virtues. For, be it observed in this connexion, we do not commonly and naturally call the virtues 'beneficial'. This is significant. The virtues are *needed*; absence of virtue is a bad thing for us. The goodness of the virtues is that they protect us from harm and *not* that they supply us with some good. (Cf. Ch. III, sect. 1 and Ch. V, sect. 10.) This, incidentally, is why pride of possessing various virtues is stupid conceit and exhibitionism in them a counterfeit of the good life.

There has been much dispute among philosophers, whether such and such *is* a virtue or not. That courage is a virtue has, as far as I know, never been disputed. But whether charity or chastity or humility are virtues *has* been put in question.

Disputes of this kind sometimes concern the *conceptual status* of the objects of dispute. For example: whether they can rightly be called traits of character or whether they are relevantly concerned with choice or with the conquest of passion. Such dispute may be of considerable interest. It may serve to sharpen our idea of a virtue or lead us to distinguish between different kinds of virtues or maybe even between different concepts of a virtue.

But the question, whether something is a virtue or not, can also have an entirely different meaning. It can ask whether something which undoubtedly is a state of character concerned with choice

151

guided by a rational principle in contest with passion, really has the *usefulness* of a virtue, *i.e.* is needed for protecting our welfare. To question whether something is, in this sense, a virtue or not may be a thoroughly sensible thing to do. This is so, because— as was already noted—it is by no means obvious that the influence of passion on the practical judgment must be obscuring, *i.e.* induce us to make choices which later we have reason to regret. If no such harm is to be expected, conquest of passion or thwarting of natural impulse becomes a pseudo-virtue. To encourage pseudo-virtues in oneself or in others is moralistic perversion. But to know whether something is or is not a pseudo-virtue, may require great psychological insight into the conditions of man.

It is here good to remember that man's needs and wants and wishes, his fears and hopes, are not immutable facts of his natural history. They are conditioned by a number of factors which are themselves susceptible to change. We need only think of the important rôle which religious beliefs have played in the formation of man's views as to what is good or bad for him, and therefore also as to what is a virtue or not. Changes in the religious outlook of an age need not affect its conception of what a virtue *is*. But they may influence the estimation of the importance of various features of character to the good life and therewith also its conception of what is a *virtue*.

10. There are various ways of dividing the virtues into groups on the basis of characteristic differences and similarities.

Thus, for example, courage and temperance may be regarded as specimens of two essentially different types of virtues. Courage normally manifests itself in virtuous *acts*, temperance in virtuous abstentions or *forbearances*. This conceptual asymmetry between the two virtues is a consequence of their different relationships to pleasure and pain, *i.e.* to the hedonic good and bad. The courageous man, when acting bravely, agrees to suffer or undertakes to do something in itself unpleasant, or maybe even painful, in order to avoid a future greater evil. The temperate man, when showing temperance, forsakes an immediate pleasure for a similar reason.

One could suggest the name *ascetic virtues* for those virtues which, because of some conceptual peculiarity of theirs, normally manifest themselves in forbearances. Temperance is thus an example of an ascetic virtue. Chastity is another.

152

Virtues are often also divided into self-regarding and other-regarding virtues. *One* way of marking the distinction between them is to say that self-regarding virtues essentially serve the welfare of the agent himself, who possesses and practises them, whereas other-regarding virtues essentially serve the good of other beings. Courage, temperance, and industry are self-regarding; consideration, helpfulness, and honesty other-regarding.

The sharpness of the distinction is not obliterated by the obvious fact that virtues, which are essentially self-regarding, may also be accidentally other-regarding, and *vice versa*. Take courage, for example. To be courageous is necessarily a good thing for the brave man himself, when he is facing danger—although, of course, what courage does to help him may become counteracted by other things which work against him. Courage can also be of the greatest importance to action which is done for the sake of others, *e.g.* in battle or when saving our neighbour from disaster. But whether a man's courage is or is not useful in the service of the good of others, depends upon the attitude which he happens to take to this good, or is compelled to take by external circumstances, such as threat of punishment if he flies. The courage which burglars or robbers display, can be much to the detriment of their neighbour's welfare. The value of courage from a 'social' point of view is therefore accidental; it depends upon the attitude, which the brave man happens to take to his fellow-humans.

The virtues we call other-regarding are essentially useful from the neighbour's point of view. The considerate man, for example, has learnt to conquer the influence of selfish impulses on his judgment as to how his action will interfere with the good of others. That he has learnt this much is already a welcome thing for his neighbour. It means that he *can* show consideration, if he cares for his neighbour's good. He has acquired the necessary mental discipline. And we would, of course, not call him considerate, unless he also cares. But there is a 'logical gap' between a man's practical wisdom and his virtue, in the case of the other-regarding virtues, which is not there in the case of the self-regarding virtues. We can explain the difference as follows:

There is a sense in which a man necessarily will, in the particular case, practise as much self-regarding virtue as he happens to possess. This follows from the relation, as we have defined it (Ch. V, sect. 10), of a man's good to that which he wants and shuns, *and* the relation of virtue to knowledge of the right course of action with a view to a man's good.

Knowledge of the right course of action in a particular situation with a view to our neighbour's good involves, however, no such necessity. For whether action is in accordance with this knowledge or not, depends upon whether one wants to do that which one's neighbour would welcome one to do, and whether one wants this or not is an entirely contingent matter.

To say that the practising of self-regarding virtue presupposes, beside an unobscured judgment, also an interest in one's own welfare is not to state a presupposition at all. For the sense in which interest in one's own welfare is presupposed is the sense in which this interest is necessarily there, *viz.* as defined in terms of that which the agent wants (welcomes) and shuns.

To say, however, that the practising of other-regarding virtues presupposes, in addition to an unobscured practical judgment, also an interest in the good of some other being *is* to state a presupposition. It can contingently be fulfilled or not.

To let the other-regarding virtues be, in the sense here explained, dependent upon contingencies, may seem to some unsatisfactory. Is there no sense then, in which practising other-regarding virtues is incumbent on man? To think that it is incumbent is to think that it is a man's duty to aspire after and observe virtues independently of what his contingent interests happen to be. With this we have arrived at the big question, how considerations of duty and norm are related to considerations of good and evil. The three last chapters of this work will be devoted to a discussion of some aspects of this problem.

VIII

'GOOD' AND 'MUST'

---

1. IT is a widely entertained opinion that value-concepts are intrinsically normative notions. This opinion is reflected in a certain philosophic jargon, which tends to confuse or to mix value-terms with normative terms. When, for example, some writers insist upon the value-free nature of science (*Wertfreiheit der Wissenschaften*), they often give as a reason that science can tell us how things *are* but not how they *ought to be*. In the spirit of Hume, philosophers talk of a Great Divide between fact and norm, between the *is* and the *ought*—but also of a Great Divide between fact and value, as if the two divides were the same. (Cf. above, Ch. I, sect. 2.)

Which is then the alleged normative nature of value? When one tries to give a clear answer to the question, one immediately runs up against difficulties.

To say that the good is something which ought to exist or ought to be pursued, is not only very vague but can easily be seen to be an untenable opinion, unless stated with heavy qualifications. Ought apples to be good? Ought good apples to be eaten? Must one choose the better of two instruments? Whom and in what way does the goodness of a good runner oblige?

A supporter of the idea that goodness is intrinsically normative would perhaps, when faced with these questions, wish to qualify his opinion and restrict it to 'moral' goodness only. Are morally good acts then morally obligatory? This is not at all obvious. It may, on the contrary, be argued that moral goodness is 'over and above' obligation and that no man is or does good merely on the ground that he does not neglect his moral duties.

But is it not clear, at least, that the morally bad or evil *must not*

155

be done? The normative flavour of the notion of moral evil is certainly more obvious than the normative flavour of the notion of moral goodness. Yet according to the opinion of G. E. Moore, to whom we owe one of the most serious efforts ever made at a formulation in precise terms of the relationship between 'good' and 'ought', evil-doing is permissible (right), provided the evil done is 'outbalanced' by the good consequences of one's action. To me this seems morally most objectionable. I am not, however, suggesting that Moore's position could be refuted by an appeal to moral intuitions. But the fact that Moore, who was an intuitionist himself, arrived at his challenging opinions, at least shows how difficult it is to tell what the connexion is between norm and value. It may even make us doubt whether there is any immediate intrinsic connexion between the two at all.

Beside the problem how norms and values are related, there is also the problem of which of the two, norms or values, is more fundamental. One sometimes distinguishes some main types of ethical theory according to the solution which the theories propose to these two problems. By an *ethics of value* ('Wertethik') one can conveniently understand a view, according to which value is fundamental and norms are somehow to be extracted from or established on the basis of value-considerations. The views of Moore and Brentano are clearcut examples of this type of ethics. (But not any ethics of value needs, as theirs, be an ethics of consequences.) By an *ethics of duty* ('Pflichtethik') again one may understand a view which regards duty (ought) as a basic idea. The ethics of Kant is the standard example. As well known, Kant thought that the good will was the only unconditionally valuable thing in the world and that this will was a will to do one's duty for duty's sake. Yet it would be rash to maintain that Kant wanted to derive value concepts from normative notions. It may even be doubted whether there has been any serious attempt in the history of ethics to do this. What has been maintained, however, is that there is a 'moral ought', which is *sui generis* and not founded on value. This is sometimes called the *deontologist* view. As one of its best and most forceful champions we may regard the late Professor Prichard.

It seems to me that the discussion of the relation between norms and values, even in recent times, has suffered from the narrowing and obscuring implications of the term 'moral'. If we want to get to know what values, as such, have to do with norms, as such, or to know the general nature of the connexion, if there is one, between norms and values, we must disentangle the two from their associations with morality and study them in the widest possible generality. We must try to link a General Theory of the Good with a General Theory of Norms. The usefulness of the 'general theories', it seems to me, shows itself most convincingly in the approach to the old problem of the relation of Good and Ought. In the new light on this relation we shall also, I would maintain, come to a better philosophic understanding of the nature of morality.

2. A General Theory of Norms is not an objective of the present inquiry. A few general remarks on norms will nevertheless be necessary in this place. I hope to be able to substantiate these remarks with fuller arguments in another investigation.

Norms, in the sense here contemplated, may be said to be prescriptions for human action. One may distinguish three main aspects of such prescriptions. I shall call the three aspects norms as *commands*, norms as *rules*, and norms as *practical necessities*. (The reasons for calling them 'aspects' rather than 'kinds' of norm or prescription, I shall not try to state in this place.)

One may also distinguish between three main ways of formulating norms in language. These three ways may, with some caution, be called 'linguistic counterparts' of the three main aspects of norms, which I mentioned. The correspondences, however, are by no means rigorously maintained in ordinary usage.

The first linguistic counterpart of norms are sentences in *the imperative mood*. For example: 'Open the window', 'Never tell a lie', 'Honour your parents.' Imperative sentences may be said primarily to answer to the command-aspect of norms.

The second linguistic counterpart of norms I shall call *deontic sentences*. These are, roughly, sentences employing the auxiliary ('deontic') verbs 'ought to', 'may', and 'must not'. 'You must not open the window', 'Children ought to honour their parents,' 'You may play in my garden.' Deontic sentences could perhaps be said to correspond primarily to the rule-aspect of norms.

The third linguistic counterpart of norms I propose to call *anankastic sentences*. These are sentences employing the auxiliary ('anankastic') verbs 'must' ('has to'), 'need not', and 'cannot'. 'I must be at the station in time for the train,' 'You need not help me

157

with this,' 'He cannot travel to-morrow.' As expressions of norms, anankastic sentences primarily answer to the aspect of norms as practical necessities.

As already said, ordinary language does not uphold a sharp distinction in meaning between the three types of sentence. The meanings of imperative and deontic sentences shade into one another. 'Open the window' and 'You ought to open the window' *can* mean exactly the same. The border between deontic and anankastic sentences is also vague. 'You may go for a walk' and 'You need not stay at home' can be alternative ways of stating the same permission. The classification of sentences (and auxiliary verbs) as 'deontic' or 'anankastic' is therefore to some extent arbitrary. (We have classified 'must' as anankastic but 'must not' as deontic.)

Anankastic sentences have a common use for expressing, beside *practical*, also *logical* and *natural* (causal, physical) necessities. Deontic sentences, too, are not infrequently used in connexion with these latter modalities. 'If the wire is to carry the weight, it ought to be at least one inch thick,' we may say. Instead of 'ought to' we could also have said 'must' or 'has to'. Of that, which is logically or physically contingent, it is just as natural to say that it *may be* thus or otherwise and to say that it *need not be* thus or otherwise.

Statements of natural necessity are not, by themselves, prescriptive of action. They are therefore not norms in our sense, though they are commonly called 'laws' of nature. But they are nevertheless often relevant to human action, and thus indirectly to norms.

We say, for example, that if the house is to be habitable, it has to (ought to) be heated. This is natural necessity—about the living conditions of human beings. It has, as such, nothing to do with a command or an obligation or even with a practical necessity to heat the house. But it may become connected with a norm. It does so, in the first place, by engendering a practical necessity. How this happens we shall soon have occasion to study.

3. First, however, some main distinctions and points relating to the aspect of norms as commands must be made.

One can distinguish between positive and negative commands. Positive commands are orders to do, negative commands are orders to forbear. Negative commands are also called prohibitions.

A command is issued by somebody—we call it a norm-*authority*. It is further addressed to some agent or agents—we call them norm-*subjects*. The command has a *content*: this is the category of act or activity, the doing or forbearing of which is prescribed. The norm as command, finally, is issued for one or several *occasions*, on which the subject or subjects have to do or forbear the pre-scribed thing.

Normally, when *a* orders *s* to do *p*, *a* can be said to want *s* to do *p*. In commanding, the authority makes, or tries to make, the subject do the commanded thing. The issuing of commands may therefore be characterized as efforts *to make agents do or forbear* things.

The issuing of commands I shall call *normative action*. The result of a normative act is the coming into existence of a certain relation-ship among agents. I shall speak of this as a normative relationship or relationship under norm.

An important aspect of normative action is the *promulgation* of the command or norm. The authority promulgates the norm to the subject or subjects, *i.e.* he makes known by means of symbols (usually language) what he wants the subjects to do or forbear.

To the promulgation of the norm is further, in many cases, attached a threat of punishment or *sanction*, in case the subjects should not comply with the order. It may be argued that, unless there is at least an implicit threat of punishment, *i.e.* of some evil consequent upon disobedience, then there is properly speaking no command either.[1] I shall accept this view.

If the norm-authority is different from the norm-subject(s), the command or norm is called *heteronomous*. This may be regarded as the normal case. If authority and subject are one and same, the command or norm is called *autonomous*. It must not be taken for granted that the notion of a self-command makes sense. I hope presently (sect. 8) to be able to show that the conception of autono-mous norms as self-commands is an analogical supplementation of the command-aspect of norms.

[1] Cf. Austin, *The Province of Jurisprudence Determined,* Lecture I, Section headed 'The Meaning of the Term Command': 'A command is distinguished from other significations of desire, not by the style in which the desire is signified, but by the power and the purpose of the party commanding to inflict an evil or pain in case the desire be disregarded. If you cannot or will not harm me in case I comply not with your wish, the expression of your wish is not a command, although you utter your wish in imperative phrase.'

4. With the statement of natural necessity, 'If the house is to be habitable, it must (ought to) be heated' may be compared the form of words, 'If you want to inhabit the house, you must (ought to) heat it.'

In the second sentence there is mention of something wanted, *i.e.* of a state of affairs which is or may be desired as an end of action. Such sentences express that which I propose to call *technical norms*. Technical norms are, roughly, the same as that which Kant called 'technical imperatives' and which he regarded as a sub-class of the broader category of 'hypothetical imperatives'.[1]

The formulations of technical norms ordinarily employ a deontic or an anankastic vocabulary. But there is no strong objection to the use of the imperative mood in them. Instead of saying, 'If you want to inhabit the house, you ought to heat it,' we could also say, 'If you want to inhabit the house, then heat it.'

What is the logical nature of technical norms? Do they express propositions? How are they related to commands? And how are they related to statements of natural necessity? These are questions of considerable complexity and difficulty.

In order to facilitate understanding of the nature of technical norms, let us first ask, what could be the *use* of the sentence, 'If you want q, you must do p.' The sentence could, for example, be used to *inform* a person of the existence of a causal tie between a certain human act and a certain consequent state of affairs, which *may* be desired as an end of action. Or it could be used to *remind* him of the existence of this tie. Or it could be used to give him a piece of *advice* or a *recommendation*.

The person who reminds or gives advice is probably not indifferent to the acts and aims of the other person. But saying to another person, 'If you want q, you must do p' or even, 'Since you want q, you must do p' would not normally signify an attempt or effort on the part of the speaker to make the addressee of his words

[1] Kant divided the hypothetical imperatives, on the one hand into 'problematic' and 'assertoric', on the other hand into 'technical' and 'pragmatical'. How the two grounds of division are related, according to Kant, is not quite clear. Problematic imperatives, broadly speaking, concern means to potential; assertoric imperatives again, means to actual ends. A man's own well-being or happiness (*Glückseligkeit*) Kant seems to have regarded as an actual and, moreover, necessary end of action. The pragmatic imperatives concern means to this peculiar end. They are therefore related to the notion of an autonomous self-regarding duty, which we shall discuss in the next chapter.

do p. Therefore speaking thus would not normally be an act of commanding. No threat of sanction on the part of the giver of the advice is implied.

In these features technical norms differ sharply from that which I shall call *hypothetical norms*. The words, 'If it starts raining, shut the window' would normally express a hypothetical command. The person who utters them is anxious to influence the conduct of the person whom he addresses, in such a way that, should a certain contingency arise, this person will perform a certain act. There is no causal connexion, however, between this act and the state of affairs.

I think it is correct to say that Kant, much to the detriment of his ethics, did not distinguish technical norms from hypothetical norms. The 'if-then'-form of words used for expressing norms of either kind seems to have influenced him into thinking that the two were essentially the same sort of rule. This is by no means the case.

Have technical norms then nothing at all to do with commanding? Consider a man who wants to attain an end q, *e.g.* to make an empty hut habitable for himself. He is deliberating about the means to this end, *i.e.* about that which he—as we commonly express ourselves—ought to do or has to do or must do in this situation. He might then say to himself, 'If you want q, you must do p.' Such soliloquies, even in the second person, occur. The 'if' is not here the conditional 'if'. It does not mean 'in case'. It could be replaced by 'since'. And that which he says to himself could also be explicated and given the form of a 'syllogism'. As follows:

> You want q.
> Unless you do p, you will not get q.
> ∴ You must do p.

The first premiss is a want-statement. The second premiss is a statement of natural necessity. It is 'purely objective'; there is no mention or even hint of wants in it.

Is the conclusion a command? One could call it a *quasi*-command which the person, who conducts the argument, addresses to himself. I shall, however, prefer to call it a statement of *practical necessity*. In it the person who reasons reaches the conclusion that his wants, *plus* a certain natural necessity, impose upon him the practical necessity of acting in a certain manner.

161

I shall call the whole argument a Practical Syllogism. The form of words, 'If you want q, you must do p', used in soliloquy, could be regarded as a contracted form of the syllogism which, skipping the second premiss, proceeds directly from the first premiss to the conclusion. The technical norm, on this analysis, splits into the three components of a want-statement, a statement of natural necessity, and a statement of practical necessity. The last, we noted, shows a certain resemblance to a command.

Not in the technical norms themselves, but in the conclusions of practical syllogisms are we confronted with that aspect of norms, which, in section 1, I called the aspect of *norms as practical necessities*.

The name 'practical syllogism' can be used and has been used to mean different things, which it is important to keep sharply apart. The great obscurity of Aristotle's doctrine of the practical syllogism is partly due, it seems to me, to a failure to uphold the relevant distinctions here.

By a Practical Syllogism one can understand a pattern of reasoning, in which both premisses and conclusion are norms. For example:

> It is permitted to do p.
> One must not leave q undone, if one does p.
> ─────────────────────
> ∴ It is permitted to do q.

Such patterns of reasoning are studied in the branch of logic which is nowadays commonly known under the name Deontic Logic.

By a Practical Syllogism one also often understands a pattern, in which one normative and one factual premiss yield a normative conclusion. For example:

> All thieves ought to be hanged.
> This man is a thief.
> ─────────────────────
> ∴ This man ought to be hanged.

This pattern, too, may be relegated to the province of Deontic Logic. But the practical syllogisms, which illustrate how wants and natural necessities engender practical necessities of action, require a theory of their own. They have so far been very little studied by logicians. A *formal* study of them will not be attempted in this work.

5. The second premiss of our practical syllogism on p. 161, 'Unless you do p, you will not get q', we called a statement of natural necessity. q is something which is or may be an end of action. p is the result of an act which is causally connected with this state of affairs q. Considering this, we can also say that the second premiss is a statement about *means* to an *end*.

There are at least two typical uses of the word 'means' (to an end).

Under the one use the term signifies a *thing* or a kind of thing. Such a thing is often also called an *instrument*. For example: To cut a cloth I may need a pair of scissors. 'By means of' the instrument I achieve an end or goal. By 'means of production' or 'means of transportation' we usually understand means in this sense of the word, or in some closely related sense.

Under another use of the term 'means' signifies an *action*. For example: By turning the key I open a door. Turning the key is an act by means of which I achieve an end, *viz.* the opening of the door. The key, too, is here a means, *viz.* a means in the sense of instrument.

There is an obvious logical relationship between the two uses of the term 'means'. Means in the second sense is very often, but not always, the same as *the use of a means* in the first sense. The turning of the key as a means of opening the door is the use of the key as an instrument.

Instruments would not be means to ends, unless they were *used*, *i.e.* unless there was human action aiming at certain goals. Because of this we can say that 'means' in the sense of action is *primary* to 'means' in the sense of instrument. (But there may be other reasons for saying the reverse.)

Means in the sense of instruments we have discussed before. Instruments, it will be remembered, are called good, when they serve well a purpose for which they are used. This is what we called 'instrumental goodness'.

Here we are concerned only with means, which are acts. The relation, which we wish to study, between means and ends is thus a relation between certain acts and certain states of affairs. Our question is now: Which conditions must those acts and those states of affairs satisfy, in order that we shall say that the former are related to the latter as means to potential ends? The question is a complex and difficult one, and our treatment of it here cannot pretend to be exhaustive.

Can an act be a means to its own *result* as an end? If, for example, the desired state of affairs is that the window be open, is then the act of opening the window a means to achieving this end? It seems to me that calling it a 'means' is *one* of the uses of the word—though perhaps not a very common one. When individual acts are viewed as means to their own results as ends, the acts are often classified as falling under different *ways of doing* this thing, *i.e.* of achieving this result in acting. These ways may then be rated as good or bad, or one as better than another. For example: Let 'going there by bus' and 'going there by train' be two ways of reaching a certain destination. I can compare the two with regard, say, to expense, time, and comfort. On the basis of this comparison I may rate the one as a better way of travelling to the destination than the other. Such an attribution of goodness to a way of doing something is, we have said before, closely related to the attribution of goodness to instruments.

The means-end relation, if we call it by that name, between an act and its result is an intrinsic relation. It has therefore nothing to do with the natural necessities referred to in the second premisses of practical syllogisms. It is accordingly not a means-end relationship of the kind in which we are now interested.

The means-end relationship between acts and states of affairs, to which the second premisses of practical syllogisms refer, is a causal or extrinsic relation. As previously observed, the relation between an act and its *consequences* is extrinsic. (See Ch. VI, sect. 3.) So is also the relation between an act and its *causal requirements* or *prerequisites*. (Cf. Ch. V, sect. 8.)

Not everything which is a consequence of action needs be an end of action. Some consequences are not foreseen at all. Others are foreseen but not yet ends, *i.e.* consequences for the sake of the production of which the act was undertaken. To those consequences which are ends, and to them only, can the act rightly be said to stand in the relation of means to end.

Often the attainment of an end requires or presupposes the performance of an act, the result of which is not the same as the end. In order to fetch a book from the top-shelf of my bookcase it may be necessary for me to step on a ladder. My climbing the ladder is here a 'necessary preparation' or a 'causal requirement' of my fetching the book. It can also, without twisting ordinary usage, be called a means to an end, the end being the fetching of the book. This is true generally of every act which is a causal requirement of the attainment of a given end.

There are thus two basic types of causal or extrinsic relationships between acts as means and states of affairs as ends:

The one is a relation between an act and its consequences. If doing p produces a state of affairs q, different from p, and if q is an end of human action, then the doing of p is a means to this end.

The other type is a relation between acts and their causal requirements. If the production of a state of affairs q requires the doing of p, and if q is an end of human action, then the doing of p is a means to this end.

I shall call means of the first type *productive* means, and means of the second type *necessary* means.

Productive and necessary means are in the following sense inter-definable:

Let the doing of p be a productive means to the end q. Then the forbearing of p will be a necessary means to the end $\sim q$. For example: If opening the window is a productive means to cooling the room, then keeping the window closed is a necessary means to keeping the temperature in the room from sinking.

Let the doing of p be a necessary means to the end q. Then the forbearing of p will be a productive means to the end $\sim q$. For example: If turning the radiator on is a necessary means to increasing the temperature in the room, then keeping the radiator closed is a productive means to preventing the temperature from rising.

A means to an end can be both productive and necessary. When this is the case, we say that the means is *the only means* to the end in question. In a room where the windows are closed, the only means of altering the temperature at will may be by regulating the radiator.

It is important to observe that the causal relation between productive or necessary means and an end of action need not be a relation of so-called universal implication between an act-category and a generic state of affairs. It can also be a 'laxer' relationship of probability. When, for example, we say that unless water is boiled, there is a risk that contagion shall spread, or that if there are more than 40 passengers on board the vessel, the passage will not be safe, the words 'risk' and 'safe' indicate a causal relationship of a probabilistic nature. Yet boiling the water can quite appropriately be termed a necessary means or precaution to prevent contagion from spreading, and not allowing more than 40 persons on board the vessel a necessary means of making the passage safe.

Productive and necessary means are both that, which in Ch. III, sect. 4 we called *favourably causally relevant* to the attainment of an end. They therefore possess, *qua* means to ends, utilitarian goodness. This value-aspect of theirs, however, is not relevant to the discussion in this chapter of the relation of value to norm.

The relations of productive means to ends are natural necessities just as much as the relations of necessary means to ends. The means-end relationship, however, to which the second premisses of practical syllogisms (on our understanding of the term) refer, are causal or extrinsic relations between ends of action and *necessary* means to those ends. It is therefore with the notion of a necessary means to an end that we are primarily concerned in the present discussion.

6. Reference to causal means-end relationships is often made when we wish to explain (interpret, understand) human action.

Suppose we are anxious to get to understand why a person behaves in a certain way or does something which is exceptional or surprising, or such that a man would not ordinarily do this 'for its own sake'. For example: We see a man running in the street and wish to know why he does this. We are told that he is running in order to catch a train.

If we accept this reply as an explanation of the person's behaviour, we assume that the agent regards his action, running, as a *productive* means towards this end.

It is, however, not certain that the reply, 'He ran in order to catch the train' will be accepted as an explanation of the person's behaviour. Why did he not take a taxi? may be our rejoinder. The man must know that this is another productive means towards his end, and probably a better (more efficient) one. What *we* wish to know is, why he used that very means which he actually did use.

Suppose now that we are told that the man *had to run*, because this happened to be the only means for him to reach the train. There was, say, no taxi available in the street or he had no money on him to pay the taxi-fare. Saying that the man *had to* run in order to catch the train, is to say that running was a *necessary* means to his end.

To explain an action by giving reference to productive means to a desired end is to leave open a question to which we may want to have the answer before we regard the explanation as complete. This is the question: Why the agent used *these very means*? If we are told that the means were necessary as well as productive, we regard the explanation as complete or exhaustive of the case.

The explanation, which makes reference to necessary means, can also be exhibited in the form of a practical syllogism, as follows:

> *x* wants to reach the train in time.
> Unless *x* runs, he will not reach the train in time.
> ∴ *x* has to run.

What this syllogism is supposed to explain is *x*'s action. It explains this by making it plain that the action was a *practical necessity* incumbent upon the agent.

A practical syllogism, when offered as an explanation of action, which has taken place in the past or is taking place in the present, I shall call a *third person* practical syllogism. When the explanation is given by the agent himself, he will normally be speaking in the first person. 'I want(ed) to reach the train in time, etc.' This I nevertheless call a third person syllogism. The agent is here speaking *about* himself, as it were viewing himself from the outside.

Is a third person practical syllogism a logically conclusive argument? This is not a futile question to ask. On the one hand, our syllogism above seems absolutely conclusive, flawless, watertight. On the other hand, one would look in vain through all the text-books and works on logic for the inference scheme, of which this syllogism could be said to be an instantiation. Its pattern is not one of the categorical or modal syllogisms, of course. It has a certain resemblance to a *modus ponens* or perhaps rather a *modus tollens* argument. But certainly it is not an ordinary *modus ponens* or *tollens* either. Shall we try to supplement it with suppressed premisses and thus make it conclusive according to the laws of 'ordinary logic'? I believe that this would be a blind alley. Nor would it help, if we expanded the second premiss into, '*x* believes that, unless he runs, he will not reach the train in time.' Shall we deny then that the syllogism is logically valid? This way out too has been suggested—but seems to me to be a mere evasion. We must, I think, accept that practical syllogisms are logically valid pieces of argumentation in their own right. Accepting them means in fact an enlargement of the province of logic. We cannot reduce the practical syllogisms to other patterns of valid inference. But we can, indeed must, say something more to elucidate their peculiar nature.

7. A man is walking in the street towards the railway station. He wants to be there in time for the train. Perhaps he is expecting his fiancée. He looks at his watch and realizes with a start that the train will be there in a few minutes time and that, if he continues at walking pace, he will be late. There is no taxi within sight. He *has to* run. And he puts himself in motion.

We could call the situation just described a first person practical syllogism—though not a syllogism in words. Let us try to give a schematic presentation of this wordless argument. A man has a certain aim. (First premiss.) He realizes that, unless he does a certain thing, he will not reach his aim. (Second premiss.) But what is the conclusion?

Shall we say that the conclusion is his insight that he has to do this thing? But what is this 'insight'? As far as I can see, the only thing here which deserves to be called an insight is the agent's understanding that, unless he does a certain thing, he will be late for the train. But this, we said, is the second premiss. If the conclusion were the second premiss repeated, the first premiss would be totally irrelevant to the argument. This it obviously is not.

Shall we say then that the conclusion of the syllogism is the man's doing of the thing, the necessity of which he has realized in the second premiss? Saying thus would be to take a view of the matter, reminiscent of one which Aristotle appears to have held. In one place Aristotle explicitly says that the conclusion of the practical syllogism is an act.[1] In other places it is not quite clear how he regarded the conclusion. It should be observed that calling an act a 'conclusion' from something is not at all odd. We very often call that which a man does, the 'conclusions' which he has drawn from a certain situation.

I would say myself that calling the conclusion of our wordless syllogism an act is *almost* right—but not *quite* right. Consider the man on his way to the station. If his running is the conclusion, *when* shall we say that the conclusion has been drawn? Suppose

---

[1] *De Motu Animalium* 701ᵃ 10–40. Cf. also *EN* 1147ᵃ 25–31. It should be remembered, however, that Aristotle's concept of a practical syllogism has a wider scope than ours.

that, after he has run one hundred yards, he has a stroke and dies? Shall we then say that he died before he had drawn the conclusion —or before he had finished drawing it? Must he 'draw' it all the way to the station? (This is almost like asking: How 'long' must the conclusion be?)

Let us go back to the case as we originally described it. The description ended in the words 'he puts himself in motion'. This, in my opinion, correctly describes the conclusion. Neither the man's insight into the necessary connexion between an act and an end, nor his doing of the act, is the conclusion of the wordless piece of argumentation, but the man's *setting himself to do* the act. Putting oneself in motion is setting oneself to run. This is what the syllogism ends in.

Is 'setting oneself to do something' action? The agent who sets himself to do something also 'puts himself in motion', *i.e.* embarks on the road to the actual performance of the act. Drawing the conclusion of a first person practical syllogism need not take the agent to the very end, at which he is aiming. But it must put him on the road to this end. Aristotle would have been *quite* right, had he said that the practical syllogism *leads up to* action. It ends, not necessarily in *doing* something, but in *setting oneself to do* something.

When the act is completed, we can ask in retrospect, 'What *made him do it*?' And the answer then is, that his wanted end of action in combination with the insight that, unless he does the thing, he will fail of his end, *made him do* it.

Sometimes the conclusion of a practical syllogism refers to the future. I want, say, to leave the town not later than the day after to-morrow. I realize that, unless to-morrow I do so and so, I shall not be free to travel the day after. Therefore I must do this thing to-morrow. The question may be raised: In what sense can deciding to-day to do something to-morrow be called 'putting oneself in motion' or 'embarking on the road to the actual performance of the act'? The answer will be: In the sense that the agent will from now on ('is from now on set to') forbear doing things, which are likely to prevent him from completing his set task to-morrow, and do things which are in their turn necessary or useful for making the decided thing come off. He will, for example, decline an invitation to lunch and finish some piece of work instead of meeting his friends. The agent who has set himself to do something in future, is like a ship moving towards a destination.

His forbearances and acts are to some extent *preformed* by his decision. He *may* become detracted from his set route but not without compelling reasons.

We have so far regarded the first person practical syllogism as a wordless argument. It *could* be accompanied by words, and sometimes *is*. The agent might say to himself, aloud or in thoughts only, 'I want to be at the station in time,' thus verbalizing the first premiss. But the essential thing is not, whether he *says* this, but that he *wants* this as an end of his action. The agent may also say to himself: 'Unless I run, I shall be late,' thus verbalizing the second premiss. Yet the essential thing is not, whether he *says* this, but that he *thinks* thus. The agent may finally say: 'I ought to run' or, which would do equally well: 'Hurry up, there is no time to be lost,' thus verbalizing the conclusion. But again, it is not the *words* which matter, but that he *sets himself* to do it.

In first person practical syllogisms words are 'decorations', 'frills', 'inessential accompaniments' only. Essential to it are the *wanting* of an end, the *understanding* of a natural necessity, and the *decision* to act. The way in which these three components unite in the syllogism I shall call *practical necessitation*—necessitation of the will to action through want and understanding.

'Want' and 'understanding', these are words related to 'passion' and 'reason'. We are here in the neighbourhood of the problem, discussed with so much fervour and ingenuity by Hume, whether reason alone can move man to action. Hume said reason cannot move, but passion is the mover. With this view he coupled an, in many respects, deep-cutting attempt to found obligations on interests. But I think it is right to say that Hume did not fully realize the rôle which reason plays in the origination of obligations. He did not see clearly through the logical mechanism of the practical syllogism. To show why something is an obligation founded on interest, is not to show that it is something we ('really', 'innermost') *want to do*, but that it is something we *have to do* for the sake of that which we *want* (to be, to do, to have, to happen).[1]

---

[1] It may, of course, be argued that, if an end is wanted, then use of the means, which are seen to be necessary for the attainment of the end, will *a fortiori* be wanted too. Cf. Kant, *Grundlegung zur Metaphysik der Sitten* (2nd ed.), p. 46: 'Wer den Zweck will, will (sofern die Vernunft auf seine Handlungen entscheidenden Einfluss hat) auch das dazu unentbehrlich notwendige Mittel, das in seiner Gewalt ist. Dieser Satz ist, was das Wollen betrifft, analytisch.' It is interesting to note that Kant regarded the proposition as analytical.

We said at the end of the preceding section that practical syllogisms are logically conclusive arguments—but that it was difficult to see, *how* they are this. The non-verbal first person syllogism provides the clue. If practical syllogisms are logically conclusive, then the practical necessitation of the will to action must at the same time be a logical necessitation. This I think it is. Assume that the man in our example wants to be at the station to meet his fiancée, that he quite clearly sees that, unless he runs, he will be late (and that if he runs, he has at least a good chance of arriving in time), but that he does nothing to hurry up. What shall we then say about the case? *One* thing which we might say is this: Our man was so unwilling to run (perhaps he finds it undignified) that, having realized that only by running he could arrive in time, he altered his aims. 'I would rather be late than run,' he says. He, of course, *wanted* to be at the station in time. He still *wishes* he could have been. Arriving in time to meet the train is, moreover, an 'in itself' wanted thing to our man; if a God appeared and took him to the station in time, he would *welcome* this. But he no longer wants this as an *end of his action*. Therefore he is not moved to act.

To regard practical syllogisms as logically conclusive arguments is, I would say, to knit or tie together in a peculiar way the concepts of wanting an end, understanding a necessity, and setting oneself to act. It is a contribution to the moulding or shaping of these concepts. The justification of this moulding procedure is partly its conformity with actual usage and partly that which it does to meet the philosopher's craving for clarity in these matters.

8. In the conclusions of first person practical syllogisms, I shall maintain, we encounter the *autonomous norms*. (Strictly speaking, we encounter *a* concept of autonomous norm. For there are other phenomena, too, which qualify as candidates for the name. We shall not discuss them, however, in this work.)

The autonomous norms, on this view, are necessitations of the will to action under the joint influence of wanted ends and insights into natural necessities.

The concept of autonomous norm, of which we are now treating, is rather unlike Kant's. It has, for one thing, no specific connexion with so-called moral matters. Yet it is not in every relevant respect unlike the Kantian notion.

171

One point of resemblance has to do with a contrast which, in Kantian phraseology, could be called a contrast between 'inclination' and 'duty'. There is a truth hidden in the idea, which is so prominent with Kant and for which he has been severely censured by others, that action under autonomous norm or rule must in some sense go against inclination. I think the truth is that action under such rule is never undertaken, *because* we want to do it, but is forced upon us by natural necessities and the remoter objects of our wants and likings. If the act is something which for its own sake we want to do, then no autonomous norm is needed to move the will to action. When the act is, in itself, indifferent to us, the movement towards action follows smoothly upon want and insight—we do not have to say to ourselves, 'I must do this.' But when there is a practical necessity of doing something, which is, in itself, unwanted or shunned by us, then the incumbent nature of the autonomous obligation acquires prominence. It is chiefly in such cases that we resort to soliloquy and, by keeping our goal and the insight into the necessity of the act clear before our minds, urge ourselves on to action. We could say: the wider the gap between the *must* and the *want to*, the more prominent the *must*; and if there is no gap at all—meaning that we do the act from sheer inclination—then there is no autonomous necessitation of the will either.

One crucial difference again between Kant's and our notion of an autonomous norm has to do with Kant's distinction between categorical and hypothetical imperatives. The notion of a hypothetical imperative with Kant is not altogether clear. It is, anyhow, closely related to our notion of a technical norm. Of the technical norms we said (sect. 4) that they may be regarded as contracted forms of practical syllogisms. The conclusions of practical syllogisms in the first person, finally, are what *we* (here) call autonomous norms. Even though they are categorical in form, it seems obvious that this relationship of theirs or dependence upon technical norms marks them as different from the Kantian categorical imperatives and therewith from the Kantian autonomous norms.

The conclusions of practical syllogisms, which I have called autonomous norms, resemble heteronomous commands in that they both manifest efforts *to make agents do or forbear*. (Cf. above sect. 3.) This is an *essential* similarity, which connects the aspect

172

of norms as practical necessities with the aspect of norms as commands.

Are there features of autonomous norms which answer to promulgation and sanction? These two, we said (sect. 3), were essential features of heteronomous commands.

There is an *essential* feature of autonomous norms, which may be said to resemble promulgation *by analogy*. This is the agent's insight into or understanding of the causal connexion between the doing of a certain act and the attainment of a certain end. Such insight, it seems, is possible only for rational beings, who are capable of conducting arguments and who possess some knowledge of the ways actions and events in nature are causally interwoven. It is plausible to think that such insight is possible only to beings who master a language. If this is true, then another essential similarity between norms as practical necessities and norms as commands is that both presuppose language.

The conclusion of a first person practical syllogism, we said, need not be verbalized—not even 'in thoughts'—and take the shape of a norm-formulation 'do this' or 'you must (ought to) do this' addressed, as it were, by the agent to himself. But it *may* become verbalized and a form of words may be used for soliloquy, which strongly resembles the use of words for urging agents to action. This is an *accidental* feature of autonomous norms, which may be said to resemble promulgation, not by analogy, but *literally*.

There is further an *essential* feature of autonomous norms, which may be said to resemble sanction *by analogy*. If a man, who is under a practical necessity of doing a certain thing, fails to do this, then he will also necessarily fail of his end of action. The end was a wanted thing. Not to get the wanted, frustration of desire is intrinsically unpleasant, we have said before. Failure to act in accordance with the norm is thus intrinsically connected with unpleasant consequences. This *is* an analogy of punishment. But it is only an *analogy*. Punishment, properly so called, is for disobedience, and failure to carry an autonomous necessitation of the will into effect cannot properly be termed disobedience.

We are here touching upon an important difference between autonomous and heteronomous norms. With the second the agent is 'in principle' free to choose between obeying the rule and escaping the penalty and disobeying with a risk of being punished.

He *may* choose the second. But the autonomous norm comes into being with or consists in the agent's putting himself in motion as directed by his wants and insights. In a sense, therefore, autonomous norms are *ipso facto* 'obeyed'. That is: the notions of obedience and disobedience do not apply to them.

If, however, failure to complete the act in conformity with the dictates of practical necessity is due to weakness of will or to negligence or thoughtlessness in action, then it is due to something which is analogous to disobedience, and which may for that reason be regarded as deserving punishment. The agent may invent various forms of self-chastisement, *e.g.* with a view to strengthening his will-powers or to making him more careful in acting. When this happens, autonomous norms are conjoined with an *accidental* feature, which can be said to answer to sanction, not by analogy, but *literally*.

This will suffice as an answer to the question, to what extent norms as autonomous practical necessities resemble norms as commands. Our next task will be to investigate to what extent and in what way norms as heteronomous commands may acquire the aspect of practical necessities.

9. Orders are sometimes issued for no particular reason. Then they have no foundation in the ends of the norm-authority. This case appears to be comparatively rare. Orders are sometimes issued in obedience to an order to issue them. Then the question, why they are issued, is the same as the question, why the authority who issues them, obeys the order of the higher authority. Finally, orders are sometimes issued for the sake of an end.

A man x commands another man y to do a certain thing p. *Why* does x command y? The answer is often, though certainly not always, that x has some end in view, towards the attainment of which his commanding y to do p is a necessary means. x is, say, engaged in some complicated task, for the successful accomplishment of which he needs the assistance of y. y must do p, if x is to succeed. But y does not do p out of his own inclination. y may have totally different ends of *his* action. Therefore x must *make y do p*, if he is to succeed. Perhaps more gentle means than commanding are first tried, but found fruitless. Therefore x must *command y* to do p, if he is to succeed. That is: commanding y to do p is a necessary means of making y do p, which in its turn is a necessary means of

securing x's success. So x opens his mouth and gives the order
to y 'Do p'.

If the reasons why x ordered y to do p, are such that in their
light x's normative action assumes the character of a necessary
means to his desired end, then we shall say that x had a *compelling*
motive or reason for giving the order to y. The normative act
assumes this character, when we come to think that, had x *not*
given the order to y, he would not have attained his end.

That ordering y to do p is a necessary means for x either to p
itself as an end or to some remoter end q, is a statement of *natural*
necessity. If x realizes this and if he aims at p or q, then ordering
y to do p becomes a *practical* necessity incumbent on x.

In this way the normative acts of issuing heteronomous commands or orders may become practically necessitated by the ends
of the norm-authority in combination with considerations pertaining to means to those ends. When the normative act is thus
necessitated, we shall call the heteronomous norm, which comes
into existence as its result, a *well-grounded* norm. A heteronomous
norm is, in this sense, well-grounded, when the norm-authority's
normative action is guided by autonomous norm or is, as we could
also say it, autonomously necessitated. Since autonomous norms
are *ipso facto* practical necessities, they may be said to be *ipso facto*
well-grounded too.

Also obedience to (heteronomous) commands can be autonomously necessary.

It is an essential feature of the heteronomous norm, we said
(sect. 3), that it should be associated with a threat of penalty in
case of disobedience. Threat of punishment for disobedience constitutes a motive for obedience. This is not to say that orders are
always or even normally obeyed, because the subject wants to
escape punishment. But *sometimes* they are obeyed for this reason.
Then the norm-subject considers obedience to the norm as a
necessary, and usually also productive, means to escaping punishment. He *wants* to escape punishment. *Unless* he obeys, he will be
punished. Therefore he *has* to obey, *i.e.* has to do the act, which
the norm says he ought to do.

Sometimes we are anxious to obey orders, not for the sake of
escaping punishment, but for the sake of something else. The end
could, for example, simply be our wish to please the person who
gave the order. Perhaps he gave the order for the sake of attaining

some end of his and we want to help him. Then *our* want, in combination with the natural necessity of obedience to the norm as a means to *his* end, engenders an autonomous practical necessity of obedience.

It can, of course, happen that the thing we are ordered to do is the very thing we want to do. Then there is no autonomous necessitation of the will to obedience. This case is therefore uninteresting from the point of view of the making-do-mechanism of commands. But there is a case which is related to it and which is of much interest. This is, when the norm is addressed to a multitude of subjects and the state of affairs which prevails or comes into being thanks to the fact that *all* subjects obey the norm, is an end of *each one* of the subjects individually. Then obedience is necessary as a co-operative step towards the attainment of the end. This is another case of autonomous necessitation to obedience to a heteronomous norm.

10. We may now go back to the problem of the relation between norms and values.

Ends are goods attainable through action, we have said. To say, as is sometimes done, that ends demand or require us to pursue them, is metaphorical speech. There is nothing normative about ends and goods as such. Ends *are* pursued and goods wanted, or else they are not ends and goods. But the ordinances of *ananke* (that too, of course, is metaphorical talk), *i.e.* the natural necessities, may, when they become known to man, in combination with his ends force upon him the practical necessities of doing things which, for their own sake, he would not do and of forbearing things from which, considerations of ends apart, he would not have abstained. In this way norms may be said to 'hook on' to values.

If by autonomous norms we understand the practical necessitations of the will to action under the joint influence of ends and insights into causal connexions, then such norms are *intrinsically value-directed*, one could say.

The heteronomous norms as commands or orders, given by norm-authorities to norm-subjects, have no intrinsic connexion with ends. But heteronomous norms may become grounded in ends and thus assume the appearance of practical necessities. If they are that which I here call *well-grounded*, then the normative acts of issuing them are value-directed under autonomous norms.

176

Also the acts of obeying the norms can become thus value-directed.

It will perhaps be objected to our treatment in this chapter of the problem, how norms and values are related, that we have been discussing only the relation of 'good' (or rather: 'want') to 'must'. Traditional discussion of the problem has been concerned, above all, with the relation of 'good' to 'ought'. (Cf. the presentation of the problem in sect. 1.) This is true—and also that the meanings of 'ought' and 'must' can be significantly distinguished. Our discussion of the relation of norms and values has been very far from exhaustive. In defence of the adopted course of treatment I would say that I tend to think that it is only the aspect of norms as practical necessities (the anankastic or 'must'-aspect), which bears an intrinsic relationship to ideas of the good. Other aspects of the normative may become value-oriented only through the intermediary of the anankastic aspect. How this happens for the aspect of norms as commands, I have tried to indicate in sects. 8 and 9. How it may happen for the aspect of norms as rules, the deontic aspect as it could also be called (cf. sect. 2), will not be discussed here. Hints of this will be given in the last chapter.

IX

DUTY

---

1. IN the preceding chapter we introduced the notion of a *well-grounded* norm. A heteronomous command we call well-grounded, when the act of issuing it is a practical necessity with a view to the norm-authority's ends. Autonomous norms are *ipso facto* well-grounded. (Ch. VIII, sect. 9.)

We shall in this chapter study a special case of well-grounded norms. This is the case, when the ultimate end, relative to which the norm is well-grounded, is the good of some being. Of this case I shall say that it imposes a *duty* on the norm-subject.

The term 'duty' is used with a multitude of meanings in ordinary language. Here it is used as a technical term. Not everything which is called a 'duty', is a duty in our sense. Legal duties, *e.g.*, need not be. Whether so-called moral duties are or not, will depend upon the view we take of the nature of morality. But I think it is true to say that everything which is a duty in our sense, *i.e.* is a practical necessity with a view to (promoting or respecting) the good of some being, is in common speech quite naturally called a duty. Therefore our use of 'duty' as technical term is in good agreement with one of the uses of this word in ordinary language.

Duties in our sense can be suitably divided into certain main categories.

A first division is into self-regarding and other-regarding duties. The names and also the sense, which we give to them here, are familiar from traditional ethics. When a duty is self-regarding, the good, which the agent is supposed to serve by his dutiful action, is the agent's own welfare. When a duty is other-regarding, it is the welfare of some being other than the agent himself.

A second division is into autonomous and heteronomous duties.

178

A duty is autonomous when dutiful action is incumbent on the agent itself as a practical necessity—independently of whether the good, which it serves, is the agent's own or some other being's. A duty is heteronomous when dutiful action is heteronomously prescribed to the agent.

When we combine these two grounds of division, we get in all four basic types of duty, *viz.* autonomous self-regarding, autonomous other-regarding, heteronomous self-regarding, and heteronomous other-regarding duties.

There is, however, also a third way of dividing duties, which must be noted. It is their division into that which I propose to call positive and negative duties. The first are duties to *do*, the second duties to *forbear* something. The two kinds of duty thus answer to two sub-kinds of that which we have called positive and negative commands. (See Ch. VIII, sect. 3.) Of the negative commands we said that they are also commonly called *prohibitions*.

From the dutybound agent's point of view positive duties are (mainly) duties to *promote*, negative duties are duties to *respect* the good of beings. From the point of view of the norm-authority again the purpose of negative duties can be said to be (chiefly) to *protect* the good of some being.

Negative other-regarding duties are related to one of the many different concepts of *a right*. This notion of a right is a normative idea with a characteristic dual aspect. From the point of view of the right-holder, a right in this sense is a freedom or permission to act in a certain way. From the point of view of the dutybound agents again, the right is a prohibition to interfere with the right-holder's action, should he choose to avail himself of his right.

2. An autonomous self-regarding duty, according to the definitions we have given, is an autonomous necessitation of the will to do something for the sake of promoting or protecting the acting agent's own good.

Autonomous self-regarding duties must not be confused with autonomous practical necessities in general. Consider once again the example of the man, who runs to the station. (See Ch. VIII, sect. 7.) He wants to be in time for the train. Unless he runs, he will be late. Therefore he has to run. This is autonomous practical necessitation. Why is it not autonomous self-regarding duty?

Wanting to be at the station in time is usually not an ultimate end of action. A man may want this because he wants to meet someone, or because he has promised to meet someone and is anxious to fulfil his promise. These could be ultimate ends. Some such ends may actually make his action other-regarding duty. They would not make it self-regarding, unless the agent could say truly of himself that he wants to be at the station in time, because his welfare demands this. I am not suggesting that a man could never say this truly of himself. But it would certainly be an uncommon case.

There are two main types of case, when a man can be said to care for his own good and on that account to have autonomous duties towards himself.

The first case of caring for one's good gives rise to negative duties only. There are certain things which a man shuns or regards as 'in themselves' unwanted. He may sometimes be willing to suffer those things for the sake of some end which he wants to attain—as, e.g., when he decides to have a tooth pulled out. But unless he has some such end or some other wanted consequences in view, he will consider those things bad for him and try to avoid them. Now assume that he realizes that, if he does p, then some such in itself unwanted thing q will befall him. He finds, for example, that a particular kind of food, which he likes in itself, upsets him very violently. He could then adopt as a maxim or rule never to take food of that sort. He, as it were, enforces a certain prohibition on himself for the sake of protecting himself (his 'good') against something unwanted. Such self-protective self-prohibitions can be called autonomous self-regarding duties.

The second case of caring for one's own good occurs, when a man *deliberates* about his ends.

But does a man ever deliberate about his ends? *Can* one deliberate about ends? The question was discussed with much ingenuity by Aristotle.[1] On Aristotle's view deliberation is about means, not about ends. So-called deliberation about ends is about intermediate ends and therefore really about means to some ulterior ends.

It is probably right to say that the word 'to deliberate' is most commonly used in situations when we raise such questions as, '*How* shall I achieve this?' or '*Which way* shall I choose to do this?' When we raise such questions, we are sometimes deliberating

[1] See *EN*, Bk. III, Ch. 3.

about means to given ends, and sometimes about that which we have called 'ways of doing things'. (Aristotle did not distinguish the two.) But we are not deliberating about ends.

Sometimes, however, a man stops to consider questions like this: 'What consequences is my pursuit of this end going to have— beside my possibly attaining the end?' He is perhaps working hard to get a promotion in his job. 'Am I ruining my health? Is it good for me never to afford time for relaxation? And when I get my promotion, what will then happen? I shall get a higher pay, but there will also be heavier work and more responsibility and even less time than now for relaxation.'

When a man in pursuit of ends stops to reflect upon the consequences of his pursuing and/or of his attaining his ends, then he can truly be said to be deliberating about ends. This he can also be said to do when, without a view to existing ends, he asks himself the question, 'What shall I do?'

In such situations, however, a man can also be said to be deliberating about his own welfare. He asks what is good and bad for him. As a consequence of such self-searching activity he may come to aim at new or revised ends.

A man who deliberates about ends may come to see that there are certain things which he ought to do and, perhaps more often, must not do, lest he shall regret it later in life. He may come to the conclusion that he must take some physical exercise or else he will neglect his health or that he must afford some time for reading novels or listening to music or else his soul will dry up completely or, if he tends to be a spendthrift, that he must think of saving for his old age. In reaching such conclusions a man may be said to impose upon himself autonomous self-regarding duties. He, as it were, forces upon himself a certain course of action or way of living with a view to what he considers necessary for his welfare.

There cannot exist an autonomous self-regarding duty to care for one's own good (welfare) in either of the two chief ways, in which such care takes place. Self-care is the foundation and source of all autonomous self-regarding duties. To say that a man imposes upon himself the duty to care for himself is to say that his care for his own good makes it necessary for him to care for his own good. This is empty talk, unless it means that it imposes upon him specific self-regarding duties, *e.g.* a duty to care that he gets enough sleep or exercise.

3. The practical syllogism, which embodies the prototype of an autonomous other-regarding duty, is this:

> x wants to promote or respect the good of y for its own sake.
> Unless x does (forbears) p, he will not be promoting or respecting the good of y.
> ───────────────
> ∴ x must do (forbear) p.

By respecting the good of another being one may understand the forbearance of any act which, if done, would be bad for this being. On this definition, the duty to respect is necessarily a duty to forbear. By promoting the good of another being, again one may understand the doing of something which will be good for this being. On this definition, the duty to promote a being's good is necessarily a duty to act in a certain way.

It may, however, happen that a man by forbearing to act becomes responsible for damage to another man, *e.g.* because a third man *does* some harm to him. Then a duty to act (to interfere) can be called a duty to *protect* the neighbour's good, and this duty can be distinguished both from the positive duty to promote and from the negative duty to respect this good.

It may also happen that a man by forbearing to act will promote the welfare of another man, *e.g.* because this gives the other man an opportunity, which he would otherwise not have had, of doing something he likes. Then a duty to forbear (to stay aside) can be called a duty to *forsake*, and this negative duty can be distinguished from the other negative duty to respect another man's good.

There are thus in all four types of duty, which fall under the case we are now discussing: the positive duties to promote and protect another man's good and the negative duties to respect and to forsake. But forsaking can also be regarded as a negative form of promoting a good, and protecting as a positive form of respecting it. I shall therefore include forsaking under promoting and protecting under respecting. And I shall say that, *basically*, promoting is a positive and respecting a negative duty.

Autonomous other-regarding duties to promote the welfare of other beings have to do with the feeling or sentiment we call *love* in a broad sense of this word.

Other-regarding duties, both autonomous and heteronomous, which require us to respect the good of other beings, are felt to have a peculiar connexion with morality, to be the moral duties

182

par excellence. We shall in the last chapter examine this opinion more in detail.

We distinguished in a previous chapter between self- and other-regarding virtues. To try to acquire the other-regarding virtues: consideration, helpfulness, honesty, etc. can be part of the autonomous other-regarding duties of a man. To try to acquire and observe them is certainly part of the heteronomous other-regarding duties which we wish to implant in others. Of the other-regarding virtues most, it would seem, have to do with respecting our neighbour's good; but some, such as helpfulness, are obviously relevant to the promotion of this good.

When speaking of self- and other-regarding virtues (see Ch. VII, sect. 10), we noted that practising the latter presupposes an interest in the welfare of other people. This is the interest to which the first premiss of our practical syllogism above refers. Whether a man takes such an interest in another man, or in other men generally, is contingent. For this reason there can exist no such thing as an autonomous duty to love our neighbour or to want to respect his good for its own sake. Love of our neighbour is the foundation and source of any autonomous other-regarding duty we may have, *i.e.* impose upon ourselves, to promote our neighbour's good. Similarly, the will to respect his good for its own sake is the foundation and source of every autonomous other-regarding duty to respect it in this or that particular regard. Interest in another man's good for its own sake cannot be autonomous other-regarding duty, since it is presupposed in every such duty.

But is such interest even *possible*, albeit not duty? Here we are touching upon a major problem of ethics, *viz.* the problem of egoism and altruism.

4. By *interest* in or *regard* for somebody's good I shall here understand a desire to promote or respect this good.

That promoting his neighbour's welfare can be an intermediate end of a man's action presents no problem. This case simply amounts to that regard for his neighbour's welfare is a means to some ulterior end of the agent's. If the means is necessary, regard for his neighbour is forced upon the agent by autonomous practical necessity.

There are innumerable ways in which regard for the good of others can become a means to self-interested ends. The master wants his servant to work effectively for him. This the servant will not do, unless the master cares for his welfare—not to speak of the necessity of not maltreating the servant. *Ergo* will the master take heed to respect and promote the welfare of his servant to the extent he thinks necessary. This is *not* what I here call autonomous other-regarding duty, since the ultimate end, which necessitates action, is not an interest in the welfare of another being.

By the thesis of Psychological Egoism one could understand the idea that promoting and respecting his neighbour's good is never anything but (at most) an intermediate end of a man's action. Regard for the good of others for its own sake we could call pursuit of an *altruistic* end. Egoism, as here defined, is thus a doctrine which denies the existence of altruism, *i.e.* of altruistic ends of action.

The nature of this negative thesis must not be misunderstood. Egoism, as here defined, does of course not deny that promoting and respecting another man's good can be an end of action. It can even have the appearance of being an ultimate end. But egoism maintains that, if such an end is not overtly intermediate, it can become unmasked as an intermediate end.

The thesis of egoism, however, admits of several interpretations —which supporters of it have not always kept well apart. The denial of altruism can be understood as the denial of a logical possibility or as the denial that something is a fact. It is egoism as a denial of the logical possibility of altruistic ends of action, which here interests us first of all.

It is easy to see, I think, what is the nerve of the idea that action *cannot* be genuinely altruistic. It is a logical fact that any end of action whatsoever is some *agent's* end, *i.e.* is something which the agent, whose ends we are considering, wants to attain. Therefore, if promoting my neighbour's welfare is an end of my action, it is yet an end of *my* action, something *I* want, *my* interest, *for me* a good. There is a sense in which aims in acting are helplessly self-centred.

The thesis of egoism, which we are now discussing, rests on a misunderstanding of the significance of the logical facts, which we have just mentioned, about ends of action, wanting, and the good of a being. Egoism misconstrues the necessary connexion, which there exists between my neighbour's welfare as an end of my action and *my* welfare, as an impossibility of pursuing the first except as a means to safeguarding or promoting the second. This is the very same mistake as the one which psychological eudaimonism commits. (Cf. Ch. V, sect. 2, the discussion of the example on p. 90.) It is related to the self-refuting mistake, which psychological hedonism commits, when it misinterprets the necessary connexion between satisfaction of desire and pleasure as meaning that pleasure is necessarily the ultimate object of every desire.

Psychological hedonism, egoism, and eudaimonism are closely related philosophical views of human nature. They are all false. They all commit very much the same mistake. Their mistake consists in a misinterpretation of an existing necessary connexion. These necessities 'behind' the falsehoods give to the three doctrines the strong appearance of truth which they possess. A refutation of hedonism which denies the necessary connexion between desire and pleasure, and a refutation of egoism or of eudaimonism which denies the necessary self-centredness of all ends of action, is therefore doomed to fail of its object. The aim of the refutation is not to deny these connexions but to put right their significance.

When the logical mistake of egoism has been corrected, the logical possibility of altruistic (ends of) action has become established.

The admission of the logical possibility of altruism, however, is fully compatible with the view that, as a matter of fact, regard for our neighbour is never an ultimate moving force of human conduct. Apparent altruism, on this view, is always egoism in disguise.

We need not here discuss this doctrine in detail. It contains a good portion of truth. Its claim to the whole truth is founded, I think, partly on an exaggerated pessimism about human nature and partly on the logical mistake, which we just mentioned, relating to the self-centredness of ends of action. In the gloom of pessimism it becomes tempting to give to one's insight into the vileness of human nature an absolute character, which can be given to it only at the expense of committing a logical mistake.

Beside the *logical* question, whether a man *can* take an ultimate interest in the good of his neighbour, and the *psychological* question whether a man ever *is* interested in his neighbour's good except as a means to some end, there is also the *genetic* question, whether every interest in another man's good as an end was not in origin an interest in this good as a means.

185

Those who take the view that altruism must have a genetic foundation in self-interest are, somehow, *astonished* at the fact that there should exist such a thing as pure unselfishness, *i.e.* action which springs from affection, friendship, love, sympathy, or respect and which is completely untinged by calculations about its utilitarian value for the agent. That man acts self-interestedly seems not to require any explanation. But that he acts unselfishly may strike us as something of a 'mystery'.

Is unselfishness a 'mystery', once we have seen clearly through the *logical* mistake which egoism commits? I do not know what is the right answer to the question. The answer, of course, partly depends upon what we mean by a 'mystery' here. But I tend to think that the appearance of 'mystery' or of something standing in need of 'explanation', which pure unselfish action can be said to exhibit, is really nothing but a conceptual confusion nourished by the same mistake as the one underlying hedonism and eudaimonism. Therefore I am also inclined to think that action inspired by affection, friendship, and love is just as typical of human nature as action in a spirit of self-interest, and that the view of man as essentially a self-interested creature is a logical misconception. But I may be mistaken.

5. Behind heteronomous self-regarding duties there is a practical syllogism of the following type:

> *x* wants the good of *y* to become promoted for its own sake.
> Unless *y* does *p*, his good will not be promoted.
> ∴ *x* must make *y* do *p*.

The distinction between promoting and respecting and also the distinction between doing and forbearing is not, it seems, of much importance to the case which we are now considering. I shall therefore here use the verb 'promote' to cover 'promote or respect' and the verb 'do' to cover 'do or forbear'.

The conclusion of the above syllogism is an autonomous practical necessity incumbent upon *x*. *x* ought to make *y* do *p*. There are many ways in which *x* can try to achieve this. *One* way is by commanding *y*. This is the only way which interests us here. When it is resorted to, then *x* imposes upon *y* a duty to act in a manner which *x* considers good for *y*. The duty is heteronomous.

186

y or the norm-subject is not moved to action by his own wants and insights into necessities. It is *x* or the norm-authority, who is thus moved.

Thus when there is a heteronomous self-regarding duty, the norm-*subject*'s good is the norm-*authority*'s end. The authority imposes upon the subject a duty for the sake of (in the name of) the subject's welfare. But the subject, if he obeys, does not necessarily do the ordered thing for the sake of his good. He may do it simply and solely for the sake of escaping punishment. Or he may do it because he wants to please the authority, or out of respect for the authority.

6. When does commanding actually take place 'in the name of' the good of the commanded? There are some typical cases. *One* is when parents order their children to do certain things, because it is good for the child, or to forbear something because it would be bad for the child to do it. Also in the relations of teachers to pupils orders of a similar nature are sometimes given. Finally, people who are feebleminded or for some other reason incapable of looking after themselves may have to be commanded by others, who have a better understanding of their welfare.

It will be noted that the agent who issues commands to others in the name of their good, usually enjoys some recognized position of '*authority*' over those whom he commands—such as parent or teacher or guardian. It will also be noted that two of the three typical cases which we mentioned, have to do with that which we call *education*.

I shall call—partly for want of a better name—commands, which are issued in the name of the good of the commanded, *moral commands*. Of the educational purposes, which such commanding may serve, I shall speak as *moral education*. And the authority who gives such orders, I shall call a *moral authority*.

This use of the adjective 'moral', incidentally, is not unnatural or at great variance with ordinary usage—though maybe not very familiar in moral philosophy. It has no immediate connexion with so-called *moral goodness* nor with so-called *moral duty*. I am not suggesting that the duties imposed by what I call moral commands are those which we ordinarily call moral duties. The activity, however, which in common speech is called *moralizing*, largely consists in advising and recommending to other people

187

things in the name of their good, and also in drawing their attention to various ways in which people may have neglected their own welfare. Moralizing is not co-extensive with that which I here call moral commanding. But that which I here call moral commanding falls under that which is ordinarily called moralizing.

We shall distinguish between the *reasons* and the *justification* for commanding others in the name of their good.

The immediate reason for such commanding is that the norm-authority takes an interest in the welfare of the norm-subject. The immediate reason need not, however, be an ultimate reason. Sometimes a man takes an interest in the good of another man for the sake of some ulterior end of his own. This is the case of the master who cares for the good of his servants because he expects a better return of services. Sometimes a man is under a legal obligation to care for the good of others in a manner which involves commanding them. Parents and guardians have such obligations. It is an important, though not the sole, aspect of parental love that this love should be the *ultimate* reason why parents oblige their children to acts and forbearances in the name of the children's good.

Only when the ultimate reason for commanding others is an interest in their welfare, shall we say that a heteronomous self-regarding duty is being imposed.

Commanding others in the name of their good can be said to entail a claim on the part of the norm-authority to a better insight into the requirements of the welfare of the norm-subject than the norm-subject can claim for himself. The justification of this claim is part of the justification of heteronomous self-regarding duties.

It is a fact that some men have a much less developed conception than other men of that which is good or bad for themselves. This can be due to various reasons, *e.g.* to lack of experience of that which may befall a man as a consequence of his actions. Small infants can be said to have as yet no conception at all of that which is good or bad for them. Children, who already have some views in the matter, may nevertheless be completely mistaken in their views, *e.g.* strongly want to do things which they will regret, thinking that they will not. It is in such situations, when a being's conception of his own welfare either is lacking or undeveloped or distorted,

188

that men are called upon to exercise moral authority over others.

Part of the justification of heteronomous other-regarding duties is thus the superior wisdom of some men as to that which is good or bad for other men. The moral authority of parents, guardians, and teachers can normally be expected to possess this justification for its exercise.

If men necessarily pursued their real good, any claim to superior wisdom on the part of others would necessarily lack justification —and therewith also any attempt to impose heteronomous self-regarding duties. As a matter of fact, however, men often pursue things which 'on second thoughts' they consider unwanted. The test which shows that something was a constituent of a man's apparent as opposed to his real good, is that he *regrets* it. (See Ch. V, sect. 14.) To know the requirements of another man's welfare better than he does it himself is essentially the superior capacity of seeing what a man will later regret having done or neglected. The man who exercises moral authority over another, is justified in doing so only to the extent that he can say truthfully to the other man: 'There will be a day when you will have reason to be grateful for that which I did to guide you.' The important point is not whether the other man acknowledges his gratitude. Some men are by nature little inclined to be grateful even when there is a reason. The important point is that there should be reason for thinking that, had the other man not obeyed the commands, he would have been worse off in the long run, or for thinking that, had he obeyed, he would be better off than he is now. But what is 'better off' and 'worse off' is, in the last resort, for the subject himself to decide.

When the claim to superior knowledge of good and evil lacks justification, the exercise of moral authority of one man over another deteriorates into something which may be called *moral tyranny*. The subject is then forced to do things 'in the name of his good', when actually he knows better himself what is good or bad for him. To know whether the claim to superior knowledge on the part of the norm-authority is justified or not, can be most difficult. The struggle for *moral freedom*, *i.e.* for the right to act in accordance with that which one considers good or bad for oneself, against alleged moral tyranny, can greatly upset the relations between parents and children in the period before the latter come of age.

It is an important aspect of that which we call a child's 'coming of age' that the child reaches that which we shall here call *moral maturity*. An individual can be said to have reached moral maturity when there is no *obvious* justification for a claim, which others may put forward, to superior insight into the requirements of that individual's good.

With the reaching of moral maturity the moral education of men —in the form of heteronomous self-regarding duties being imposed on them—comes to an end. It is the aim of moral education not only to promote and protect the good of others during their moral immaturity, but also to facilitate the process of maturation by teaching them to care for their own welfare. But here again it is important to remember that the criterion of the present superior wisdom of the teacher is set by the future verdict of the pupil on the fruits of his teaching.

7. We now proceed to heteronomous other-regarding duties.

A man x commands another man y to do something. The command, let us assume, is well-grounded. This means that x must issue it in order to secure some end of his. If this end is the good of y and if it is an ultimate end, then the command imposes a heteronomous self-regarding duty on y. If the end is the good of some being other than y and is an ultimate end, then the command imposes a heteronomous other-regarding duty on y in relation to that other being.

The case when one man commands a second man in the name of the welfare of a third man, is a thoroughly possible and by no means unrealistic case. Nevertheless it seems to be a case of rather subordinate interest. We shall therefore here disregard it.

With this exclusion, the remaining cases of heteronomous other-regarding duties are those in which one man for the sake of his own welfare commands another man. Such duties must be distinguished from heteronomous commands for self-interested ends generally. We do not wish to say that we are imposing a heteronomous other-regarding duty on a man, if we order him to open a window because we want to have the room ventilated. But we may wish to say that an order not to disturb us, when we are working, aims at imposing an other-regarding duty.

As observed in sect. 2, one way in which a man can care for his own welfare is by taking various self-protective steps in order to escape things, which he shuns as being unwanted either in themselves or due to their consequences. It would seem that it is this way of caring for one's own good that is predominantly relevant to heteronomous other-regarding duties. Such duties, when imposed by one man on another in the interest of the first, are mainly negative duties, *i.e.* prohibitions to do things which the first man considers harmful for himself. From the norm-authority's point of view heteronomous other-regarding duties are chiefly *self-protective prohibitions*.

8. We have so far been talking as though, as a matter of course, any man *could*, if he wanted to, command any other man. The recipient of an order may disobey the order, nevertheless *he has been commanded*.

As a matter of fact, men do not often command other men. When this happens, it usually takes place in circumstances under which commanding has become somehow 'institutionalized'. Parents command *their* children, but not the children of other parents. Teachers sometimes command their pupils; for pupils to command their teachers is out of place. Officers of superior rank command officers of inferior rank; commoners do not often command one another. When I ask my friend to shut the door I do not command him; not to speak of the case when I ask a stranger for a service. When I order a book through my bookseller, this is not ordering in the sense of commanding.

Why is it that we do not command our friends or strangers? Is it because we are too polite thus to intrude upon them? *Can* we command our friends? The question is worth asking.

The fact that commanding usually takes place under some 'institutionalized' circumstances may suggest to us the idea that in order to be *able to command* one must possess something which could be called a *right to command*, enjoy some recognized position of authority. Parents have a right to command their children, children no right to command their parents. Has the highwayman, who commands 'hands up', a right to command this? Certainly not. Is he then not *commanding* 'Hands up'? He certainly is.

We have said before (Ch. VIII, sect. 3) that to a command is essentially tied a threat of punishment in case of disobedience. This threat must not be empty or a mock threat. It must be an effective threat. That it is effective does not mean that it necessarily

191

secures obedience. Nor does it mean that disobedience is without exception punished. I shall not here discuss in detail, what constitutes the efficacy of a threat of punishment.

It thus follows that the possibility of commanding is essentially tied to the possibility of effectively threatening the recipient of the order with punishment in case of disobedience. This second possibility again depends upon that which I shall call the *relative strength* of the agents concerned. Effective threatening is, on the whole, possible only when the individual who threatens, is *stronger* than the individual who is being threatened. Thus the possibility of commanding is founded upon the *superior strength* of the commander over the commanded.

This concept of strength stands in need of elucidation. It is not the same as that which is ordinarily understood by 'physical strength', though it is related to it. A big, strong man may not be able to command a small, weak one, because the second can run away and put himself out of reach of the punishing arm of the first. But then it must be remembered that running, too, is part of a man's physical powers.

Our strong man can, of course, continue to shout out commands to the small man and even accompany his orders by the most fearful threats. Is he then not 'issuing commands'? If he is not convinced that his words will not impress the small man, he can rightly be said to be *trying* to command him. If he *knows* that his shouting and threatening is all in vain, we could say that he is not commanding but only giving vent to his wishes and his anger. We could also, if we wanted, distinguish between *commanding*, which would consist merely in the use of words combined with a certain intention, and *effectively commanding*, which would combine intention and the use of words with an *effective* threat of punishment. Then we could say that it is only effective commanding, which constitutes normative relationships of the kind we are here studying, between men.

The notion of strength, which is essential to the possibility and existence of normative relationships among men, I shall define as capacity of affecting through one's action the good of other beings favourably or adversely. By saying that two agents are of roughly equal strength we here mean that they have roughly the same capacities (powers) of influencing the welfare of one another. By calling one stronger than another we mean that the first can do more for promoting but also more for injuring the good of the second than the second can do with regard to the good of the first.

It is obvious that capacity of favouring and capacity of injuring someone's welfare need not be proportionate. The fact that one man can do more good to another than this other man can do to him does not exclude the possibility that the second man can do more harm to the first than the first can do to the second.

To the capacity of commanding, the capacity of visiting another man with evil is of more importance than the capacity of doing good to him. This is so, because commanding is essentially connected with punishing disobedience but not with rewarding obedience. The superior strength, necessary for commanding, is therefore essentially a superior power of causing suffering to others. That such should be the logical foundation of heteronomous law and heteronomous duties may seem brutish, but must, I think, be accepted as fact.

One man may *accidentally* enjoy superior power or strength, in the sense defined, in relation to another man. Such accidental superiority can then be used for commanding. *Blackmail* is a species of commanding, which is based upon accidental superiority of strength.

Consider two men 'by themselves', *i.e.* in abstraction from such relationships which they may have to other men and which may be relevant to their capacity of doing good or harm to one another. For example: the one man is king and can command his bodyguard to seize the other man, if he does not obey the king's orders. Then abstract from this and think of the king without his bodyguard. Abstract also from such accidental superiority, which one man may have over another. For example: the one man has a rifle. Abstract from this, or endow in thought the other man with a rifle too. The balance of strength, which remains after these abstractions, I shall call the *natural relative strength* of the two men.

Such logical fictions as this about the powers of men in a state of nature may strike one as old-fashioned and unrealistic. They were much in favour with writers of the 17th and the 18th centuries. They may be grossly unrealistic as hypotheses concerning the conditions which existed before the conventions, customs, and norms of society had 'perverted' the 'natural' ways of life. As abstractions for the purposes of studying concepts, these fictions may be both legitimate and useful. It is to be regretted that an exaggerated respect for the 'naturalistic' study of man by anthropologists, historians, and psychologists has made philosophers generally abandon these fictions, of which the supreme product is the Contract Theory of the State.

It is a fact of fundamental importance alike to moral, legal, and political philosophy that men are, by nature, roughly equally strong, *i.e.* endowed with roughly the same natural powers of affecting the welfare of one another favourably and adversely. I shall express this fact by saying that men are, by nature, *approximate equals*.

There are, of course, noteworthy natural inequalities too. Some of these inequalities are founded in physical, others in intellectual superiority, some in both.

There is, first of all, the physical and intellectual superiority of adult people over children before the latters' coming of age. On *it* the normative relationship between parents and children is ultimately based. It should be noted that the natural limits to the normative authority of a father or mother over children other than their own are not set by the *children* of other parents, but by the *parents* of other children.

There is further a certain inequality, at least in physical strength, between the sexes. Whether it is relevant to normative relationships is arguable. It certainly has been considered relevant in some quarters.

Here must also be noted the fact that physical strength, up to a point, declines with increasing age. This decline, however, is, up to a point, compensated for by an increase in the mental power which we call 'wisdom'—maybe not in matters purely intellectual, but certainly in matters pertaining to the good of man.

Of the normative relationships between parents and children it is characteristic, not only that it exists 'naturally', *i.e.* on a basis of natural superiority in strength, but also that it dissolves 'naturally', *i.e.* as a consequence of the children's growing up to become the approximate equals of their parents. It is an interesting and deeply significant fact about man that children become their parents' equals in strength *roughly* at the time when they reach that which I called moral maturity, *i.e.* become capable of caring

194

for their own welfare. The basis of parental normative authority thus vanishes roughly at the time when its exercise loses its justification.

At least as important as the fact that men are approximate equals by nature is the fact that men can add to their strength by joining forces with other men. The *ability to co-operate* for ends is not a uniquely human ability. But the rôle which this ability plays in the creation of normative relationships among men, has no counterpart elsewhere in the animal kingdom. For it is on this possibility of joining forces that much of social life on the human level depends and above all the great fabric of commanding power we call the state.

The significance for normative relationships of man's capacity to join forces with other men is twofold. Firstly it can overrule all natural (and accidental) inequalities, which may exist among individual men. If there are two men, x and y, on a desert island and x is the stronger, there may also develop between them a relationship which we could call that of master to servant. x commands and y, on the whole, obeys. If there are three men x and y and z and x is strongest, x *may* succeed in making himself master of both y and z. His superior strength may partly consist in his skill to kindle unfriendly relations between y and z and thus prevent them from joining forces against him. But if y and z join forces, it is most likely that they shall be able to withstand any attempt on the part of x to tyrannize over them.

Here we find the second respect in which man's ability to co-operate is important. It can create 'artificial' inequalities on a basis of 'natural' equalities. It is on such created inequalities that *institutionalized* normative power of some men over other men mainly rests. The 'ruler', in the widest sense of the word, is not necessarily stronger than each of his subjects. He is almost certainly weaker than even *two* of them jointly. Yet he can command each of his subjects because, should one of them be recalcitrant and refuse to obey orders, there will be others who join hands with the ruler to punish the recalcitrant.

Thanks to the fact that men are approximate equals by nature the possibilities of the human individual to command and therewith also to impose heteronomous duties on other individuals are narrowly restricted. But thanks to the power of co-operation heteronomous normative relationships yet play an all-pervading rôle in the life of human communities.

Inequalities of strength based on men's capacity to co-operate are the foundation of *legal* duties and the reign of *law*. These inequalities, however, may also serve the establishment of *moral* duties and the reign of *justice*. How this happens I shall try to show in the next chapter.

X

JUSTICE

1. IN the preceding chapter we stressed the importance of the two facts that men are approximate equals by nature and that they can join hands to co-operate. Thanks to the first, the possibilities of individual men to exercise normative authority over other men are narrowly limited. The significance of the second fact, we said, was twofold. Thanks to it men can withstand and overrule any 'tyranny', which one man may attempt to exercise over his equals by commanding them. But thanks to it men can also subjugate their natural equals and exercise joint normative authority over them. Both consequences of men's capacity to join strength are simultaneously at work in society. The significance of both can be summed up in the words 'society is stronger than the individual'.

Let us raise the question: What *makes* men join hands in co-operative efforts?

One thing which makes men co-operate is the practical necessity, autonomously incumbent upon each of the members of a group of men, of working together for the attainment of a common end. That the end is common shall mean that each of the men in the group wants a certain state of affairs p to exist. That working together is necessary shall mean that, if any one of the men stays away from work, the end will not be attained.

This case of co-operation under autonomous necessity is an extreme case. But it is an important prototype.

If ends are goods attainable through action, an end which is common to several agents can be called a *common good*. Not everything, however, which is a common good, *i.e.* a good for each member of a group of men, is also a common end. That something is a good for a man means that it is something which is, in itself

197

welcome to him. But not everything a man welcomes, if it befalls him, is an end of his action. Hence, though common ends are also common goods, all common goods are not also common ends.

Co-operation is for some end. This end can be a common good of *all* the co-operants. We shall call this the first case. Or it is a common good of *some* of them. We call this the second case. Or it is a good for *none* of them. This is the third case.

In the first case there are two possibilities. Either the men have to work for the common good under autonomous practical necessitation, or some can stay aside and let the rest work, or relax and let the rest work harder.

The first of these two possibilities answers to the prototype case which we have already described.

The second possibility means that a group of men have a common end, but that it is not necessary that they *all* work for it. We can in every such case distinguish a minimum number of *necessary co-operants* and a maximum number of *possible bystanders*. This division gives rise to a number of problems, which we cannot discuss here. We give only one example: Three men have a common end of their action. The co-operation of two of them is necessary in order that the end shall be attained. But one man can stay aside and look on, when the other two work. Assume that x and y work and that z stays aside. To make z participate in the work for the common good of the three men may then become another common interest of x and y. Since they are two and z is one, they will probably be able to order z to co-operate with them. If z remonstrates, they may jointly proceed to punish him. The co-operation of x and y in commanding z is co-operation in the sense of our prototype case.

We proceed to the second case. Then the end of co-operation is a common good of some but not of all of the co-operants. For example: Three men co-operate for a result p. Two of them are anxious that p shall be. For the third, however, p is not a good, Perhaps he co-operates because he has been commanded by the other two and is anxious to escape punishment. If this is the case, then making the third man work is another common interest of the first two men—beside the attainment of p. The co-operation of the two for this common end again is co-operation of the prototype case, *i.e.* of the case when men are under autonomous necessitation to co-operate for a common good. If, however, the group of men in pursuit of the first common good is great, then co-operation of a few of them may be sufficient for commanding some men from outside the group to labour for their end. Then the problem of co-operation for commanding outsiders becomes a case of the problem of co-operation in a group, which may be divided into necessary co-operants and possible bystanders. This problem we already discussed.

Consider finally the third case. Here the end of co-operation is not an end of any man in the group of co-operants. If this is the case, their co-operation serves as a means to some end of a being or of some beings outside the group. Use of this means may have to be secured by commanding the men to work. Then the problem of co-operation for a common end will arise for the men, for whose ends the co-operants are assumed to work. This problem falls under our first case.

By these considerations I have wanted to indicate, how that which I called a prototype case of co-operation for a common good holds a crucial position among a variety of cases of co-operation. I would maintain that all cases, which are not in themselves of this prototype and in which co-operation has to be secured by commanding, rest—in the last resort—upon *autonomously necessitated co-operation for a common good.*

There are, however, forms of co-operation, which do not necessarily serve the attainment of a common good. We now turn to a study of some such cases.

2. Let it be assumed that x and y join hands to attain an end of x's, which is not also an end of y's. x could not attain his end alone. He needs the assistance of y. Let us rule out the possibility that x can command y to serve him. Since men are approximate equals, the assumption that the one cannot command the other is thoroughly realistic. Let us further rule out the possibility that y wants to help x, because he wants to promote the good of x for its own sake. Since men, even if they are not unlimitedly egoistic, are not overwhelmingly altruistic either, this assumption is thoroughly realistic too. Is there then any motive left which could *make y co-operate?*

There is at least one possible motive left: hope of reciprocal service in return. y could argue: if I do not help x to attain p now,

199

x will probably not help me to attain q on another occasion. If I help x now, there is at least a good chance that he will help me then, considering that *he* may need *my* assistance on some other occasion. Hence it is in my interest to help him.

This form of co-operation may be said to hinge logically upon three facts. The first is that men are approximate equals and cannot normally exercise commanding authority over one another. The second is that men far from always pursue the good of their neighbours as an ultimate end of their own. The third is that men are to some extent dependent for their welfare upon the assistance, *i.e.* co-operation, of others. Co-operation, which is not for a common good, can yet be to mutual advantage.

Co-operation, which is to mutual advantage but not for the attainment of a common good, is *exchange of services*.

Exchange of services, be it observed, need not take the form of co-operation. y does something alone, say p, which is wanted or welcomed by x. p is thus a good for x. x, in return, does something, say q, which is wanted by y. The exchange of services which has taken place can be called an *exchange of goods*.

Exchange of services and of goods plays an important rôle in the conceptual genealogy of the normative ideas known as *agreement*, *contract*, and *promise*. I shall not, however, discuss them here.

When exchange of services or of goods takes place, people can be said to work in turns for the *promotion* of one another's good.

Hope of reciprocal service or of a good in return can thus be a motive for co-operation and for promoting another man's good generally. But it can also be a motive for *respecting* it.

A man may gain an advantage for himself by harming his neighbour, *i.e.* by doing something which his neighbour thinks unwanted. A man cannot command another man of roughly equal strength to respect his good. But if the other man harms him, he may be able to 'pay back', revenge himself and thus return evil by evil. *Revenge* may be regarded, logically, as a preform of *punishment*, and threat of revenge as a preform—on the level of rough equality of strength among agents—of normative relationships. One could say that revenge and retaliation are what punishment 'logically' deteriorates into, when approximate equals try to command one another.

To return evil by evil is also an exchange of services or of goods of its kind. One could call it an exchange of 'negative' services or goods. Such exchange is not to the mutual advantage, but to the mutual disadvantage of the agents, who engage in this sort of commerce. But the reciprocity of disadvantage is at the same time a ground for a reciprocity of advantage, *viz.* the mutual advantage gained from *not* doing evil to one another. Thus respect for the neighbour's good can be to the mutual advantage of agents, who are approximate equals by nature and therefore cannot effectively exercise normative authority over one another.

The principle called the Golden Rule is sometimes given the following formulation: Do to others what you want them to do to you, and don't do to others what you do not want them to do to you.

When the principle is formulated in this way, it is presupposed that one man regards as wanted and unwanted *roughly* the same things as those which any other man regards as wanted and unwanted respectively. This presupposition is largely fulfilled. But it is no logical necessity. There are exceptions to it. Something which *I* shun, another man may like. Then it is not to be seen why the fact that I do not want it should be a motive for not acting in such a way that *he* gets this thing. Similarly, it is not to be seen why I should do him something he does *not* want, although I may want him to do this for me. But if we both want and shun similar things, then we can exchange services to our mutual advantage by doing to one another what we welcome and not doing to one another what we shun.

If the Golden Rule is formulated in a way which is independent of the presupposition of similar wants, it would run as follows: Do to others what they want you to do to them and don't do to others what they do not want you to do to them. The utilitarian defence of this principle would then be that its adoption by all agents is to their mutual advantage.

The rule consists of two parts. We could call them the *positive* and the *negative* parts. The positive part urges us to promote, the negative part to respect the neighbour's good.

There is a noteworthy asymmetry between the parts. That the adoption of the negative part of the rule by all agents would be to their mutual advantage is *a priori* clear. Everybody would then gain the advantage of never being harmed by anybody else. That the adoption of the positive part of the rule by all agents must be to the mutual advantage of all is not in a similar way clear. Some men are more demanding on their neighbour's services than other men. If one man unlimitedly works for his neighbour, there is simply no time for his neighbour to return the service. If promoting the good of one another shall be to mutual advantage, there must be some 'check' on the demands which men have on their neighbours' good services.

I shall not here discuss at length how this check is provided. I only suggest that it *may* be provided by the negative part of the rule. This would mean that a man must never demand of his neighbour greater services than those which the neighbour can render without detriment to his own good. By demanding more he may become responsible for harm to the neighbour and thus sin against the negative part of the Golden Rule.

These last considerations support the view that the negative part of the principle holds a more fundamental position than the positive part. I shall henceforth in this chapter discuss only the negative part, *i.e.* the rule which urges us to respect our neighbour's good.

The big problem before us is this: How can respect for our neighbour's good become duty? In order to see how this is possible, we must try to link considerations relating to mutual advantage with considerations relating to co-operation for a common good.

3. Consider a number of men 'in a state of nature'. They occasionally do harm to one another; not often merely for the sake of harming, more often perhaps as an act of revenge for some evil they have suffered from others, usually however because pursuit of some end of theirs is causally incompatible with respect of the neighbour's good. Since some of them do harm, some of them also suffer harm. Some of them may never do and often suffer, others again often do and never suffer; but even those who escape harm from their neighbours may suffer under the inconveniences of having to take various self-protective measures. The more evil a man does, the more reason he has to fear evil himself.

Suppose the men come to agree that each of them has to gain more from *never being harmed by anybody* else than from *sometimes harming somebody* else. I shall call this a *basic inequality* of goods.

The men who agree or subscribe to the basic inequality, I shall speak of as constituting a *community*. Observance of the rule never

202

to harm anybody (in the community) I shall speak of as the adoption of a *practice*. We can call it 'the practice of not-harming'.

A member of the community who adopts the practice, can be said to make a 'personal sacrifice'. He gives up any such advantage which he may gain from doing harm to others. It is not certain that, by giving up this advantage, he will gain the greater advantage of never being harmed by anybody. But it is certain that, if every member of the community relinquishes the smaller advantage of sometimes harming somebody else, then they will all gain the greater advantage of never being harmed by anybody (in the community). Universal adoption of the practice is thus a necessary and sufficient condition for universal attainment of the greater good of the basic inequality. For being to the *mutual advantage* of all its members, universal adoption of the practice is also a *common good* of the community.

Escaping harm from others I shall call each member's *share* in the community's greater good.

Universal adoption of the practice of not-harming can be called the *price*, which the community has to pay for the greater good. Individual adoption of the practice, *i.e. not doing harm to others*, can be called each member's *due* or *due share* of the community's price for the greater good.

In order that the greater good of the community shall exist, it is (logically) necessary that all members pay their due. But in order that an individual member shall get his share in the greater good of the community, it is not (logically) necessary that he pays his due. To this end it is in fact *not* necessary that anybody pays. The only thing which is necessary, is that nobody does harm to *him*. If, however, everybody else pays his due, it *is* (logically) necessary that he will get his share. For, that all the rest pay their due means that they adopt the practice of never harming anybody else in the community. If they do this, the one remaining man can be sure of getting his share in the greater good, independently of whether he pays his due or not. He can therefore try to add to the greater advantage of never being harmed by anybody also the smaller advantage of sometimes harming somebody—try to get the best of both worlds so to speak. If he adds to the greater advantage of getting his share also the smaller advantage of skipping his due, he will necessarily deprive some of his neighbours of their share in the greater good. This I propose to call *parasitic action*.

The problem before us is to show how, in spite of the possibility of parasitic action, adoption of the practice which is conducive to the greater good of the community, nevertheless may become a practical necessity.

4. Assume that a man harms one of his neighbours for the sake of some advantage, *i.e.* end of his. The man who has suffered harm may wish to *revenge* himself. We need not here discuss whether revenge is or is not in origin associated with ends in acting or with primitive ideas of retributive justice. Revenge can, in any case, be said to have a natural, self-protective purpose.

Let us suppose that people never joined hands with others to revenge a wrong, unless they had been wronged themselves. Even then it is easy to see how threat of revenge may assume an accumulative deterrent effect on prospective evil-doers. Fear of revenge need not deter x from harming y and z individually. It may nevertheless deter him from harming them both. For, if revenge on x becomes a common interest of both y and z, they may co-operate and successfully revenge themselves. Even if x is stronger than each of them individually, it is unlikely that he will be stronger than both of them jointly. This is a consequence of the fact that men are approximate equals by nature, and that they can co-operate for common ends. Fear of revenge may therefore work as an effective deterrent at least against evil-doing on a larger scale, *i.e.* involving several wronged agents. It may thus go at least some way towards making observance of the practice of not-harming a practical necessity.

I shall call evil caused by revenge for evil done the *natural punishment* of evil-doing. It can also be called the natural sanction attached to the practice of respecting one's neighbour's good.

The step from these logical preforms of law to the establishment of normative relationships is not difficult to imagine. Let there be three men x, y, and z, who constitute a community by subscribing to our basic inequality of goods (see sect. 3). x and y are both anxious that z shall pay his due, for otherwise they will not get their share in the greater good of the community. x and y can command z, being jointly stronger. If commanding z turns out to be necessary for making him pay, co-operation in commanding becomes autonomously incumbent on x and y. Thus x and y impose upon z the (heteronomous other-regarding) duty of paying.

Similarly x and z impose the same duty on y, and y and z on x. Thus the very same interest which makes each one of the three co-operate with one of the other two against the third, *viz.* anxiety to get one's share in a greater good which benefits them all, becomes the power which forces each of them to pay their due. We can imagine the men as thoroughly selfish, void of any sense of justice or morality whatsoever. They have not the slightest desire to pay their due for their share. But the greedier they are on their share, the stronger will the normative pressure become under which they are themselves to pay their due. This is a fascinating mechanism. In co-operating for the common end of imposing heteronomous other-regarding duties on others, men come to get these same duties heteronomously imposed upon themselves.

The considerations which we have conducted, show how men's self-interested pursuit of a common good may engender a practical necessity of adopting a practice which is to the mutual advantage of them all.

5. Fear of revenge or of the punishing arm of heteronomous law is, of course, far from being the only motive which may make men adopt the practice of not doing harm to their neighbours. The circumstances, under which there is an advantage to be gained from harming others, are *special* circumstances. In the life of some men they do, perhaps, not often arise. Observance of the practice of not-harming because of lack of motives or opportunity of harming is, of course, not more to the moral credit of men than observance from a motive of self-interest.

The reasons why a man wants to respect a *particular* man's good, may be some particular relationship in which the two stand to one another. Depending upon the nature of this relationship, the reasons can be self-interested or altruistic. Perhaps he expects some good in return from that particular man. Or perhaps he just loves him and therefore is anxious to respect that other man's good 'for its own sake'. (I am here thinking of that *aspect* of love which consists in an unselfish regard for the good of another being.)

Could unselfish regard for the good of *all* men be a reason why a man never does evil to his neighbour? It must not be considered self-evident that, since a man can love some or other of his neighbours, he can love them all. Love of man is different in kind from love which is a relationship between particular men. One could

205

call the second, with Kant, *pathological* love. 'Pathological', of course, does not here mean 'sickly'. It refers to the foundation of this kind of love in a peculiar sentiment which one human being feels for another. We cannot exclude the possibility that a man felt this sentiment for every other man whom he happens to meet on his life's journey. His love of *men* would yet be different from that love of *man* which, independently of relationships among individuals, makes a man respect his neighbour's good 'for its own sake' or treat his neighbour 'as an end in itself'.

In order to get a firmer grasp of this 'abstract' love of man, let us go back to our problem of the greater good of the community and the individual's share and due.

We have seen how wanting one's share can engender a practical necessity of paying one's due. But we also know that paying one's due is not, as such, a necessary means to getting one's share as an end. It becomes a necessity only thanks to the intervention of heteronomous norm-pressure, one could say.

Suppose a man refuses to receive the smaller of two advantages, if he can have it only at the expense of another man losing the greater advantage. He gives as a reason for his refusal, that his receiving the advantage would hit his neighbour harder than it would benefit himself. Is such comparison of goods possible? We have touched upon the problem before. We then suggested that a balancing of goods against one another is possible only from the point of view of one and the same valuing being. Therefore, if a man thinks that an action of his injures another man more than it benefits himself and on that ground abstains from this act, then he respects the good of that other man as though it were his own. This peculiar respect for the good of another being *as one's own* is a motive which, without the intervention of heteronomous norm-pressure, will put a man under an autonomous necessity to pay his due for his share in the greater good of a community, of which he is a member.

It would be quite wrong to call this attitude to one's fellow humans self-interested. It would be misleading, if not wrong, to give to it the name of self-love. But it could be called a man's *love of himself in his neighbour*. This is the 'abstract' love of man, which I was contrasting with the 'pathological' love of one man for another.

6. I have tried to show under what conditions there could exist

a duty to abstain from evil-doing. We must now stop to reflect on the nature of the argument which we have been conducting.

That something is duty, we have said, means that it is a practical necessity with a view to the welfare of some being or beings. To ask under which conditions something or other is duty, entails asking what the wants of men must be in order that something or other shall be a practical necessity.

It is not off-hand clear, which wants of men would necessitate abstention from evil-doing. *Mere* wanting to escape harm from others cannot affect this—for one thing because men cannot as individuals command one another to reciprocal respect of one another's good. Wanting not to harm others would not make abstention from evil duty—wanting the very thing is not practical necessity of doing the very thing. These considerations show that our problem is not trivial.

The method which we employed for its solution was a general method. The derivation of the duty to abstain from evil was only an illustration of how the method works in a particular case. We shall now describe the method in abstraction from this particular application of it.

We started from the assumption of a community of men, who agree about that which we called a basic inequality of goods. A certain good G_1 is for them (individually) greater than a certain other good G_2. This basic inequality is subject to the following three conditions:

(i) If all men in the community relinquished the smaller good G_2, then all of them will get the greater good G_1.

(ii) It is logically possible for a man to get both goods, the greater and the smaller one, for himself.

(iii) It is logically necessary that, if one man gets both goods for himself, then some other man will lose the greater good.

The existence of the greater good for one man we called his *share* in the greater good of the community. Giving up the smaller good by one man we called his paying his *due*. In this terminology, the first condition means that the greater good of the community will exist, if each member pays his due. The second means that it is possible to get one's share without paying one's due. The third means that, if a man gets his share without paying his due, another man will lose his share.

To get both goods for oneself or, which means the same, to have one's share without paying one's due, can be regarded as a basic form of *injustice*. The idea of justice has many roots and has accordingly assumed many conceptual forms. We shall not here discuss the varieties of justice. The only form of it with which we are concerned is embodied in the following principle: *No man shall have his share in the greater good of a community of which he is a member, without paying his due*. (It is essential that 'greater good', 'share', and 'due' are defined in such a way that having one's share without paying one's due logically entails that some other member of the community loses his share in the good.)

This Principle of Justice I would regard as the cornerstone of the idea of morality.

The Principle of Justice has as many applications as there are communities of men, for whom a basic inequality of goods satisfying our three conditions holds true. I shall call any such community a *moral community* of men and a duty to act in accordance with the Principle of Justice a *moral duty*. Thus, *e.g.*, in the community of men who have more to gain from never being harmed by anybody else (in the community) than from sometimes harming somebody else (in the community), a duty to abstain from evil-doing would be a moral duty. This restriction of a moral duty to a moral community we must discuss presently (see sect. 7).

The problem is now: How can action in accordance with the Principle of Justice become duty in a moral community?

This can happen in two ways. We can call them the outer and the inner way. The first imposes the moral duty as a heteronomous other-regarding duty on the members. The second imposes it as an autonomous other-regarding duty.

Self-interest is sufficient as a moving force behind heteronomous moral duties. This is so, because men's anxiety to get their share in a greater good of the community can engender a practical necessity for them to pay their due. The logical mechanism works as follows:

Wanting one's share in the greater good of the community is a motive for joining hands with other members to enforce a duty to pay their due on such members, who might otherwise be un-willing. It is not a motive why one should pay one's due oneself. But fear of revenge or of punishment for breaking the very same laws, which are upheld by one's anxiety to make others pay, *is* such a motive. We can imagine a community, in which everyone is anxious to add the smaller of the two goods of the basic in-equality to his share in the greater good, but is prevented from doing so by his even greater anxiety to prevent anybody else from trying the same unjust trick lest *he* should become the victim. It should namely be observed that from subscribing to the basic in-equality of goods *it follows* that one's anxiety to get one's share is *greater* than one's anxiety, should one feel it at all, to profit from injustice. This is the very 'point' of the inequality: it provides a check on a man's desire to treat others unjustly in the form of his even greater desire to be treated justly by others. We can, in other words, make us a picture of a society, in which justice and morality are 'kept going'—even perfectly—through mere self-interest. It is essential that such a society *could* exist. In it men would observe their moral duties—but not from what we would call moral motives.

I shall say that an agent acts from a *moral motive*, when he ob-serves his moral duty, neither from a self-interested motive such as fear of revenge or punishment, nor from an altruistic motive such as love or respect for the neighbour, whose welfare might become affected through his action, but from a will to secure for all the greater good which similar action on the part of his neigh-bours would secure for him. Action prompted by a moral motive is thus beyond both egoism and altruism. The moral will is, in a characteristic sense, a *disinterested and impartial will to justice*. Its impartiality, however, consists in treating your neighbour as though his welfare were yours and your welfare his. Therefore the moral will is also a love of your neighbour *as yourself*.

When action takes place from a moral motive, observance of the Principle of Justice has become autonomous other-regarding duty.

The question may be raised: *Are* moral duties, in the sense defined, ever heteronomously imposed? Or is the possibility 'purely theoretical'?

The answer is that the possibility is *not* 'purely theoretical'. It is an important aspect of the working of the huge normative power, which we call the state, that it serves the interests also of moral communities of men. It would be a great misunderstanding to regard the laws of the state as essentially void of a moral content. The very example of a moral duty which we have been discussing, *viz*. the duty to abstain from evil, is probably the most important single concern of the laws of all states. What may nevertheless make us think of the law of the state as essentially different from 'the moral law' is probably not so much the fact that there are branches of law which are not immediately concerned with matters of public or private welfare, as the fact that, although laws of the state need not be void of a moral content, the power of the state as an authority of norms is founded on self-interested co-operation of men for common ends and not on a disinterested will to observe the Principle of Justice.

Since self-interest *can* be the safeguard of morality, why should a man ever act from a moral motive? To raise this question is to express astonishment at the fact that men should pursue other than self-interested ultimate ends. But even if one cannot give reasons why men should act morally from moral motives, one can try to make a man respect the good of another as if it were his own by the use of arguments, which *look like* an appeal to ends. One can ask questions like this, 'What right have you got to put yourself in a privileged position? If you get your share without paying your due, then somebody else, who is equally anxious to get his share, will necessarily be without it. Don't you see that this is unfair.' One could almost call this appeal to a man's sense of justice an appeal to a man's sense of symmetry. 'If my wants are satisfied at the expense of another man's, then why not his wants at my expense?' This is like saying: 'For symmetry's sake you must want to be just. And for justice's sake you must make yourself pay your due for your share in the good of the community.'

Such argumentation as this need not be without effect upon men. To resort to it is not cheating. But it is not an appeal to further ends, for the sake of which we should aim at acting justly. It is making the nature of justice as an end clearer by making us see logical relationships between concepts.

That which is here called action from a moral motive has a certain resemblance to that which Kant calls action from a motive of duty (*Handeln aus Pflicht* as distinct from *pflichtmässiges Handeln*). The resembling features are those of disinterestedness and impartiality, and the detachment of the moral will *both* from self-interested concern *and* from altruistic sentiment.

The moral will is a will to do to others something which we want others to do to us. It is not, however, a will to do this, because we count upon or demand a return of service. It is a will to do this because we think it but fair that we too should contribute to the agreed good of all. One could say that the moral will is a will to observe the principle known as the Golden Rule from a motive, which comes at least very close to that which is a Christian love of our neighbour. But one could also call it a will to treat our fellow humans as ends in themselves. Here is another resembling feature with the ethics of Kant.

7. Someone may wish to raise the following objection against the argument which we have been conducting: This argument makes the existence of moral duties depend upon the wants of men. It may not be futile or uninteresting to try to describe the peculiar nature of the wants behind such duties. What men want, however, is contingent. Is it not a most unsatisfactory position in moral philosophy to let questions, whether something or other is moral duty, depend upon such contingencies?

There are, moreover, two ways in which moral duties, on our understanding of the term, depend upon the wants of men. The first is that moral duties exist only within moral communities defined in terms of that which I have called a basic inequality of goods. The second is that, even within the moral community, the moral duty exists only to the extent that it is either autonomously imposed by the member upon himself or heteronomously imposed upon him by others.

The restriction of moral duties to members of a moral community may seem very narrowing. This impression, however, is deceptive. Let us go back to the basic inequality in the example which we discussed, and consider how big the moral community might be, which it determines.

The moral community under consideration consists of all those who have more to gain from never being harmed by anybody else than from sometimes harming somebody else.

Some men may stubbornly refuse to acknowledge that they have more to gain from never being harmed than from sometimes harming and yet be mistaken. But they *may* also be right. In order to see under which conditions they would be right, we must inspect more closely the nature of the goods, which are balanced against one another in the inequality.

It is conceivable that a man never suffers any harm from his neighbours all through his life. It is also conceivable that such a man has done harm to some other man for the sake of attaining some end and that he attained his wanted end and never regretted it. This man has then gained an advantage from harming his neighbour without having suffered a corresponding loss in the form of revenge or punishment. Since our assumption was that he never suffers harm from anybody else, there is no such harm which he could balance against this advantage so that he might say to himself: 'I should have rather been without that which I gained from harming my neighbours than have had this harm done to me.'

If these are the assumptions, does it follow that the basic inequality does not hold good for our man? This does *not* follow. All that follows is that this man actually gained more from harming others than he lost from being harmed by others. But this possibility is not denied in the basic inequality. It says that a man has more to gain from not being harmed than from harming. Therefore, in order to decide whether the basic inequality holds true for our man, we must also consider how much he has gained from escaping harm. How shall this quantity be estimated?

The harm which, on our assumption, the man has escaped, is the harm which would have resulted to him had his neighbours never hesitated to wrong him, when this could have been to their advantage. Escaping this harm is the advantage which a man *has to gain* from never being harmed by anybody.

The advantage against which this has to be put in the scale is *not* the advantage which, on our assumption, the man actually gained from doing harm to somebody. It is an advantage greater than that, *viz.* the advantage which would have resulted had he never hesitated to wrong his neighbour for the sake of anything which was coveted by him. This is what a man can be said to *have to gain* from sometimes harming others. Unless our assumption is that the man is very ruthless, we shall have to admit that he probably did not gain the full measure of what he had to gain from doing evil.

In considering whether the basic inequality in our example is true for a man or not, we have thus to balance against one another the following two—negative and positive goods: On the one hand, the loss which a man can be expected to suffer, if others take as much advantage from harming him as they can. On the other hand, the gain which a man can be expected to harvest, if he takes as much advantage as he can from harming others.

Having thus made clear the nature of the goods, which are balanced against one another, we go back to the question, whether the basic inequality is true for all men or not. The question is, in other words, whether the moral community which the inequality defines will comprise the whole of mankind.

To this question is relevant that which we have said before about the approximate natural equality of men and about the possibility of overruling natural inequalities by co-operation.

If there existed a giant among men, who could treat the rest of mankind as insignificant worms, who can do nothing to harm him, then this man would not belong to the moral community as determined by the basic inequality in our example. Men sometimes imagine that they are such giants—metaphorically speaking. They are usually soon taught that they are not. Also when the lesson is ineffective, the truth may nevertheless be that they too have more to earn from escaping harm, which could befall them, than from harming others.

Yet it is hardly an *a priori* necessity that an individual man should be weaker than all other men jointly. (I say 'hardly', since we may wish to deny the name of 'man' to a being of superhuman powers.) Suppose a man invents some fearful weapon, to which he alone has access and by means of which he can wipe out any number of men who withstand his wishes or encroach upon his privacy. He could be a kindly man and never want to do harm to anybody. *Could* he be just and moral? I shall not attempt to answer the question. As long as he keeps his secret weapon and is aware of the superiority, which it confers upon him in relation to the rest of humanity, he, in any case, does *not* belong to the moral community, which is determined by the basic inequality in our example.

The fiction of the superman, although logically possible, is yet highly unrealistic, someone may say. Is it *highly* unrealistic? I would ask. Substitute, in our example, a team of men for an individual— and the example is less unrealistic. Substitute a state—and we shall

213

recognize it as thoroughly realistic. The basic inequality from which we derived the moral duty to respect the neighbour's good, holds true for *practically all* individual men. It is therefore, even if not logically necessary, yet practically certain that the moral community, which it defines, will comprise the whole commonwealth of men. This is a consequence of men's natural equality and powers of co-operation. On the level of relationships between states the same basic inequality is not undisputably true. Therefore it is not practically certain that the moral community, which it defines, will comprise the whole commonwealth of nations. For, although states can co-operate, they are not individually approximate equals. For this reason, too, the problems of justice and morality in state-relationships are, to a great extent, *logically different* from the problems of justice and morality in the relations of individual men.

I hope to have succeeded in showing that the restriction of the moral duty, which we derived, to a community of men is of no practical importance. For it is a practical certainty that no man can put himself outside the community as we have defined it.

But what about the imagined superman, who is not in the community? Is it not his moral duty, too, never to do evil to his neighbour? *Must* it not be everybody's duty? I would answer *No*. The superman *cannot* be commanded to respect his neighbour, *i.e.* fear of punishment is no motive for him to obey such a 'command'. Moreover, he cannot even feel *that* love of man, which puts him under the autonomous law of respecting all other men. For this love 'of thy neighbour *as thyself*' is conditioned by the similarity of needs and wants and powers of men. If a being stronger than all men together shows benevolent concern for the welfare of humans, this would be more like an act of *mercy* than an act of *justice*.

8. In conclusion, I wanted to raise the following question: In which sense, if any, can justice and observance of moral duty be said to possess a 'utilitarian justification'?

The Principle of Justice, as we formulated it, says that no man must have his share in the common good of a community, of which he is a member, without paying his due. Assent to this principle autonomously imposes a moral duty on the members of the community to adopt the practice of paying. The same duty may also become heteronomously imposed.

Observance of a moral duty, on this view, is a kind of 'public utility'. This means: To do one's moral duty is a necessary condition for the existence of a common good of a community, of which the dutybound agent is a member. In this sense, justice and the observance of moral duty, trivially, has a utilitarian foundation.

From this does not follow, however, that the man who acts as justice and moral duty demand, will fare better than the man who acts unjustly and neglects his moral duties. If all men in the community act justly, they will all get a profit from their good conduct, which is necessarily—this follows from membership in the community—greater than any profit they could have gained from acting unjustly. But, as we have seen, it is also possible for a man to add to the profits of justice the profits of injustice—at the expense of another man's loss of the first profit. This is a fearful possibility and its occurrence cannot be ruled out by logical argument. Of course, to try to draw the extra profits of injustice and retain the profits of justice is an extremely difficult game and it is probably right to say that few are successful at playing it. It is even logically impossible that *all* men could thus profit from both justice and injustice. (This can be deduced from the conditions, which the basic inequalities have to satisfy.) But *some* can, theoretically.

The possibility of adding to the blessings of the reign of justice the profits of unjust action, in short: the possibility of that which we have called parasitic action, constitutes an important sense in which justice and morality can be said to be *essentially* void of a utilitarian justification.

Justice and morality are of public utility in a sense in which, for reasons of logic, injustice and immorality could never be. But injustice and immorality can be of private utility. If any attempt to increase one's well-being by immoral means would necessarily be doomed to be unprofitable, then moral action would be what it *is not*, *viz.* a practical necessity under considerations pertaining to the agent's own welfare alone. Moral action would be autonomous self-regarding duty.

There have been many attempts to 'reduce' the moral imperative to self-regarding duty. This attempted reduction is, I think, *one* of the roots of the idea that there will be a last judgment, when the unjust shall suffer and the just triumph.

I fear I cannot share this optimism—if it be called by that name —in the ultimate triumph of justice. Injustice may as a matter of fact become revenged. Or it may become punished. But from the standpoint of a secular morality it must remain a contingent matter, whether the unjust man will prosper or perish.

INDEX

217

International
Library of Philosophy
& Scientific Method

Editor: Ted Honderich
Advisory Editor: Bernard Williams

List of titles, page two

International
Library of Psychology
Philosophy &
Scientific Method

Editor: C K Ogden

List of titles, page six

ROUTLEDGE AND KEGAN PAUL LTD
68 Carter Lane London EC4

International Library of Philosophy and Scientific Method
(Demy 8vo)

Allen, R. E. (Ed.)
Studies in Plato's Metaphysics
Contributors: J. L. Ackrill, R. E. Allen, R. S. Bluck, H. F. Cherniss, F. M. Cornford, R. C. Cross, P. T. Geach, R. Hackforth, W. F. Hicken, A. C. Lloyd, G. R. Morrow, G. E. L. Owen, G. Ryle, W. G. Runciman, G. Vlastos
464 pp. 1965. (2nd Impression 1967.) 70s.

Armstrong, D. M.
Perception and the Physical World
208 pp. 1961. (3rd Impression 1966.) 25s.

A Materialist Theory of the Mind
376 pp. 1967. about 45s.

Bambrough, Renford (Ed.)
New Essays on Plato and Aristotle
Contributors: J. L. Ackrill, G. E. M. Anscombe, Renford Bambrough, R. M. Hare, D. M. MacKinnon, G. E. L. Owen, G. Ryle, G. Vlastos
184 pp. 1965. (2nd Impression 1967.) 28s.

Barry, Brian
Political Argument
382 pp. 1965. 50s.

Bird, Graham
Kant's Theory of Knowledge:
An Outline of One Central Argument in the *Critique of Pure Reason*
220 pp. 1962. (2nd Impression 1965.) 28s.

Brentano, Franz
The True and the Evident
Edited and narrated by Professor R. Chisholm
218 pp. 1965. 40s.

Broad, C. D.
Lectures on Psychical Research
Incorporating the Perrott Lectures given in Cambridge University in 1959 and 1960
461 pp. 1962. (2nd Impression 1966.) 56s.

Crombie, I. M.
An Examination of Plato's Doctrine
I. Plato on Man and Society
408 pp. 1962. (2nd Impression 1966.) 42s.
II. Plato on Knowledge and Reality
583 pp. 1963. (2nd Impression 1967.) 63s.

Day, John Patrick
Inductive Probability
352 pp. 1961. 40s.

International Library of Philosophy and Scientific Method
(Demy 8vo)

Edel, Abraham
Method in Ethical Theory
379 pp. 1963. 32s.

Flew, Anthony
Hume's Philosophy of Belief
A Study of his First "Inquiry"
296 pp. 1961. (2nd Impression 1966.) 30s.

Fogelin, Robert J.
Evidence and Meaning
Studies in Analytical Philosophy
200 pp. 1967. 25s.

Gale, Richard
The Language of Time
256 pp. 1967. about 30s.

Goldman, Lucien
The Hidden God
A Study of Tragic Vision in the *Pensées* of Pascal and the Tragedies of
Racine. Translated from the French by Philip Thody
424 pp. 1964. 70s.

Hamlyn, D. W.
Sensation and Perception
A History of the Philosophy of Perception
222 pp. 1961. (3rd Impression 1967.) 25s.

Kemp, J.
Reason, Action and Morality
216 pp. 1964. 30s.

Körner, Stephan
Experience and Theory
An Essay in the Philosophy of Science
272 pp. 1966. 45s.

Lazerowitz, Morris
Studies in Metaphilosophy
276 pp. 1964. 35s.

Linsky, Leonard
Referring
152 pp. 1967. about 28s.

Merleau-Ponty, M.
Phenomenology of Perception
Translated from the French by Colin Smith
487 pp. 1962. (4th Impression 1967.) 56s.

International Library of Philosophy and Scientific Method
(Demy 8vo)

Perelman, Chaim
The Idea of Justice and the Problem of Argument
Introduction by H. L. A. Hart. Translated from the French by John Petrie
224 pp. 1963. 28s.

Ross, Alf
Directives, Norms and their Logic
192 pp. 1967. about 25s.

Schlesinger, G.
Method in the Physical Sciences
148 pp. 1963. 21s.

Sellars, W. F.
Science, Perception and Reality
374 pp. 1963. (2nd Impression 1966.) 50s.

Shwayder, D. S.
The Stratification of Behaviour
A System of Definitions Propounded and Defended
428 pp. 1965. 56s.

Skolimowski, Henryk
Polish Analytical Philosophy
288 pp. 1967. 40s.

Smart, J. J. C.
Philosophy and Scientific Realism
168 pp. 1963. (3rd Impression 1967.) 25s.

Smythies, J. R. (Ed.)
Brain and Mind
Contributors: Lord Brain, John Beloff, C. J. Ducasse, Antony Flew,
Hartwig Kuhlenbeck, D. M. MacKay, H. H. Price, Anthony Quinton and
J. R. Smythies
288 pp. 1965. 40s.

Science and E.S.P.
Contributors: Gilbert Murray, H. H. Price, Rosalind Heywood, Cyril Burt,
C. D. Broad, Francis Huxley and John Beloff
320 pp. about 40s.

Taylor, Charles
The Explanation of Behaviour
288 pp. 1964. (2nd Impression 1965.) 40s.

Williams, Bernard, and Montefiore, Alan
British Analytical Philosophy
352 pp. 1965. (2nd Impression 1967.) 45s.

International Library of Philosophy and Scientific Method
(Demy 8vo)

Wittgenstein, Ludwig
Tractatus Logico-Philosophicus
The German text of the *Logisch-Philosophische Abhandlung* with a new
translation by D. F. Pears and B. F. McGuinness. Introduction by Bertrand
Russell
188 pp. 1961. (3rd Impression 1966.) 21s.

Wright, Georg Henrik Von
Norm and Action
A Logical Enquiry. The Gifford Lectures
232 pp. 1963. (2nd Impression 1964.) 32s.

The Varieties of Goodness
The Gifford Lectures
236 pp. 1963. (3rd Impression 1966.) 28s.

Zinkernagel, Peter
Conditions for Description
Translated from the Danish by Olaf Lindum
272 pp. 1962. 37s. 6d.

International Library of Psychology, Philosophy, and Scientific Method
(Demy 8vo)

PHILOSOPHY

Anton, John Peter
Aristotle's Theory of Contrariety
276 pp. 1957. 25s.

Bentham, J.
The Theory of Fictions
Introduction by C. K. Ogden
214 pp. 1932. 30s.

Black, Max
The Nature of Mathematics
A Critical Survey
242 pp. 1933. (5th Impression 1965.) 28s.

Bluck, R. S.
Plato's Phaedo
A Translation with Introduction, Notes and Appendices
226 pp. 1955. 21s.

Broad, C. D.
Scientific Thought
556 pp. 1923. (4th Impression 1952.) 40s.

Five Types of Ethical Theory
322 pp. 1930. (9th Impression 1967.) 30s.

The Mind and Its Place in Nature
694 pp. 1925. (7th Impression 1962.) 55s. See also Lean, Martin

Buchler, Justus (Ed.)
The Philosophy of Peirce
Selected Writings
412 pp. 1940. (3rd Impression 1956.) 35s.

Burtt, E. A.
The Metaphysical Foundations of Modern Physical Science
A Historical and Critical Essay
364 pp. 2nd (revised) edition 1932. (5th Impression 1964.) 35s.

6

International Library of Psychology, Philosophy, and Scientific Method
(Demy 8vo)

Carnap, Rudolf
The Logical Syntax of Language
Translated from the German by Amethe Smeaton
376 pp. 1937. (7th Impression 1967.) 40s.

Chwistek, Leon
The Limits of Science
Outline of Logic and of the Methodology of the Exact Sciences
With Introduction and Appendix by Helen Charlotte Brodie
414 pp. 2nd edition 1949. 32s.

Cornford, F. M.
Plato's Theory of Knowledge
The Theaetetus and Sophist of Plato
Translated with a running commentary
358 pp. 1935. (7th Impression 1967.) 28s.

Plato's Cosmology
The Timaeus of Plato
Translated with a running commentary
402 pp. Frontispiece. 1937. (5th Impression 1966.) 45s.

Plato and Parmenides
Parmenides' *Way of Truth* and Plato's *Parmenides*
Translated with a running commentary
280 pp 1939 (5th Impression 1964.) 32s.

Crawshay-Williams, Rupert
Methods and Criteria of Reasoning
An Inquiry into the Structure of Controversy
312 pp. 1957. 32s.

Fritz, Charles A.
Bertrand Russell's Construction of the External World
252 pp. 1952. 30s.

Hulme, T. E.
Speculations
Essays on Humanism and the Philosophy of Art
Edited by Herbert Read. Foreword and Frontispiece by Jacob Epstein
296 pp. 2nd edition 1936. (6th Impression 1965.) 32s.

Lange, Frederick Albert
The History of Materialism
And Criticism of its Present Importance
With an Introduction by Bertrand Russell, F.R.S. Translated from the German
by Ernest Chester Thomas
1,146 pp. 1925. (3rd Impression 1957.) 70s.

International Library of Psychology, Philosophy, and Scientific Method
(Demy 8vo)

Lazerowitz, Morris
The Structure of Metaphysics
With a Foreword by John Wisdom
262 pp. 1955. (2nd Impression 1963.) 30s.

Lean, Martin
Sense-Perception and Matter
A Critical Analysis of C. D. Broad's Theory of Perception
234 pp. 1953. 25s.

Lodge, Rupert C.
Plato's Theory of Art
332 pp. 1953. 25s.

The Philosophy of Plato
366 pp. 1956. 32s.

Mannheim, Karl
Ideology and Utopia
An Introduction to the Sociology of Knowledge
With a Preface by Louis Wirth. Translated from the German by Louis Wirth and Edward Shils
360 pp. 1954. (2nd Impression 1966.) 30s.

Moore, G. E.
Philosophical Studies
360 pp. 1922. (6th Impression 1965.) 35s. See also Ramsey, F. P.

Ogden, C. K., and Richards, I. A.
The Meaning of Meaning
A Study of the Influence of Language upon Thought and of the Science of Symbolism
With supplementary essays by B. Malinowski and F. G. Crookshank
394 pp. 10th Edition 1949. (6th Impression 1967.) 32s.
See also Bentham, J.

Peirce, Charles, *see* Buchler, J.

Ramsey, Frank Plumpton
The Foundations of Mathematics and other Logical Essays
Edited by R. B. Braithwaite. Preface by G. E. Moore
318 pp. 1931. (4th Impression 1965.) 35s.

Richards, I. A.
Principles of Literary Criticism
312 pp. 2nd edition. 1926. (17th Impression 1966.) 30s.

Mencius on the Mind. Experiments in Multiple Definition
190 pp. 1932. (2nd Impression 1964.) 28s.

Russell, Bertrand, *see* Fritz C. A.; Lange, F. A.; Wittgenstein, L.

8

International Library of Psychology, Philosophy, and Scientific Method

(Demy 8vo)

Smart, Ninian
Reasons and Faiths
An Investigation of Religious Discourse, Christian and Non-Christian
230 pp. 1958. (2nd Impression 1965.) 28s.

Vaihinger, H.
The Philosophy of As If
A System of the Theoretical, Practical and Religious Fictions of Mankind
Translated by C. K. Ogden
428 pp. 2nd edition 1935. (4th Impression 1965.) 45s.

Wittgenstein, Ludwig
Tractatus Logico-Philosophicus
With an Introduction by Bertrand Russell, F.R.S., German text with an English translation en regard
216 pp. 1922. (9th Impression 1962.) 21s.
For the Pears-McGuinness translation—*see page 5*

Wright, Georg Henrik von
Logical Studies
214 pp. 1957. (2nd Impression 1967.) 28s.

Zeller, Eduard
Outlines of the History of Greek Philosophy
Revised by Dr. Wilhelm Nestle. Translated from the German by L. R. Palmer
248 pp. 13th (revised) edition 1931. (5th Impression 1963.) 28s.

PSYCHOLOGY

Adler, Alfred
The Practice and Theory of Individual Psychology
Translated by P. Radin
368 pp. 2nd (revised) edition 1929. (8th Impression 1964.) 30s.

Eng, Helga
The Psychology of Children's Drawings
From the First Stroke to the Coloured Drawing
240 pp. 8 colour plates. 139 figures. 2nd edition 1954. (3rd Impression 1906.) 40s.

Jung, C. G.
Psychological Types
or The Psychology of Individuation
Translated from the German and with a Preface by H. Godwin Baynes
696 pp. 1923. (12th Impression 1964.) 45s.

International Library of Psychology, Philosophy, and Scientific Method
(Demy 8vo)

Koffka, Kurt
The Growth of the Mind
An Introduction to Child-Psychology
Translated from the German by Robert Morris Ogden
456 pp. 16 figures. 2nd edition (revised) 1928. (6th Impression 1965.) 45s.
Principles of Gestalt Psychology
740 pp. 112 figures. 39 tables. 1935. (5th Impression 1962.) 60s.

Malinowski, Bronislaw
Crime and Custom in Savage Society
152 pp. 6 plates. 1926. (8th Impression 1966.) 21s.
Sex and Repression in Savage Society
290 pp. 1927. (4th Impression 1953.) 28s.
See also Ogden, C. K.

Murphy, Gardner
An Historical Introduction to Modern Psychology
488 pp. 5th edition (revised) 1949. (6th Impression 1967.) 40s.

Paget, R.
Human Speech
Some Observations, Experiments, and Conclusions as to the Nature, Origin, Purpose and Possible Improvement of Human Speech
374 pp. 5 plates. 1930. (2nd Impression 1963.) 42s.

Petermann, Bruno
The Gestalt Theory and the Problem of Configuration
Translated from the German by Meyer Fortes
364 pp. 20 figures. 1932. (2nd Impression 1950.) 25s.

Piaget, Jean
The Language and Thought of the Child
Preface by E. Claparède. Translated from the French by Marjorie Gabain
220 pp. 3rd edition (revised and enlarged) 1959. (3rd Impression 1966.) 30s.

Judgment and Reasoning in the Child
Translated from the French by Marjorie Warden
276 pp. 1928 (4th Impression 1966.) 28s.

The Child's Conception of the World
Translated from the French by Joan and Andrew Tomlinson
408 pp. 1929. (4th Impression 1964.) 40s.

International Library of Psychology, Philosophy, and Scientific Method *(Demy 8vo)*

Piaget, Jean *(continued)*
The Child's Conception of Physical Causality
Translated from the French by Marjorie Gabain
(3rd Impression 1965.) 30s.

The Moral Judgment of the Child
Translated from the French by Marjorie Gabain
438 pp. 1932. (4th Impression 1965.) 35s.

The Psychology of Intelligence
Translated from the French by Malcolm Piercy and D. E. Berlyne
198 pp. 1950. (4th Impression 1964.) 18s.

The Child's Conception of Number
Translated from the French by C. Gattegno and F. M. Hodgson
266 pp. 1952. (3rd Impression 1964.) 25s.

The Origin of Intelligence in the Child
Translated from the French by Margaret Cook
448 pp. 1953. (2nd Impression 1966.) 42s.

The Child's Conception of Geometry
In collaboration with Bärbel Inhelder and Alina Szeminska. Translated from the French by E. A. Lunzer
428 pp. 1960. (2nd Impression 1966.) 45s.

Piaget, Jean and Inhelder, Bärbel
The Child's Conception of Space
Translated from the French by F. J. Langdon and J. L. Lunzer
512 pp. 29 figures. 1956 (3rd Impression 1967.) 42s.

Roback, A. A.
The Psychology of Character
With a Survey of Personality in General
786 pp. 3rd edition (revised and enlarged 1952.) 50s.

Smythies, J. R.
Analysis of Perception
With a Preface by Sir Russell Brain, Bt.
162 pp. 1956. 21s.

van der Hoop, J. H.
Character and the Unconscious
A Critical Exposition of the Psychology of Freud and Jung
Translated from the German by Elizabeth Trevelyan
240 pp. 1923. (2nd Impression 1950.) 20s.

Woodger, J. H.
Biological Principles
508 pp. 1929. (Reissued with a new Introduction 1966.) 60s.

867 PRINTED BY HEADLEY BROTHERS LTD 109 KINGSWAY LONDON WC2 AND ASHFORD KENT

Date Due